OUTSTANDING
CUSTOMER
SERVICE

Implementing the Best Ideas
from Around the World

OUTSTANDING CUSTOMER SERVICE

Implementing the Best Ideas from Around the World

Colin G. Armistead

Graham Clark

FINANCIAL TIMES

IRWIN PROFESSIONAL PUBLISHING

Burr Ridge, Illinois
New York, New York

Originally published as *Customer Service and Support: Implementing Effective
Strategies* by Pitman Publishing, a division of Longman U.K. Ltd., copyright 1992.

This edition of *Outstanding Customer Service and Support: Implementing the Best
Ideas from around the World* is published by arrangement with Pitman Publishing,
London. The Financial Times and FT are trademarks of the Financial Times, Ltd.,
London.

Sponsoring editor: Cynthia A. Zigmund
Project editor: Beth Yates
Production manager: Jon Christopher
Designer: Larry J. Cope
Compositor: Northern Phototypesetting Co. Ltd.
Typeface: 11/13 Palatino
Printer: Book Press, Inc.

Library of Congress Cataloging-in-Publication Data

Armistead, Colin G.
   Outstanding customer service : implementing the best ideas from
around the world/ Colin G. Armistead, Graham Clark.
      p.   cm.
   Includes bibliographical references and index.
   ISBN 1–55623–629–8
   1. Customer service—Management   2. Consumer satisfaction.
I. Clark, Graham.   II. Title.
HF5415.5.A76   1994
658.8'12—dc20   93–29974

Printed in the United States of America

1 2 3 4 5 6 7 8 9 0 BP 0 9 8 7 6 5 4 3

DEDICATION

This book is dedicated to our wives, children, and pets, who were deprived of our attention during the time we were writing, and to all the customer service and support managers who have contributed either directly or indirectly to our research.

Preface

INTRODUCTION

This book is about managing change in customer service and support organizations. It has been written as the result of years of research and is clear to us that the pressure for change in customer service and support will not slacken over the next years. Some of the key reasons are:

- Customer demand for ever more reliable products. Service in the sense of reacting to breakdowns will tend to disappear, with more emphasis on routine maintenance and ultimately no service at all.

- As companies emphasize product image in marketing, service and support, operations must be consistent to give the desired result. As service and support personnel may meet the customer more often than sales people, they must be fully briefed about what role they are to play.

- There will be an increasing trend to identify yet more ways in which the customer needs support to ensure maximum use of the purchase. "Total Solutions" and "One-Stop Shopping" are examples of this.

- Product life cycles will continue to shorten, placing more pressure on the service and support organization's ability to support more products.

- The need to ensure that the customer is inconvenienced as little as possible will put yet more pressure on response times, in particular, the rapid movement of materials through the network.

- Customers continue to expect better levels of service in all senses of the word. They will expect to be dealt with courteously and promptly and will expect to be fully informed at all times.

We are sure that if customer service and support organizations are to meet these challenges then they should aspire to be world-class service providers and compare themselves with service providers across the spectrum of services. We ourselves recognize world-class service organizations by how much they fulfill the following criteria:

- World-class services give a high level of customer satisfaction, judged on value for money.
- World-class services have a high level of customer retention over time.
- World-class services have a very good "service image." People talk about their experiences with them.
- World-class services have their costs under control.
- World-class services find people want to work for them.
- World-class services display a high-level of innovation in the services offered, and the way they are delivered.
- World-class services give clear and often unconditional guarantees.
- World-class services cope with change.

We see some organizations in the customer service and support area who are well along the path to being world-class. Caterpillar, Hewlett Packard, Rank Xerox, Hitachi, and Otis are all companies we would put in this category of able aspirants to the title.

WHO IS THE BOOK WRITTEN FOR?

We have written the book primarily for managers who have to provide support to customers and also possibly for service equipment of some form. Typically, their jobs require them to make provision across a network to give geographical coverage, and they may do this using their own resources or they may have to manage the process through intermediaries. Let us give some examples:

- *Andrews Engines* are built for power generation and sold worldwide. The role of the customer service and support managers is to ensure the supply of spares and, when necessary, engineers on site.
- *Domestic Products* makes kitchen appliances, including washing machines, dishwashers, and driers. It provides customer service and support through a network of offices from which service engineers work.

- *COM* makes computers from mainframes to PCs and peripherals. It provides customer service and support to consumers and business customers through a network of telephone response centers, giving support and field engineers for site visits. It also sells some products through agents whom they have to manage.
- *BL Cars* manufactures and sells automobiles through agents whom they must manage to maintain consistency of the customer service and support activity.
- *ACME Stores* sell electrical products in a network of stores. They provide and manage customer service and support for products postsale.
- *International Power* generates and distributes electricity and provides customer service and support to its domestic, industrial, and commercial customers.

We have also found, however that in discussing our work with managers from other service sectors, they find the ideas and approaches that are presented in the book useful and relevant to their work. These managers could be from retail banking, insurance, financial services, travel and leisure, distribution and public sector services.

Six Steps for Improving Customer Service and Support

Step 1: Know and understand what must be done well.

This statement reflects that the world is changing, and customer service and support must change with it. Merely being good at yesterday's task is not sufficient. Changes in products, the competitive environment, the customer expectations, mean that success can only be achieved by recognizing the implications for the organization.

The measures used by customers to assess success will have changed. Having an excellent service organization, able to respond to equipment failure in less than two hours, may have been the recipe for success yesterday, but today customers assume that you will perform to this level as a matter of course, and the winners are those organizations who are able to provide equipment that rarely fails, and have found new ways to create customer confidence.

The "excellent" organizations are those that are constantly re-sponding to the changing demands of the environment, under-standing the implications of change for each detail of their opera-tion.

Step 2: Build value in delivering service.

In this book we discuss some aspects of service delivery. It is worth emphasizing some key principles here:

- Pay attention to each detail of delivery, managing the processes, materials, people, and information to give a consistent result.
- Analyze the operation from the customers' viewpoint, understanding their needs and their perceptions of how well they are being served.
- Work hard at forming strong links at each point of the chain or service delivery: front line staff to customers, front line staff to back room process personnel or support staff.

The objective is that there should be a clear and consistent link between "what needs to be done well" (step 1) and how it is performed (step 2).

Step 3: Balance resources.

The best organizations manage to walk the tightrope of achieving consistently good service standards while keeping costs at such a level that preserve good margins. This level can only be achieved by a better understanding of how to match supply and demand by:

- Knowing the effective capacity of the service and support organization, the rate at which demand can be consistently satisfied.
- Forecasting future demand to ensure that appropriate resources are provided.
- Knowing the point at which resources become profitable (break-even point) and the point at which extra demand results in a deterioration in customer perceived quality levels.
- Building flexibility into systems and people to improve response to variability in demand.

- Limiting the negative effect on customer satisfaction that occurs when demand outstrips supply by reducing the chance of it happening and preparing contingency plans for those increasingly rare occasions.

Step 4: Create a structure for quality.

In recent years much has been written about the various aspects of quality, from Customer Care to Quality Assurance, from systems and procedures to Quality Circles and TQM. Whichever approach proves itself to be the most useful for your situation, the fact is that quality must be managed, rather than allowed to find its own level.

Developing a structure for quality means developing actions that range from clear management commitment to quality, to the dedication of resource to quality improvement, the use of measurement and data gathering, motivation and reward, involvement, creativity quality assurance systems: there is no one right approach. Sometimes, detailed systems and procedures must be put in place, which are then brought to life by employees who are motivated to deliver top quality service. In other situations, the route lies in recruiting and training the best people and underpinning their actions with broad systems to give coordination to their efforts.

Do not forget that Continuous Improvement is a vital element of quality management, and if encouraged may yield significant competitive advantage.

Step 5: Work on resource productivity.

As products, whether they be goods or services, mature, the opportunities for price increases diminish. Any differentiation through improved customer service must be paid for largely by increased efficiency or effectiveness.

This first step will require a review of productivity measures currently in place, ensuring that they reflect the priorities of the business. The recent interest in activity-based costing is a recognition that simply spreading overheads over direct costs may give an inaccurate assessment of the contribution of each service product.

Identifying the major elements of resource cost may allow the organization to compare itself against similar customer service and support departments – probably those who are not competitors –

to question whether some areas might be more effective. This activity of benchmarking is becoming more common as customer service and support managers find that the issues and problems faced are very similar across most industry sectors.

Finally, the organization must work hard at continuously improving the effectiveness of systems and people. Many organizations are discovering the value of looking at how the amount of time that work spends in the system can be reduced on the principle that work expands to fill the time available. Others are finding that the value chain analysis described later shows up areas where a marginal increase in one resource yields far greater savings in other resources.

Step 6: Manage change.

This book is largely about the need to recognize change and to ensure that the customer service and support function moves with it. Recognizing change, however, is only part of the task. People must be carried with you if change is to be carried out successfully. The next section indicates some areas to be considered if change is to be managed.

The Black and Decker Service Division

Black and Decker United Kingdom, is unusual in the industry in that it has always maintained its own network of service points, although also supported by numbers of agents often acting as "drop-off" points for equipment to be repaired at a central location.

In the 1970s there were 15service points in industrial locations in the United Kingdom. The approach to service at this time was said to be functional, the service points being workshops rather than consumer oriented, often located on industrial estates. By the mid-1980s the network had grown to 25, but Black and Decker recognized that this was not sufficient to meet the needs of the professional users in geographically remote areas. Agents were appointed to deal with the needs of the professionals with collection points in retail outlets arranged for the domestic user.

Company senior management was concerned that, whereas a reasonable service was being given when necessary, the company possibly was not receiving some more positive benefits to be derived through better customer contact. A full review of the current service operation was carried out by managers drawn from all functions within the business, not just service management, to ensure that the review was as objective as possible.

A mission statement was evolved on two levels:

1. *Primary*: "To administer the warranty policy and satisfy the product related needs of all our customers."

2. *Secondary*: "To provide any other related service requirement, conveniently and efficiently, in line with corporate policies and marketing objectives."

This mission statement was translated into a set of objectives for the next three years that were both general and specific. General objectives included the aim to administer the warranty policy in such a way as to be seen to be equitable to the customer and to enhance the company image by making sure that customer contact was both friendly and efficient, while a specific objective was to provide access to a company-owned service point within 30 minutes' travel to 90 percent of the population.

Active participation from all service division personnel was encouraged through formal presentations and "Total Customer Service" seminars. Senior management visited every service point to discuss proposed plans and to review "mini business plans" developed by the local staff. This element was felt to be the most significant in managing the transition in the service division.

Over three years some significant improvements were carried through. These were:

1. The number of locations where on the spot repairs can be made have been increased, with a reduction in time and cost. The result was increased demand.

2. The support for professional users has been improved, with a four-hour "urgent" service and also a loan service.

3. Information from the repair centers and through warranty claims has been fed back to product development for improved reliability.

4. Retail design consultants were used to develop a new concept for service centers to be incorporated in new locations, increasingly sited in the high street rather than industrial estates.

5. The quality program "Total Customer Service" has improved customer service. This service is monitored by a continuous program of customer questionnaires and response to complaints.

6. Staff flexibility has resulted in productivity gains in excess of 20 percent.

7. A new information system was designed with full input from all service personnel that has improved the speed and quality of decision making.

The service division recognized the need for change and took positive steps to manage it, setting clear objectives across the business. The key to the results has been the involvement of management from across the Black and Decker business and active participation of all service division personnel.

A WORKSHOP APPROACH TO CHANGE IN SERVICE AND SUPPORT

We have found it useful to adopt a workshop for groups of managers and frontline staff to build up an understanding of the business, identify the implications of change, and, consequently, to move a plan that is the result of the combined efforts of those involved.

The aim is to address the three main factors in the customer service triangle, namely, strategy, systems, and the sparkle provided by the people. Each topic is introduced, briefly explaining the area to be addressed, but much of the value we have found comes from the participants working together to answer questions specifically related to their organization. This approach takes place in syndicate groups with feedback, questioning, and summary of issues.

The process consists of seeking answers to some basic questions: What business are we in?

1. What are our customers really buying from us? What value are we giving them?

2. What makes us different from our competitors?

3. How do we want to compete in the future?

4. How do we build *value* in our service delivery, and where are the cost drivers?

5. What tends to go wrong with our delivery of customer service and support, and how serious is it?

6. How can we maintain the best balance of service intensity and the capacity to satisfy this demand?

7. How can we build a structure for quality in our customer service and support?

8. How can we best measure and improve resource productivity?

9. Is our culture consistent with the way in which we want to do business in the future?

In seeking answers to these questions we use the techniques and more detailed questioning contained in the earlier chapters. Within the lifetime of one workshop a resolution of all the questions will not be reached: we find that organizations often do not have the information at hand to be able to answer all the questions, and this can lead to actions to redress the gap. The asking of the question may reveal that areas of service delivery that had previously been considered to be all right are inadequate for the changing circumstances. The end of the process centers around action plans that include the search for new data and information and changes to the service delivery and the operational control of quality, capacity, and resource productivity.

POSTSCRIPT

We believe that delivering excellent customer service and support will be a key task for all organizations in the next few years. This goal will not be achieved by customer service and support managers alone. Organizations must become more and more integrated, ensuring that the efforts of product designers, manufacturing people, sales and marketing, and customer service and support combine to deliver what the customer wants.

We hope that this book assists in this process of integration by explaining the challenges and problems of customer service and support.

Colin Armistead
Graham Clark

Contents

Preface   *vii*

Chapter One
WHAT IS CUSTOMER SERVICE AND
SUPPORT?   1

Customer Service and Support—A Vital Activity! 2
Customer Service and Support—Another Layer of
Guilt? 4
Customer Service and Support—The Benefits, 5
The Scope of Customer Service and Support, 8
After Sales Support Starts Long Before the Sale, 9
After Sales Support at the Point of Sale, 9
Integrating Product Design and Customer Service and
Support, 10
The Customer Service Triangle, 13
Customer Service and Support Strategy, 15
Do You Know Your Service Task? 16
    Customer Service Dimensions, 17
    Demand Dimensions, 19
    Efficiency Targets, 19
    Constraints, 19
Key Actions, 20

Chapter Two
STRUCTURES FOR CUSTOMER SERVICE AND
SUPPORT   21

Are We in Control of the Structure? 21
    A Service and Support Story, 21
    The Showdown, 23
The Military Model, 23
    The SAS (Special Air Services), 24
    The Regulars, 25
    The Territorials, 26
    The Mercenaries, 27
    The Enemies, 28

Do We Have a Choice of Structure? 29

How Do We Use the Military Model? 29

What Influences Service Intensity? 30

    The Product(s), 30

    The Type of Customer Service and Support, 31

    The Users, 32

    The Service and Support Personnel, 32

    The Internal Support, 33

Why Should We Want to Control Customer Service
and Support? 34

Factors Driving a Wish for High In-House Control, 35

Is It To Be the SAS, Regulars, Territorials, Mercenaries, or
the Enemies? 35

    A Consumer Products Manufacturer, 38

    A Domestic Goods Manufacturer, 38

    A Capital Goods Manufacturer, 39

    A Computer Manufacturer, 39

Key Actions, 40

Chapter Three
THE ELEMENTS OF CUSTOMER SERVICE
AND SUPPORT   41

The Dimensions of Time, 42

    How Fast Is the First Response? 42

    Two Examples of Initial Response, 43

    Principles of Initial Response, 45

When Is the Job Completed? 45

    The Service Level Trade-Off, 46

    Decreasing Service Times, 47

    Centralized Service Functions or "Close to Customer? 49

Maintaining Maximum Uptime, 50

    Increasing Reliability, 50

    Preventive Maintenance, 51

    Replace or Repair? 52

Remote Diagnostics and Predictive Maintenance, 52
Supporting Customers, 53
  Can the Customer Use the Product Effectively? 54
  Does the Customer Need Training? 54
  Is the Customer Happy? 55
  Does the Customer Need Anything Else? 56
Money Matters, 57
Setting Customer Service and Support Priorities, 57
Key Actions, 58

Chapter Four
MARKETING AND MARKET RESEARCH   60

Are We a Marketing Oriented Organization? 60
Marketing for Customer Focus, 62
What Is the Customer Buying? 63
Are All Our Customers the Same? 65
Segmenting the Market, 66
Do We Want to Be Part of a Market? 69
Positioning Customer Service and Support, 69
Reviewing the Marketing Mix, 71
The Product/Service/Support Combination, 71
Getting to the Customers, 72
How Much Do We Charge? 73
  Value of Customer Service and Support, 74
  Costs, 74
  Setting the Price, 75
People and Delivery Process, 76
Techniques for Understanding Customers, 76
  The Use of Questionnaires, 77
  Interviews, 77
  Secondary Information, 77
Extending the Marketing Role: Enhancing the Image, 78
Key Actions, 79

Chapter Five
CUSTOMER SERVICE AND SUPPORT
DELIVERY—MANAGING THE CONTACT
WITH CUSTOMERS   80

Configuration: Identifying the Contact Points, 82
    The Front Office—Back Room Framework, 82
    Face-to-Face Customer Contact, 84
    Telephone Contact, 85
    Paper Contact, 87
    Locating Close to Customers, 88
Determining the Resources, 89
    People: The Right Service Providers, 89
    People: Managing the Customers, 91
    Facilities: Setting the Scene, 93
    Customer-Friendly Information Systems, 93
    Equipment: The Balance between Technology and People, 94
    Materials: First-Time Fix, 95
    Managing the Balance of Resources, 96
Customer Process Flow, 96
    How Much Does the Customer See? 99
    Where Does It Go Wrong? 99
    How Does the Customer Feel? 100
Key Actions, 100

Chapter Six
MANAGING YOUR HUMAN RESOURCES   103

How Much Do You Value Your People? 103
The Role of the Service and Support Manager, 105
    The Systems Architect, 107
    The Role Model, 108
    The Psychologist, 109
    The Team Builder, 109
What Managerial Competences Do You Need? 110

Business Development, 110
Analysis, 110
Managing, 111
Staff Management, 111
Do You Give Your People a Chance? 112
What Do Our People Need to Do Their Jobs? 113
The Dangers of Burnout, 115
Imposed Systems or Empowered Organizations, 114
Building the Service Team, 117
The Pathway to Effectiveness for Teams, 118
The Team Coach, 119
Key Actions, 120

Chapter Seven
CAPACITY MANAGEMENT   123

Why Is Capacity Management Important? 123
What Do We Mean by Capacity? 124
How Much Capacity Do We Have? 126
How Flexible Is Our Capacity? 127
What Are Our Patterns of Demand? 127
The Elements of Demand, 127
Forecasting Demand, 128
Creating the Balance, 129
The Chase Capacity Strategy—Altering Capacity, 130
The Level of Capacity Strategy—Altering Demand, 133
The Coping Strategy, 135
How Do We Plan and Control Resources? 136
Customer Response Centers, 137
Visits for Preventive Maintenance, 137
Visits for Breakdowns, 138
Support Activities, 138
Workshop Repair, 139
Using the Network, 140
Key Actions, 140

Chapter Eight
MANAGING SERVICE QUALITY   141

Why Is Quality Management So Important? 143

   Quality and Customers, 144

   Quality and Employees, 145

   Reducing Quality Cost, 146

Defining Quality, 147

   Dimensions of Product Quality, 148

   Dimensions of Service Quality, 151

   How Do We Set the Right Standards? 153

   How Can We Make Sure We Deliver the Right Quality? 156

   The Role of Management, 156

   Using the Quality Techniques, 158

   Involving the People, 158

   Developing the Quality System, 160

   Putting the Quality Triangle Together, 161

Key Actions, 163

Chapter Nine
IMPROVING PRODUCTIVITY   164

What Are Your Trade-Offs? 164

Why Is Managing Resource Productivity So Difficult? 165

Understanding Productivity, 165

   Measuring Outputs, 166

   Measuring Inputs, 167

   Deciding on the Level for Measurement, 167

How Can We Approach the Complexity of
Measurement? 168

Which Measurement at Which Level? 169

   How Accurate Is Our Costing? 171

How Many Measures? 171

How Can We Compare Branch Performance? 172

How Can We Improve Our Resource Productivity? 173

Volume, 174

Variation in Demand, 175

Variety of the Service and Support Mix, 175

What Are the Barriers to Improving Resource Productivity? 175

How Can We Break the Barriers and Improve Resource Productivity? 176

Understanding the Process, 177

Measurement, 177

Trade-Off Resources, 178

Key-Actions, 179

Chapter Ten
MANAGING THE INFORMATION   180

Do We Need a New Information System? 180

Developing Strategic Information Systems, 182

Combating the Threat of New Entrants, 182

The Threat of Substitute Products or Services, 182

The Effect of Industry Rivalry, 183

The Threat of Strong Buyers and Suppliers, 184

Opportunities for Advantage through Information, 184

What Information Can Be Provided? 186

Financial Systems, 186

Customer Management Systems, 186

Quality Systems, 187

Resource Management, 187

People Management, 188

The Trigger-Input – Process-Output Model, 188

Two Organizations That Have Recognized the Value of Information, 189

Otis Elevator, 189

Caterpillar, 191

Key Actions, 192

Chapter Eleven
MANAGING THE MATERIALS   193

The Cost of Inventory, 194

Why Do We Need Inventory? 194

    Fluctuation, Safety, or Buffer Stocks, 196

    How Can We Improve Our Inventory Service Level? 196

    Anticipation or Seasonal Stocks, 199

    Lot-Size Stocks, 199

    Transportation or Pipeline Stocks, 200

How Do We Manage Inventory? 201

    How Much Inventory Have We Got? 201

    Can the Task Be Simplified? 201

    Managing the Manufacturing-Service Interface, 202

    Maintaining a Service Focus in the Manufacturing Function, 204

    Material Requirements Planning, 205

    Managing the Bits and Pieces, 205

    Forecasting Demand, 208

    Commit the Inventory As Late As Possible, 209

    Can the Just-In-Time Philosophy Be Used? 210

Managing the Service Supply Chain, 211

    What Must the Supply Chain Produce? 211

    What Is Needed to Make the Supply Chain Work? 212

    Is Supply Chain Management Worth It? 214

    What Can the Service and Support Manager Do? 214

Key Actions, 215

Chapter Twelve
MANAGING THROUGH INTERMEDIARIES   216

Why Use Intermediaries? 217

    Close to Customer, 217

    Local Knowledge, 217

    Skill Shortage, 218

    Low Service Income, 218

    Demand Exceeds Supply, 219

What Approach Should Be Adopted to Controlling
Intermediaries? 219

Economic Rewards, 219

Strong Arm Tactics, 220

Providing Expertise to Support Intermediaries, 221

The Quality Reputation—Building a Relationship, 221

Manufacturer's Rights to Realistic Controls, 222

How Can the Network Be Improved? 223

Establish Clear Performance Expectations, 223

Minimize Network Disputes by Design, 224

Select the Right Intermediaries, 225

Positive Motivation, 225

Train the People, 226

Regular Evaluation, 226

Customer Complaint Management, 227

Meeting Deliveries from Parent to Intermediary, 228

The Retailer's Viewpoint—Getting Control, 228

The Case of Earthmovers Ltd., 229

Key Actions, 230

Chapter Thirteen
RECOVERY STRATEGIES: THE KEY TO
CUSTOMER RETENTION   231

Why Should We Bother About Service Recovery? 231

Customer Satisfaction, 232

Profitability, 233

What Do These Results Tell Us? 235

What's Involved in Developing Recovery Strategies? 235

Getting Better at the Basics? 236

What Are Coping Strategies? 237

Using Resources to Best Effect: Escalation, 238

Measurement of Customer Satisfaction, 239

Empowering the Service Providers, 240

Key Actions, 243

Chapter Fourteen
INTERNATIONALIZATION: MANAGING
THE NETWORK   244

What Is Changing in the International Scene? 244

Physical Barriers, 245

Technical Barriers, 245

Monetary Barriers, 245

The Impact of Global Organizations, 245

Awareness of Service Excellence, 245

What Will the Changes Mean for Customer Service
and Support? 246

What Are the Options for Service and Support
Networks? 248

Service Intensity, 249

Location of Service and Support Resources, 249

Composition of Service and Support Teams, 250

The Level of Integration of the Network, 250

How Can We Manage the Supply Chain? 251

What Upgrades in Information Systems Are Needed? 253

What Is the Affect on Human Resource Policies? 253

Can An International Network Help with Capacity Management? 254

Can We Maintain Quality? 255

How Can We Decrease the Risks from Expansion? 256

Key Actions, 256

Bibliography, 259

Index, 263

Chapter One

What is Customer Service and Support?

Introduction

In this chapter we introduce the area of customer service and support, outlining its scope, and indicating why customer service and support is so important.

The three main themes running through this book are:

Theme 1: Customer service and support is an activity that has been undermanaged in the past, but professional service and support management is emerging. As a result, the quality of support perceived by customers is generally rising. Delivering an appropriate level of customer service and support will be a major business challenge for many organizations in the 90s.

Theme 2: Customer service and support is a rapidly changing task for companies, and therefore there is urgent need for organizations to review their activities in light of competitive pressures, in the knowledge that if the task is well done, customer service and support may win business.

Theme 3: Customer service and support must be fully integrated into every activity if it is to be managed effectively from design through production to initial sale and finally to repurchase.

The problem for many suppliers is that there are few occasions where the competence of the organization can be demonstrated to its customers. Broadening the scope of its customer service and support activity may increase the number and meaningfulness of such contacts. As Drucker says, the aim of the organization is to create and keep customers. Indeed, there are examples of companies that have managed to bridge the gap between the phasing out of an old product and the launching of a new product, keeping their customer base by giving superlative customer service and support.

The final benefit also comes directly through stronger customer relationships. To improve the quality of goods and services, it is generally agreed that the organization must listen to customers. For all its bias, analysis of customer complaints will provide invaluable information that the company will ignore at its peril. On the other hand, surveys indicate that the vast majority of unhappy customers do not complain, they simply walk away. Increased customer loyalty provides motivation to give useful, quality feedback for improvement.

CUSTOMER SERVICE AND SUPPORT—A VITAL ACTIVITY!

It has taken some organizations a long time to realize that it is not sufficient to manufacture a superb product for customers to beat a path to their door and, perhaps more important, to keep returning. How many times have you made or listened to statements like "I'll never buy another . . ., their After Sales Service is useless?" There is little doubt that the quality of customer service and support plays a major part in the decision process about which product is to be purchased or repurchased. Figure 1–1 illustrates some of the influences that customer service and support activities may have on the customer relationship and therefore on sales.

Unfortunately, customers may not appreciate all the finer technical points of the design of our product even though they represent many hours or years of the finest research and development. They will, however, notice quickly how often the product fails, how easy or difficult it is to repair, and whether in the process of dealing with your company they felt they were well treated or were given the impression that they were little more than a nuisance. Unfair? Of course it is, but customers don't have the technical expertise to enable them to assess product performance. Customers can only draw conclusions from how well or poorly they feel the company performs in those areas that affect them directly or in those activities they feel they understand. I may not understand all the workings of the internal combustion engine, but I do

FIGURE 1–1
Building the Customer Relationship

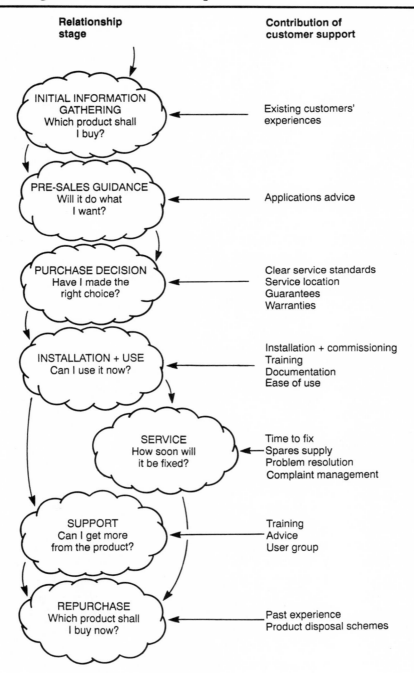

Relationship stage	Contribution of customer support
INITIAL INFORMATION GATHERING Which product shall I buy?	Existing customers' experiences
PRE-SALES GUIDANCE Will it do what I want?	Applications advice
PURCHASE DECISION Have I made the right choice?	Clear service standards Service location Guarantees Warranties
INSTALLATION + USE Can I use it now?	Installation + commissioning Training Documentation Ease of use
SERVICE How soon will it be fixed?	Time to fix Spares supply Problem resolution Complaint management
SUPPORT Can I get more from the product?	Training Advice User group
REPURCHASE Which product shall I buy now?	Past experience Product disposal schemes

know that I am not happy when my car comes back from the garage with oily fingerprints all over it.

For many companies a shift in emphasis has taken place over the last 10 years. The old stance was one of providing a product whose quality was adequate, and then providing a spares and maintenance service almost out of necessity because the product would require repair at some stage. This approach to service tended to be rather low key and functional rather than seen as a major strategic activity. To be fair, there were a few lone voices, particularly those belonging to people with a high degree of customer contact, saying that more positive steps should be taken to look after customers, but these were largely ignored. Today, much has changed. To use a somewhat overworked cliché, the task is "no longer fix the product, but rather fix the customer."

If anything, the danger is that customer service and support has become a cliché in itself. Every organization subscribes more or less to the idea that customers should be cared for. The danger is that the management thinks that it happens just because a new, customer-focused language appears. Companies are beginning to understand that it is as vital to manage the customer as it is fundamental to manage the costs and quality of a manufacturing process. No improvements happen without direct action to change the way things are done, and this is true for customer service and support.

CUSTOMER SERVICE AND SUPPORT — ANOTHER LAYER OF GUILT?

It is almost too obvious to say that we should all be customer-focused, that our strategies, our systems, and our people should all have some sort of distinguishing mark that proclaims that they have passed the customer-friendly test. Writers and speakers such as Tom Peters, Sir John Harvey-Jones, and the quality gurus have done a good job in persuading us of the need to really understand what customers need from us. The danger is that this new vision does not set us and our employees free, it merely adds another item to the list of things we ought to do better:

- Our goods and services ought to be delivered right first time.
- Our goods and services ought to cost less than they do.
- We ought to be better at cash flow management.
- We ought to be better at involving and empowering people.

The list is endless. Are we now going to add yet another?

- We ought to be better at customer service and support.

Nothing is easy. If it were, there would be no need for a book such as this, which sets out to challenge the question, but also aims to provide some guidelines about how necessary improvements in customer service and support can be achieved.

CUSTOMER SERVICE AND SUPPORT—THE BENEFITS

Hopefully, our assertion that excellent customer service and support is vital has begun to come through. It would be useful now to emphasize just how important it is by outlining some of the benefits experienced more or less by companies that have paid attention to this area.

We have mentioned the first benefit, which is the one of greater customer confidence. Customers judge the quality of the product by what they can see and understand. There are many examples of companies with good products that have been let down by the quality of documentation, invoices, and, of course, telephone techniques! We visited one of the United Kingdom's best-known factories, which has a deservedly high reputation for manufacturing excellence, to be greeted by a security guard eating fish and chips out of a paper bag. This image is almost certainly not the one this company would wish to portray, and it was made worse for us because we weren't offered any!

How many companies spend considerable sums on carefully grooming their image through marketing campaigns for it to be destroyed because something relatively trivial has been overlooked? On a more positive note. tackling all the aspects of customer contact and requirements rightly gives the impression of an organization that knows what it is doing. Confident customers are easier to manage, causing less disruption, and requiring less assurance when they feel that things are in control.

Good customer service and support should ensure that the customer gets maximum value from the purchase. It would be sad if a customer spent a significant amount of money on a product, only to use a small percentage of its facilities or potential. Computer manufacturers and software suppliers are surely a good example of organizations with this problem. The word-processing package used to write this book is perhaps only 10 percent understood and used by the authors. Good customer service and support should enable customers quickly and easily to experience full use from their purchase. Customer service and support demands must be considered throughout the business cycle from the earliest design stage right through to giving clear documentation and easy access to advice. Anyone who has tried to understand a computer manual will agree with this. Ensuring maximum value in use will help prevent what marketing experts term *postpurchase dissonance* or, in other words, asking "what did I spend all this money on this for?"

Another benefit from good customer service and support is that, in many cases, it is profitable. In this respect one must be careful to distinguish between service and support. Purchasers of capital goods and the more expensive consumer goods such as motor cars and washing machines are prepared to recognize that such complex items are likely to need repair and maintenance at intervals. For many years some manufacturers have made significant profits here, to the extent that the original equipment may be sold at a loss to capture the service business.

Total service revenue may be several multiples of the initial purchase price as well as commanding a greater margin. A cross-industry survey indicated that in 1990, over 75 percent of organizations were making profits out of service and support, with an average margin of approximately 25 percent. Customers are not foolish, and a greater understanding of lifetime costs has contributed to a trend toward more reliable products and, hence, lower service revenue per product.

There is benefit in moving closer to customers and hence understanding their needs. Apart from developing better quality goods and services through incorporating genuine customer priorities, there is an increased possibility of discovering new business opportunities. An example of this benefit would be the software supplier who has developed a major activity in management education as they identified a need to educate their customers, rather than merely train them how to use their programs. A supplier of industrial fasteners has developed a profitable business in managing the whole of this area for its customers, removing from them the need for administration and control systems and, in some cases, storage space.

As markets mature, two major forms of differentiation are those of image and service. Automobile companies, for example, have discovered that customers find it difficult to distinguish between competing offerings as they often have a similar shape, are based on similar specifications, and are in the same broad price range. Customers make their decisions on the availability of a particular color, the specification of the sound system, and the location and competence of the dealer. In this case the customer service and support activity is central to the company's competitive strategy.

If the manufacturer attempts to differentiate by image, customer service and support is again involved. It may be that the company wishes to project an upmarket image or, alternatively, a young, healthy, sporty image. In either case the company must be very careful to ensure that service and support are reviewed to match the customers' differing expectations. This is an issue often faced by the automobile companies who have to support a range of products from economy to executive motoring and may choose to separate the two service activities to end confusion.

Competent customer service and support should lead to increased customer loyalty. Marketing guru Ted Levitt likened the relationship between purchasers and vendors to that between husband and wife. If there is good evidence of care and concern "after the sale" is over, the relationship will be strong and repurchase likely. If, on the other hand, it is clear that the vendor is looking for the first sale alone, no relationship is built, and there will be a predictable reaction when repurchase is sought.

THE SCOPE OF CUSTOMER SERVICE AND SUPPORT

A primary focus of customer service and support is to ensure that the customer has maximum use and derives maximum value from the purchase. In this book we are concentrating on the area that may be identified as *After Sales Service and Support*. As such, we recognize, but not discuss in great detail, other activities that fall under the general heading of serving customers. Two such areas deserve mention here.

The general area of logistics or distribution is often referred to as *customer service*. This term is generally taken to mean managing the channels of sale from order receipt through to shipment, ensuring that the end consumer of the product experiences the greatest balance of availability and price. This activity has particular relevance to after sales support as a distribution network for the original product should also be capable of shipping spare parts to ensure rapid service completion.

The term *customer service* is often used by people to cover the process of dealing directly with customers. Much has been written on the general topic of customer care, ranging from telephone techniques to how to deal with difficult customers. Jan Carlzon of the airline SAS popularized this area in using the term *Moments of Truth*, pointing out that the customer judges the whole organization by the part that is visible to him. This aspect of how customer service and support is delivered and its impact on customers must not be overlooked, and we return to it later.

Some areas that are clearly covered by customer service and support are:

- Field service.
- Maintenance contracts.
- Warranties.
- Customer help and advice.
- Education and training.
- Product repair.
- Dealer management.
- Availability of spares.

AFTER SALES SUPPORT STARTS LONG BEFORE THE SALE

Although the focus of this book is After the Sale, the story starts long before then, as Figure 1–1 (*see* p. 3) illustrates. Many companies today are learning that the only way to manage quality is to ensure that it is designed into products and processes from the outset. The focus here is often not only that the capability and demands of the product manufacturing process will be incorporated in design philosophy, but also that service and support requirements must be considered at this stage

Caterpillar set increasingly tough targets for the time needed to dismantle an assembly to replace a wearing part. Rank Xerox realized that the service engineer might effectively rebuild the photocopier a number of times, and, therefore, the emphasis should now shift from manufacturability to serviceability.

In some industry sectors, of course, the service task has changed because as products have become so reliable, service requirements have very much reduced. This change is particularly true in the electronics sector where Mean Time Between Failure (MTBF) may be as great as four years when compared with the economic lifetime for the product of eight years. The product therefore requires repair only once in its life, and the emphasis now moves to design for supportability, where aspects such as ease of use and speed of training are considered.

AFTER SALES SUPPORT AT THE POINT OF SALE

It was stated earlier that professional customer service and support may make the difference in the purchase decision. This assertion has been true for much of the computer industry and the photocopier industry for some years. The electrical retailer Comet has recently emphasized the existence of its own after sales service as a selling point that differentiates it from other high street chains.

A problem may arise when sales staff, overeager to make a sale, overpromise. "Of course our service engineers can respond within 1 hour!" and of course, the reality is very far from this. The sad thing is that there may have been no need for this overpromise in the first place. A promise that the customer will not believe is not required, while confidence that the customer will not be abandoned but supported at reasonable cost is required.

Many customer service and support organizations are now presenting a tailored approach at the time of sale to develop a package that reflects that the same level of service may not be required throughout the customer's business. Providing the highest level of service only to the critical points may be cost effective to customer and support organization alike.

INTEGRATING PRODUCT DESIGN AND CUSTOMER SERVICE AND SUPPORT

Unfortunately, it is all too common for products to be designed without any regard for how they are to be supported after the sale. A detail of design that may save a small amount in production costs may cost the organization far more in support costs. But we have also discovered that many organizations also commit the opposite error, designing customer service and support strategies as if the product itself was almost incidental or assuming that one standardized approach will work well for all products.

Figure 1–2 illustrates some of the ways that product design and customer service and support strategies can combine to meet differing requirements. The concept is based on three product determinants:

Purchase price. This is the initial price or cost of ownership of the product. Low cost purchases are likely to be replaced on failure, high value goods are more likely to be repaired. Lifetime costs are likely to be considered by purchasers of high cost products.

Reliability index. We define this as the inverse of the number of times the product will fail in its expected, or economic, lifetime. Thus, this Index will have a value of unity for those disposable products that the customer is happy to discard on failure. It will approach unity for some high-value products in critical areas and therefore designed for reliability first and cost

FIGURE 1-2
Integrating Product Strategy and Support Strategy

Reliability index $\left(\dfrac{Economic\ lifetime}{MTBF}\right)$	Purchase Price	Cost of Customer to Downtime	Product Design Philosophy	Customer Support Task	Example
$\dfrac{6\ months}{6\ months} = 1$	Low	Low	Low cost Design for manufacture	Replacement, or warranty claims Complaint management Distribution support	Ballpoint pen
$\dfrac{8\ years}{4\ years} = 2$	Medium/high	Medium/high	Reliability Features Ease of use	Customer training Rapid service response if required Predictive maintenance	Medical electronics
$\dfrac{7\ years}{1\ year} = 7$	Medium	Medium	Serviceability Value engineering Lifting	Cost-effective service Spares policy Dealer managements	Automobiles
$\dfrac{36\ months}{1\ month} = 36$	Medium	High	Serviceability Modularization for replacement	Rapid response Customer involvement Network management	Photocopier

second, or having those products relatively few mechanical parts and so are inherently reliable.

Cost of downtime to the customer. This may be measured in financial loss or perhaps may include some estimate of annoyance or inconvenience where the customer depends on the product. Thus, a pen that fails is unlikely to cause financial loss or great inconvenience to the customer as alternatives are almost always available, allowing the customer to cope until a refill is purchased. On the other hand, a manufacturer may depend on a particular machine, and any downtime will reduce profitability.

Figure 1–2 illustrates a few common scenarios that show how product design and customer service and support tasks must combine. It is important to recognize that there are a number of strategies to be adopted. There is no single right way to serve the customer because a company may have a number of products, ranging from low to high price, with varying degrees of reliability and criticality. Although the service and support organization will develop its own style and broad philosophy for customer service and support, the detail of the task can and must change from product to product and possibly from customer to customer.

It should be noted that products change over time, and thus support strategies must reflect such changes. A particular situation to be aware of is increasing reliability as products mature. If the increase in reliability is dramatic, as in many electronically based products, the organization must recognize the point where the emphasis must change from being focussed on service and repair, through to customer service and support.

One of the objectives of this book is to enable managers to analyze their own situation to develop a coherent service and support strategy that matches the broad goals of the organization.

For a service and support strategy to be managed effectively, we believe that it is critical for many organizations to recognize that service and support is a major business activity alongside finance, marketing, and manufacturing. Indeed, we have seen the appointment of some service directors to the main boards of companies as they recognize the need to coordinate the customer service and support activities throughout the organization.

Some key activities are:

- Developing a financial and strategic assessment of the value of customer service and support to the long-term success of the organization.
- Ensuring that the requirements of service and support receive sufficient priority in product design and manufacturing.
- Developing a source of information about customer need and perceptions for business development.
- Communicating the changing nature of the service and support task to the business.
- In many cases, managing the service and support function as a business in its own right.

THE CUSTOMER SERVICE TRIANGLE

We have found the customer service triangle, developed by Albrecht and Zemke, to be useful in providing a framework for the first review of support activities (Figure 1–3).

The customer is at the center of this triangle because every activity must be seen in its impact on customer satisfaction, understanding how the customer views the organization's performance rather than accepting an internal view. The following points illustrate how a customer service and support organization can apply practices and principles to the service triangle.

Strategies. The customer service and support manager must develop realistic statements about the role of support, the way that it is to be measured, and the priorities for improvement. The strategy must express the value of service and support to the customer and identify those aspects that create a competitive advantage for the organization. It must be said that a strategy is not a wish list but a fully resourced statement of intent.

Systems. Having clarified the strategy, the systems employed by the customer service and support organization must be reviewed in light of any changes in content or emphasis in the service task. Systems to control quality, information, materials, and productivity are included here. A principle to be observed is to ensure that key measures that have significant impact on customer

FIGURE 1–3
The Service Triangle (Albrecht and Zemke)

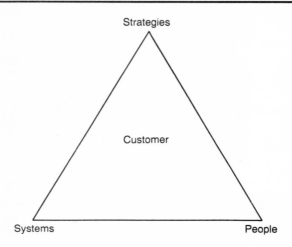

satisfaction, as for example response time, are consistently achieved because the system has sufficient capacity to do so.

People. The people are those who deliver the service. They will be more effective if they are aware of the scope of the task, and this can be achieved through a consistent service strategy. They will be committed to it if they have had the opportunity to contribute to its formulation. The service providers will also be more effective if thc systems used help rather than prevent service.

The Service Provider–Customer Team. Customer perceptions of service quality are generally enhanced where there is a bond between provider and customer. The provider will tend to try harder because the customer is appreciative, and the customer may be more forgiving of detail problems because it is apparent that the provider is trying hard.

The aim of this book is to look at the elements of this customer service triangle and to allow the reader to identify actions under each category that must be taken if the performance of the customer service and support organization is to improve rather than deteriorate.

CUSTOMER SERVICE AND SUPPORT STRATEGY

Strategy formulation is very much about direction, and the strategy compass Figure 1–4 is a powerful way for us to look at the direction and health of the business. All businesses compete on perceived added value (PAV) in the eyes of customers and price. If there is no perceived added value, then price is the only means of competition. Increasing PAV may command higher prices, but it is also likely to bring with it higher operating costs to provide enhancements.

The strategy compass shows direction of movement against axes of PAV and price. Looking at the four primary directions in Figure 1–4, note the following trends:

1. *North*–Increasing PAV without increasing the price. Consequently, there must be a reduction in some operational costs to support the cost of increasing PAV if margins are not to fall.

2. *East*—Increasing price without increasing PAV. This move is dangerous since customers will realize what is happening sooner or later and look for another supplier.

3. *South*—Decreasing PAV while holding price constant. Again, this move is dangerous as a continuing strategy since customers will look elsewhere for other service providers.

4. *West*—Holding PAV constant while decreasing price. This strategy needs an increase in efficiency and, hence, lower costs to be sustained—hoping for increased volume with a decreased margin.

Any movement into the southeast quadrant brings with it the threat of long-term failure. Movement into the northwest quadrant requires increases in efficiencies to deliver increased PAV, while reducing the price.

If we set our company at the center of the compass, we can then position the other players in the sector relative to it and discuss the consequences for adopting strategies in different directions on

FIGURE 1–4
The Strategy Compass

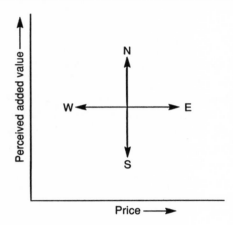

PAV and price. If we choose to move from the central position, care has to be taken because we may be moving into a completely different market sector. We can illustrate this with a simple example. If a pizza chain moves upmarket into the area of a cordon bleu restaurant or downmarket into the fast-food business, it will have to reassess its PAV relative to the competitors in the new sectors.

DO YOU KNOW YOUR SERVICE TASK?

Achieving of the goals set by our strategic direction can only be put into operation if we know our service task, which lays out the things we need to do well in service delivery. The service task is the link between the competitive strategy and the service delivery structure, systems, processes, and people, and is made up of four elements.

1. *Customer Service Dimensions*

Service and support organizations need to be clear on two aspects of customer service: the factors that give competitive advantage and are customer catching, and the factors that a customer might expect to find in an equivalent customer service and support operation. Hygiene factors are those elements of service and support that customers assume we will deliver, such as knives and forks in a restaurant. If expected levels of service for hygiene factors are not met, a loss of business might result. We use the customer service profile (Figure 1–5) as a means of evaluating both the competitive factors and sensitive hygiene factors, and to establish how well they are being delivered relative to the competition.

The profile includes a generic list of customer service and support dimensions, although others can be added for specific organizations. The process is in four stages:

1. Decide the main dimensions from the list that give competitive advantage by differentiation and allocate 100 marks among them. We find it is usual to have only four or five dimensions and to award not less than 10 marks to any one dimension.

2. Decide which are the most sensitive hygiene factors and mark these with an "H". Hygiene factors carry a mark of zero on the scoring as they do not contribute to competitive performance.

3. Assess current performance relative to the main competitors on a scale from −3 to +3 for both the competitive and hygiene factors. Establishing the weighting will often call for the use of marketing information gathered as part of marketing monitoring for a customer satisfaction index (see Chapter 5).

4. Arithmetically multiply the weighting scores by current performance to give a total score for the customer service dimension. Hygiene factors score zero since they do not lead to differentiation and perceived added value.

We will need to have a service delivery system that is capable of meeting the competitive customer service dimensions consistently while ensuring that we do not fall down on the hygiene dimensions like response and spares availability in Figure 1–5.

FIGURE 1–5
Customer Service Dimensions Profile

Attribute	Weight (W)*	Competitive position (R)
PRODUCT	☐	☐
Reliability (MTBF)	40	+1
Response (MTTR)	H	0
Warranty	10	−1
Serviceability		
Instalability		
Price		
SUPPORT	☐	☐
Customer training	20	+1
Consultancy		
Documentation	10	−1
Advice		
SERVICE	☐	☐
Maintenance contract	10	−1
Time to fix	H	+1
Service price		
Spares availability	H	0
Flexibility of response		
(Standard v. Gold Star)		
PROCESS	☐	☐
Ease of contract		
Customer feeling in control		
Customer care		
Service personnel	10	+1
Responsiveness		
Trust/confidence		
Vans		
TOTAL	100	

Rating relative to competitors
−3   −2   −1   0   +1   +2   +3
Inferior   On Par   Superior

*Hygiene factor W = 0

2. *Demand Dimensions*

We need to know the demand for service and support so that we can plan the capacity of the resources needed to match demand at the customer service level we want to achieve and also at costs we can afford. We have found it useful to think about demand in three ways:

1. The volume of demand over time (e.g. 3000 calls per month).

2. The variety of services, such as preventive maintenance, upgrades, breakdowns.

3. The variation in the nature and the volume of demand with time. For example, preventive maintenance is constant throughout the year, breakdowns tend to peak in the winter months and in the early part of the week, and upgrades come intermittently throughout the year.

3. *Efficiency Targets*

Anyone can deliver good service at any cost. However, the world is not so generous, and service and support managers must give good customer service and meet productivity targets set for them. Typical targets may be number of calls per day for an engineer, productivity time for an engineer, or inventory turns for spares.

4. *Constraints*

In this element of the service task, we capture major constraints that make life difficult but are not within the power of the customer service and support manager to change such as inadequate information systems.

We have found that service managers who know the service task for each segment of their market (something we will talk about in Chapter 4) are more successful than those who are vague about it.

In our work with service and support organizations, we have found that the best ones review each facet of their operations. They are clear about the strategic direction to be adopted and the way that the success of their strategies can be measured. The best organizations are not content with the current performance but are seeking to improve it.

Service and support cannot be effectively managed in isolation from the rest of the business, and the demands of customer service and support must be an integral part of the programs and the thinking of the other management disciplines.

KEY ACTIONS

1. Write down the role of customer service and support in your organization.
2. Write down the value of customer service and support in your organization.
3. List any changes in customer service and support you see taking place because of changes in products or markets.
4. Plot your organization and your main competitors for your main product on the strategic compass and indicate the direction of movement.
5. List the elements of the service task for your main product groups.
6. List the implications for your service task of the direction of movement for you on the strategic compass.
7. Identify all the people in your organization who should be involved as part of a team to review your customer service and support strategy.

Chapter Two

Structures for Customer Service and Support

Introduction

In this chapter we introduce the structures for customer service and support operations and explain the characteristics of each. We describe how customer service and support operations change their structures over time and name the main reasons that cause the changes.

ARE WE IN CONTROL OF THE STRUCTURE?

The structure of the organization we have for delivering customer service and support has a great influence on our ability to achieve the aims of a service and support strategy. This strategy includes satisfying the needs of our customers and meeting our own goals for costs and quality. Getting the right structure requires a knowledge of the service and support strategy and the choices open to us for the service and support organizational structure. Just as in the formulation of service and support strategy, it is important for us to make definite choices, which is more likely to happen when customer service and support is regarded as an important element of the business rather than a necessary evil.

A Service and Support Story

Let us see what often happens for a manufacturing company. Spec Pumps, making electrical pumps, was set up by a group of engineers who left one of the major pump manufacturers to develop and market a range of specialist pumps for use in the oil industry. Initially the support and service was given by the owners, who had designed the product and so knew the capabilities of the product inside out. The company was successful, and the pumps started to be used by all the major oil companies. Now the original owners found they could no longer spend a lot of their time on customer service and support because they were involved in other areas of the business.

A decision was made to recruit a team of engineers who would carry out the service and support activity. Some were recruited from their competitors, while others came from outside the industry. The company spent time and money training the new team. Also, with the growth of the business they found they had to locate the team in several geographical locations. Now they started to get requests from their major customers for training of their own engineers to be able to carry out their own servicing.

Spec Pumps continued to be successful in the market and introduced new ranges of pumps that had a wider use in other industrial sectors. After exhibiting pumps at several trade fairs they found they were being approached by some suppliers of industrial equipment, and they saw this as an opportunity to start to sell through agents. One or two of the agents already offered a service arrangement to their customers and were keen to include the servicing of Spec Pumps products in their offering. Spec Pumps was happy to go along with this arrangement, as by this time customer service and support resources were under pressure.

Finally the customer service and support manager, who had by this time taken over in Spec Pumps, became aware that an increasing number of the major companies were looking for companies who could service not only the products they supplied, but also pumps supplied by other manufacturers. Also, competition for this work was coming from companies who were not manufacturers themselves but who offered service and support for a range of products from different manufacturers.

So now Spec Pumps was faced with customers supported and products serviced by a mix of different types of people. There were Spec Pumps' own service engineers sometimes assisted by the experts in the company when things went wrong, by some of the customers' engineers, by their agents, and finally by outside specialist service companies. The question is "Was Spec Pumps in control of what was happening to its customer support?"

The Showdown

Spec Pumps was surprised to find that in a survey carried out by a trade magazine rankings for customer service and support were much lower than expected. A committee set up an internal investigation as well as one of the company's customers and agents. They found that their own engineers were aware of a growing unhappiness with their performance. Routine maintenance was not being carried out and breakdowns were becoming more frequent. Agents were complaining about the way Spec Pumps was supporting them, spares were not available when needed, and delivery was unreliable. Customers spoke of the good service they had experienced from Spec Pumps in the past but now felt they could not reach the company when they were in trouble and had, on many occasions, turned to other third party service companies to help them out. They considered Spec Pumps' service to be expensive for what they received and were considering switching future purchases to other manufacturers. Matters came to a head when Spec Pumps launched a new range of pumps that were not well received, one of the main criticisms being that the company seemed to take no account of faults in the earlier products.

Clearly, Spec Pumps had not given enough thought to the consequences of the way in which delivery of customer support had changed over time for staff and for customers. Costs of the provision of the service and support seemed high for the revenues generated, and there was no payoff in revenues and profits from the operation. Also measurement of performance was not good enough for the company to be clear of the true position. The time had come to rethink and understand what had happened.

THE MILITARY MODEL

Before we are in a position to make choices about which is the best structure for delivering customer support, we need to understand the different ways in which this activity can be organized. We have found it useful to use military terms to describe five different structures. Each of the structures has strengths and weaknesses, and we will try to bring these out as we describe each in turn. The structures are based on the service delivery.

The terms we have used are based on groups in the British Army as follows:

1. The SAS—A commando unit sent into difficult situations to operate on its own initiative.
2. The Regulars—Rank and file soldiers.
3. The Territorials—These are part-time soldiers, trained by us, but only devoting part of their working life to the army.
4. The Mercenaries—These are on your side, but only because we pay them. Their prime motivation is money.
5. The Enemies—The competition!

The SAS (Special Air Services)

The SAS, a group of highly specialized engineers, know the products in great detail from design to the way in which they are used. Some of the group may have been involved in the original design of the product or in using the products in the field. Also, they may have worked with competitors' products. Examples of the SAS would be microprocessor specialists and CNC machine tool engineers.

Strengths of the SAS

- Highly skilled, often graduate engineers.
- Motivated to learn about new products.
- Able to work together in teams to solve problems, although they tend to be loners.
- Committed to support of the product to maintain uptime.
- Interested in improving the performance of the product.
- Able to appreciate the need for design changes in the product.

Weaknesses of the SAS

- An expensive resource.
- A limited resource at times of growth in the market.
- Often more interested in the product than in supporting the customer.
- More focused on solutions than on the control of costs.
- Sometimes difficult to manage.

The Regulars

The Regulars are the service engineers who are able to carry out routine activities of repair and maintenance. They are often dispersed at several locations to be close to customers. Service engineers operating from a service center and traveling to customers in a service van that contains a range of equipment and spares are typical of the Regulars. Examples of Regulars are photocopier engineers, telecommunications engineers, and field engineers for utilities.

Strengths of the Regulars

- A visible sign of the company for customers.
- Trained in the service and application of the company's products.
- Able to train the customers in the use of the product.
- May be better at customer management than the SAS.
- More customer contact, so they are able to identify sales leads.

Weaknesses of the Regulars

- Costly resource because of their numbers and the facilities needed to house them and their equipment.
- Consistency of service delivery may vary across the whole service network.
- May be more interested in the service of the product rather than support of the customers.

- May be less likely to be committed to taking ownership of problems and achieving targets like first-time fix and product uptime.
- Problems of motivation and career progression.

The Territorials

The Territorials are the engineers or specialists in the customers' own service and maintenance organizations who are the customers for the products. They carry out some, if not all, of the service activities on the product, but they need support with training, availability of spares, and information and advice from the original supplier. Many large organizations still retain central maintenance departments, for example, manufacturers who repair machinery, hospitals who employ buyer/engineers who purchase and maintain capital equipment, and public utilities who also service their own equipment.

Strengths of the Territorials

- They know how the product is being used in their company.
- Able to carry out maintenance at a time when the equipment is available, which helps to decrease downtime.
- They are committed to high uptime of the product in use.
- They may be committed to long-term use of the supplying company's product if they are well supported.
- They cost the supplying company little in the service of the products, but costs may be incurred by having, for instance, a support engineer located permanently in the organization.

Weaknesses of the Territorials

- They may not be committed to long-term use of the products from the supplying company if they are not well supported.
- They need training in the service aspects of the products by the supplying organization both initially and as products are upgraded and engineers change.
- They may not give feedback on inherent design faults in the products that affect serviceability and performance.
- They may be affected by union restrictions, for example, mechanical fitters not being able to touch electrical connections.

The Mercenaries

The Mercenaries are the agents and dealers who both sell the products and offer service and support to the customers. The Mercenaries may do these activities just for one supplier or act for a number of suppliers, depending on the products and the industry sector. The higher the price of the products the more likely they will act for only one supplier. For example, the dealers for heavy earth-moving equipment are tied to main manufacturers such as Caterpillar, Komatsu, or JCB, whereas dealers for white and brown goods, washing machines, fridges, televisions, and videos will act for a number of suppliers. In between, the car dealers may or may not act for more than one supplier. Here the trend is toward single supplier agents.

Strengths of the Mercenaries

- They can give wide geographical coverage for customer support.
- They may know the needs of their own customers very well through local market knowledge.
- They are tied to the supplier company by contract.
- They present a lower direct cost to the supplying firm.
- They allow rapid expansion of the network by using someone else's money. This funding can be very important for international expansion.

Weaknesses of the Mercenaries

- They may not be committed to the supplying firm's products or targets for levels of customer service and support.
- They need resources from the supplying company to manage them. This help may be from marketing and sales or from a separate customer service function. If there is no clear responsibility for the control of dealers and agents, problems can result.
- They need training in the servicing of the product and in its application.
- They may not give reliable feedback to the supplying firm on the performance of the product in field operation.

- They are often limited in management expertise. They may be good dealers but limited at service and support.

The Enemies

The Enemies are the third party operators who provide customer support for a range of products like computers, local garages for automobiles, and local electrical repairers for brown and white goods. While they provide service and support for products, they are, for the most part, beyond the control of the original manufacturer. Often they will not be known to the original manufacturer. Their performance, however will change on the customer's view of the product.

Strengths of the Enemies

- If they have originally worked for the supplying firm or have had good experience with their products, they may be committed to the products over time.
- They may be able to provide support and service for products that are no longer manufactured.
- They present no cost to the supplying firm for customer support and service except for the costs associated with managing the mercenaries themselves.
- We may still derive some revenue from the activities of the enemies by way of the sale of spares.
- They may be the only alternative in areas where service intensity is very low.

Weaknesses of the Enemies

- They may have no commitment to the original supplier and may comment unfavorably to the customers.
- They give little or no feedback to the supplying firm on the performance of the product in the field.
- They may take revenue for customer support from the original supplier by direct competition.
- They may be incompetent and give a poor image of the product.

DO WE HAVE A CHOICE OF STRUCTURE?

We can see that Spec Pumps ended up with products being supported by a mixture of all the military structures. Did the company want this to happen? Even if it did we saw that it brought with it problems and costs and possible loss of future sales. So while there may be choices, we can also see that there may be pressures that make it difficult to keep in control—even when there is a commitment to customer service and support.

What then are the main reasons that cause organizations to change their mix of support provision? We think that the overriding influence is the change in service intensity or service demand. What do we mean by service intensity? It is the number of separate service or support events per unit of time for all customers and all products that a service and support organization has to deal with. Typically, service intensity may be measured by the number of calls per day into a response center.

As with Spec Pumps we find that customer service organizations might start off using the SAS structure, but as the service intensity increases they have to incorporate some Regulars if they want to deliver the customer support themselves. If by design or default there is no customer support offered, customers are left to DIY and act as Territorials or, if the sector is attractive enough, Enemies take over.

Even when the customer service and support is kept in-house, however, there may be a move to the use of Mercenaries to do the job of customer support if the service intensity increases rapidly. These changes can occur without the organization thinking through the consequences, as the Spec Pumps example illustrates.

If service intensity is so important, we need to understand the reasons that cause it to change over time.

HOW DO WE USE THE MILITARY MODEL?

The Military Model is about change. We can probably quickly identify where we are currently positioned; however, what will happen in the future? What changes can we see that will affect either our wish to alter our level of in-house control or the level of service intensity we need to deal with? Later we examine some of the reasons we see as being drivers for in-house control and which influence service intensity.

For the moment, however, one factor that we do recognize as being important in determining structure for customer service and support relates to the stage of a product in its life cycle. It is recognized that all products and services go through four stages in a life cycle: launch, establishment, maturity, and decline. We could see that in the launch and establishment stages we would wish to have the SAS/Regular structure. This structure would perhaps be carried on into maturity, although at this stage we might be discussing the merit of relinquishing in-house control to Mercenaries, and perhaps in decline leaving everything to the Enemies.

WHAT INFLUENCES SERVICE INTENSITY?

If we are to be in control of our own destiny for customer support, we need to understand the factors that influence changes in service intensity. We can see service intensity being affected by five main factors:

1. The product(s).
2. The type of service and support.
3. The user.
4. The service and support personnel.
5. The internal support for the customer service and support function.

Let us look at the influence of each of these in turn.

The Product(s)

The products will affect the service intensity in a number of ways.

- The initial price of the product will determine if there is a tendency to replace the product when it fails or service it. We have found there is a cutoff point at about $1,520 between the two, with more expensive and probably more complex items being serviced. Increased servicing will tend to increase service intensity.

- The complexity of the product will tend to bring with it increases in service intensity for both customer support and service requirements.
- The more reliable a product, the lower the service intensity. We have seen in some sectors a dramatic reduction in service intensity over the years. Mainframe computers and medical instruments are good examples of this trend.
- The newness of a product in the field will tend to drive up service intensity, especially if faults that have a safety implication are discovered. An electrical supplier found a fault in a newly launched storage heater and had to repair the fault in 5,000 heaters already installed in customers' premises within five days.
- The initial price as compared to lifetime costs for the product has an effect in the following way. If our customers are willing to pay more for a better and more reliable system, it might, in the long run, save them money in callout costs and reduce the service intensity. A security company found that as it had to compete more on price it was forced to use cheaper components in its alarm systems which were more prone to failure; hence, there was an increased service intensity for them.
- How much operation of the product is dependent on other products not sold by the supplier can increase service intensity. A failure reported to a computer company may be caused by other equipment in a network for which it is not responsible.

The Type of Customer Service and Support

By type of service and support we mean what is offered to the customer. Important elements of service and support that have an effect on service intensity are:

- The type of warranty that is given with the product. The more comprehensive the warranty the more it is likely that customers will need service and support.
- How much preventive maintenance is carried out as part of a service contract will influence the incidence of failure and, hence, service intensity.

- The use of remote sensing and diagnosis, as well as remote fixing, will tend to reduce service intensity on service engineers by cutting the need for them or by increasing the chance of first-time fix. Consequently, service intensity will fall.
- Use of additional support like help lines to give quick solutions to problems that could otherwise escalate and consume more resources.

The Users

The users, as all customer support managers appreciate, have a great influence on the service intensity. Some of the main aspects we need to consider are:

- How much users have to be trained in the use of the product. The higher the chance of users not doing what they should do, the higher the service intensity. Users changing over time adds to this problem. Whereas the original user may have been trained as part of an initial installation, commissioning, or sales activity, the newcomer is a novice, and things go wrong more often or more advice is needed. Also, with many users, for example, photocopiers, the role of the key operator becomes important as the main link with the service and support activity.
- The cost of a service call to the user will influence the propensity to call the support organization.
- The location of the product in a user's premises may lead to difficulties for the service personnel in finding the equipment. This situation can lead to repeat visits and, hence, increased service intensity.

The Service and Support Personnel

The way in which service and support personnel approach their task and their commitment to meeting service levels affects service intensity in the following ways:

- Competence of personnel to perform the full range of tasks without calling for unplanned assistance is important. The service function of a major utility company found that at a time when it had a large proportion of new service engineers the service intensity rose because of a reduction in the achievement of first-time fix.
- The commitment by service personnel to first-time fix may be influenced by the way in which service and support personnel are rewarded. Many service organizations we have looked at measure performance of their personnel on calls per day without any reference to whether these achieved first-time fix. Poor achievement of first-time fix tends to drive up service intensity and, of course, adds cost through overtime charges.
- The commitment of service personnel to ownership and resolution of problems affects service intensity. The personnel giving support on software and hardware problems in a response center originally worked as individuals handling a number of enquiries from customers. There was a tendency for them to keep some jobs on the go for many days until they were resolved. The result was many additional calls from the customers inquiring about progress. Reorganization of the personnel into teams gained common ownership and a faster resolution of problems so reducing service intensity.

The Internal Support

The ability of the rest of the organization to support the service and support operation will influence service intensity because:

- Poor supply of spares will frustrate the achievement of first-time fix and raise service intensity.
- Poor supply of information on product use or customer records will mean increased contact with the customers or users for each service or support incident. This lack has implications for the way in which the design and manufacturing, and marketing sales and accounts functions are linked to the customer support and service activity.

From this list of factors that influence service intensity we can highlight the following four points in summary:

1. Service intensity for a particular product should decrease as the product design evolves over time, so the product becomes inherently more reliable. Many customer service and support companies for consumer products and the low value end of capital goods target and track the level of service intensity.

2. Service intensity would be expected to increase with the number of products in the field and the variety of products.

3. Service intensity will be expected to increase with failure to achieve first-time fix.

4. Service intensity is affected for many support and service providers by how much planned maintenance can be carried out to prevent subsequent failures.

WHY SHOULD WE WANT TO CONTROL CUSTOMER SERVICE AND SUPPORT?

We have seen that there are a large number of factors that change service intensity. However much each factor alters service intensity, either causing increases or reductions, the overall effect for many organizations is for service intensity to increase over time. Like Spec Pumps, they start to use a mixture of the military structures. Spec Pumps problems were due to the loss of control of the customer service and support activity for their products. While they were using predominantly the SAS and Regulars structures, they had relatively good control; however, once they started to use the Mercenaries and then Enemies the control started to slip away from them.

So, are there good reasons why we might want to keep tight control over the customer service and support activity? We describe the control as in-house control. We have been able to identify some factors that firms talk about in relation to the level of in-house control. Essentially we are looking at those things that cause a company to look for a high level of in-house control and that cause problems as the level of control slips. Reasons for loss of in-house control may be intentional or because the business has taken its eye off the ball.

FACTORS DRIVING A WISH FOR HIGH IN-HOUSE CONTROL

Important reasons that cause organizations to look for high in-house control that we have seen in practice are:

- To be able to fulfill warranty obligations.
- The product is complex, so a high level of skill is required to give service and support.
- There is uncertainty about the performance of the product. Maybe it is in the early stages of launch, so all problems of field performance have not yet been identified.
- There are very real concerns about the threat to life in the event of product failure.
- The firm has decided that its competitive strategy includes the delivery of strong service and support, and it wants to project this as its image.
- The firm wishes to maintain close contact with its customers and users of the products to gain feedback on performance that can be incorporated into future designs.
- The firm wishes to maintain close contact with customers to protect future sales.

IS IT TO BE THE SAS, REGULARS, TERRITORIALS, MERCENARIES, OR THE ENEMIES?

How can a firm decide which is the best structure for customer service and support activities, given the demands for in-house control and the effects of service intensity? We use the framework shown in Figure 2–1 that shows the relationship between service intensity and the level of in-house control for the military structures for customer service and support.

We have found in practice that firms that lie in the area of high in-house control and with relatively low service intensity exhibit the following characteristics:

1. The volume of products to be supported in the field is relatively low.

FIGURE 2–1
Customer Support Organization

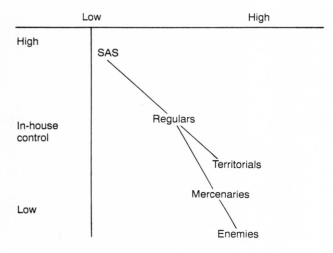

2. Service is carried out either by the manufacturer's own personnel, that is to say, a mixture of SAS and Regulars, or by the customers' staff, Territorials, who have been trained by the manufacturer.

3. The cost of the service and support is relatively high.

4. The quality, experience, and technical competence of personnel employed is higher than those required for high-volume products.

5. Time factors are very important for service levels. First-time fix, time to fix and rapid response are all important.

6. Additional services that add value to the service and support such as customer training, education, and consultancy are commonly part of the package.

7. Marketing of the service and support where it actively takes place emphasizes professional competence.

In contrast we have found firms who have low in-house control and have high service intensity exhibit the following characteristics:

1. The number of products to be supported is high both in variety and in the volume of the individual products.

2. There is a shift to the use of third-party service and support providers, the Mercenaries, with the emphasis placed on supporting the agents or dealers rather than the end customers or users.

3. Distribution networks for the sale of the products are highly developed.

4. High volume and low-priced products are designed for replacement rather than repair. Where service is still required and economic, products are designed to simplify and speed up the service task.

5. Service in the form of customer care and support is seen as the route towards competitive advantage. The emphasis is more on the way that service and support are delivered, that is, the process, rather than on the content of the service and support package.

6. The total organization is larger, and the delivery of service and support to the end customer or user more complex. Consequently, more effort is given to thinking through a strategy for the operation to try to get better control over the activity.

As we have seen, the tendency is for service intensity to increase for a particular company, and consequently, for it to move down the diagonal in Figure 2–1. This move results in a loss of in-house control by adding Mercenaries to the service and support provision. The trade-off for this loss is a reduction in costs of providing the level of customer service and support that is borne by the company.

We have found that the most powerful use of the framework is to consider future events that might change either the level of service intensity or the level of in-house control that might be needed. We have seen instances of organizations who have made a conscious decision to increase in-house control despite a current high level of service intensity.

It is perhaps helpful to look at the experience of some organizations that are typical of what we have seen recently.

A Consumer Products Manufacturer

This company produces largely high-volume consumer products with the addition of some more specialized products for the professional market. Its service and support function was, at best, average.

Immediate contact with consumers is limited as most products are purchased from major retailers or discount stores. The company had a limited range of repair workshops to handle repairs, but these were mostly to be found in inconvenient locations. Other service activities were handled by appointed agents, and some repairs were carried out by the customers.

The company decided it wanted to differentiate itself on customer service and support. It put together a three-year plan. The repair shops were moved into better locations and renamed Service Centers, staff members were trained, and the facilities were given a consistent image.

By taking these actions, the company was attempting to increase the level of in-house control by reducing the dependence on Mercenaries and loss of business to Enemies. At the same time the morale of the Regulars already employed was raised. It was realized that these changes could not be achieved without incurring extra costs. Higher productivity targets were set specifically for inventory.

A Domestic Goods Manufacturer

Some years ago this manufacturer was under significant cost competition and saw an opportunity to cut costs, allowing service agents around the country to take responsibility for customer service and support. The customer service and support function was cut to a minimum.

It was soon discovered that this decision left service to be controlled by Mercenaries and Enemies, which, although cheaper in the short term, was disastrous for customer service. The long-term quality costs were tending to rise, and most of the service agents no longer held the more expensive spares, so customer downtime was dramatically increased.

The company has moved to bring the support activity back to a role for Regulars and Mercenaries, who are closely controlled.

A Capital Goods Manufacturer

This company supplies a wide range of precision instruments to research and other professional institutions. Its products are largely differentiated by their performance, and the customer service and support operation is recognized for its expertise. The customer service and support requires highly qualified engineers, so the structure is toward the SAS area.

The threat to this company comes from Mercenaries and Enemies, who at one stage were possibly employed and trained by the company. These groups may offer a lower cost service to a narrow range of customers. The danger for the customers is the equipment may not be fully maintained. This danger may be hidden, however, from those who make decisions about service contracts as they are not the users of the equipment. The decision makers are largely driven by cost constraints.

The company must maintain control of the service and support activities because there are safety implications if the equipment is faulty. This problem has required the company to concentrate on supplementing the technical expertise of the SAS group with inter-personal skills to reinforce the support aspect.

A Computer Manufacturer

This company's traditional business has been in the manufacture of mainframe and minicomputers with a strong customer service and support operation for after sales service and support. The company has relied on a mix of SAS and Regulars to deliver the customer service and support.

The move by the company into PCs and other peripherals increased the number of products in the field, which potentially increased service intensity. The cost of increasing the SAS/Regular organization would have been difficult in the short term and also probably uneconomical because of the lower contract charges. Consequently, the company turned to the Mercenaries structure and delivered the customer service and support through a network of agents, most of whom were responsible for the sale of the original equipment.

The change in the way in which the company delivers its total customer service and support activities has meant learning new skills in managing the Mercenaries to maintain the high standards associated with the company's original image.

KEY ACTIONS

1. Determine your current mix of service and support provision using the terms of the Military Model.
2. Identify any problems with your current mix of service and support provision.
3. List the factors you see that may significantly change the service intensity in the future.
4. List the factors you see that might cause you to want to change the degree of in-house control you exert over customer service and support to your customers or end users of your products.
5. Write down the ideal structure for your own company now and in the future.

Chapter Three

The Elements of Customer Service and Support

Introduction

In this chapter we describe the major areas of customer service and support in more detail, recognizing that not all elements will apply with equal force to every situation. Indeed, some may not apply at all—disposable products, for example, clearly do not require a repair service.

The position adopted by the organization on the Military Model (Chapter 2) will influence the degree of importance placed on each element. As this position shifts in response to changes in the service and support task the emphasis placed on each element will also change. In reading this chapter you should question whether the performance of your organization is to the standard required for your current competitive position.

In the chapter on service strategy, we described the approach to developing a customer service and support profile, identifying competitive and hygiene factors. These are grouped under four main headings:

1. Product related.
2. Service and repair related.
3. Support for the customer to use the product.
4. Process issues, describing how the customer is dealt with.

The product related issues are largely a matter for initial design, Mean Time Between Failure (MTBF) being determined at this stage. No classification is absolutely perfect, MTBF also being affected by the quality of service and repair. Indeed, we would encourage you to add dimensions to the original list if you believe they are critical to the performance of your organization.

In this chapter, therefore, we describe elements of customer service and support under the broad headings of time, maintaining uptime or availability for the customer, and support for customers. These descriptions should enable you to identify your competitive priorities.

THE DIMENSIONS OF TIME

Largely, all organizations are judged on their ability to respond quickly, whether it be the speed of acknowledgement of the presence of a customer need in the first instance, or the ability to deliver a completed service faster than the competition. The customer service and support manager will ignore the opportunity to improve time effectiveness at his peril.

Apart from the customer's perception of the organization is being influenced by time performance, the internal effectiveness of the organization will obviously be improved by better time productivity.

How Fast Is The First Response?

The first principle to be observed is surely that the customer must be able to make contact quickly and easily with the person who can deal with their request. Customers want to make one telephone call or write one letter and know that having made contact, their problem will be taken care of quickly and efficiently. In other words, customers want to know that they have no longer got a problem because the organization will deal with it.

Because we believe that managing customer contact is vital, we have devoted Chapter 6 to the subject of service delivery design. Following are some brief examples of effective approaches.

Toll-free or 800 telephone numbers.   These numbers are widely advertised to ensure that customers know how to contact the organization. The person answering the telephone will be able to deal with a wide range of inquiries from invoice problems to organizing response to breakdowns. It is likely that this person will be given basic product training as well as training in telephone techniques to boost customer confidence.

Customer help line.   This device is often employed by software suppliers who want their customers to have confidence that they will be able to use the product effectively from day one. For those who are not computer literate, it is, of course, important that the program will run, let alone be used to full power, and the support employee must deal sympathetically with what may seem trivial as well as deal with the more interesting technical problems.

Applications advice. For more complex products or systems it may be a selling point to be able to offer a "what do you need to get the required result" service prior to the sale. There is a real advantage to having this advice divorced as much as is feasible from the selling activity. There is an understandable fear that the salesman will oversell, whereas technical experts tend to be embarrassingly honest in what they say. This honesty may result in a smaller initial order, but it will probably yield long-term rewards.

Warranty claims. Many companies are now offering genuine money back guarantees. Doubtless a genuine, no strings attached, no quibble guarantee can build customer confidence that may tip the balance at the point of sale. For a consumer product, although we may wish they were not needed, warranties provide an excellent source of quality feedback, provided that customers are encouraged to complain.

Call back. Some service organizations make it routine to call back the customer as soon as possible after receiving the service request to give the estimated time of arrival of the engineer. This response reassures the customers that something is happening and assists them in organizing their time better. It is worth calling back relatively quickly even if nothing definite can yet be arranged, which may allow the customer to explore other options. This second approach is not recommended to be used frequently.

Two Examples of Initial Response

During a study tour investigating service quality in the United States, we visited the customer service telephone response center of Georgia Light and Power. To sustain rapid response, they have organized the staff into small teams, each led by a supervisor who is able to monitor how well each person is doing, assess the waiting time for calls yet to be answered, and who is available to deal with more difficult problems as the need arises. They have used a powerful blend of technology in the form of a computerized call management system, combined with effective human resource management in the shape of good teamwork, and strong management support and example. The end result is that customers can contact Georgia Light and Power quickly and easily with high levels of problem resolution.

The organization sometimes experiences problems as, for example. when storms bring down powerlines, which leads to a surge in calls inquiring about restoring of power. Although response center staff often come in voluntarily to cope with this temporary overload, the call waiting times tend to increase. To alleviate this load somewhat. a recorded message indicates that Georgia Light and Power is dealing with the problem and normal service will he resumed shortly.

There is a view that customer service departments are only good because the product is bad and somebody must deal with the resulting problems. Needless to say, this is not our view. All organizations must capitalize on each customer contact, knowing that there are relatively few opportunities to make a positive impression. This contact is particularly important for manufacturers of consumer goods, most of whom sell through intermediaries or retailers and rarely meet the final consumers.

For this sector, warranty claims must be well administered. We recently had some problems with a Britax child safety seat. Anyone who has had problems with a product knows that the thought of packing up the goods to send them back to the factory is probably enough to deter them from complaining. It is easier to go out and buy another (competitor's) product. Britax customer service was easy to contact and extremely helpful, promising a replacement would be delivered by courier two days later. All we needed to do then was to put the damaged seat in the replacement box and take it to the nearest post office. The replacement arrived on time, and we immediately noticed that the faulty area had been redesigned to prevent the problem from reoccurring. Two points emerge from this example. Britax made it clear that their warranty meant something, and it was easy to deal with them. Rapid feedback from customers has enabled them to respond to problems not discovered at the prototype stage, and this tends to build rather than destroy customer confidence.

Principles of Initial Response

The principles that can be drawn from these examples are:

- Make it easy for the customer to contact the right person to solve their problems quickly.
- Make sure that the customer knows that the problem will be taken care of as soon as possible.
- Make sure that you acknowledge the customer's presence as soon as possible.
- Make sure that you make a meaningful response as soon as is feasible, explaining what will happen, and when.

WHEN IS THE JOB COMPLETED?

Although the wish of all customers may be to own products that never break down, perfection is not yet within the grasp of many. Electronically based products are moving to a state where there are few if any repairs needed. For products that are mechanically based and relatively complex, some breakdowns may occur during the economic lifetime, but even so, the frequency of unforeseen problems is reducing rapidly, and many customer support providers would see the emphasis on preventive maintenance rather than dealing with failure.

There are some products that must never break down. These will include equipment such as life support machines and computers that control critical operations. The approach to this problem is to build *redundancy* into the products and systems. Thus, *never fail* computers have a number of boards that duplicate functions enabling the computer to continue operating at virtually full power even when a board has failed. In fact, it is part of the sales demonstration to remove boards as the machine is running, showing that nothing disastrous happens. Clearly, this type of product is expensive to manufacture and purchase.

Apart from relatively inexpensive consumer items, most products need some form of service, maintenance, or repair at intervals in their lifetime, although this interval may well be increasing.

The customer support manager must decide on the level of service support to be provided.

The Service Level Trade-Off

Successful managers will need to understand the trade-offs that currently exist. The customer may well wish for immediate service at very low cost, though most would probably agree that this is impractical. The danger with using the term *trade-off* is that it can imply that the organization is complacent, not wishing to improve. The consistently successful organizations are those that refuse to accept trade-offs and work hard to decrease them, while in the short term they understand how best to manage the trade-off to gain advantage.

The service manager must understand the customer's priorities. In setting the level of support to be provided, there are two cost dimensions to be considered:

- The cost of providing a higher level of service support to the customer.
- The cost to the customer of the product not being available, which, of course, includes an assessment of the likelihood of there being alternatives readily available. If the electric toaster fails, toast can still be made using the oven grill or perhaps by lighting a fire.

In other words, there comes a time when improving on service response time is either too expensive or irrelevant to the customer. Response times in the computer service industry provide a good example of the change that takes place over time. Over the last 20 years acceptable target response times have successively decreased from 24 hours to 8 hours and finally to 2 hours. We visited one company that set a target of 1 hour 20 minutes, and measured its average achievement at 1 hour 18 minutes.

In general, though, there is no real pressure now to decrease response times still further, the emphasis being on the ability of the service despatcher to give an accurate time of arrival on site, with all the necessary information and spares to be able to solve the problem in that one visit. In fact, there has been a distinct move toward a certain amount of response time "tailoring" to provide for rapid response to ensure maximum uptime in critical areas of the customer's business with lower level response elsewhere. This strategy enables the service organization to provide very rapid support where it matters most at a lower overall price to the customer. If relatively few sites are now designated as truly critical, this should allow sufficient focus to ensure key response times are maintained.

To ensure that there is no misunderstanding, we must emphasize that being able to quote an exact time of arrival does not mean that you can be as late as you like. Clearly there are still minimum response times to be achieved, but the message is that it is becoming less likely that you will gain competitive advantage beyond a given point by improving response.

Figure 3–1a shows a typical distribution of actual response times against a target time of four hours. Although the average performance may be acceptable at four hours, the spread of response means that some customers will receive an inferior service. By providing a split-level service as shown in Figure 3–1b, the average performance is unchanged, but customer-sensitive applications will be better supported. If this better premium service can be linked to a lower level of guaranteed response for non-critical applications, say five hours in this case, customer satisfaction levels should rise at marginal cost to the service provider.

Decreasing Service Times

Most service providers must find ways of decreasing their Mean Time To Repair (MTTR) for reasons of improving efficiency and increasing uptime for the customer.

The MTTR is an objective shared by all service providers, but it becomes a key task as overall demand on the customer support organization increases. Those service organizations that have vast armies of Regulars (service engineers) or depend for their service on a network of Mercenaries (dealers) are likely to set increasingly tight targets for MTTR and to devote significant effort to designing serviceability into the product.

In our 1987 survey of after sales service in United Kingdom manufacturing, we found that in the electronics sector, MTTRs averaged around two hours and that organizations were working

FIGURE 3–1a
Response Time Performance: Standard Four Hour Response

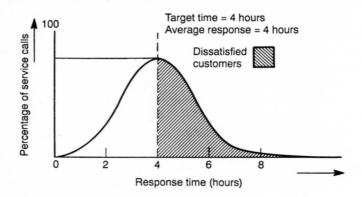

FIGURE 3–1b
Response Time Performance: Two-Level Response

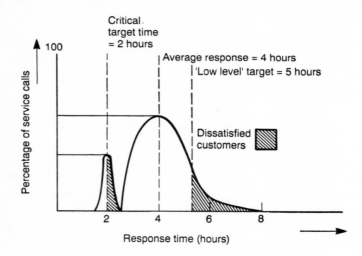

hard to decrease this still further. For more complex products, especially those with numbers of mechanical or electromechanical systems, MTTRs averaged over 14 hours, and some companies reported times considerably longer than these. An extreme MTTR value would be several months for something like a power station turbine or boiler overhaul.

Most manufacturers claim to consider service demands in finalizing designs, but a survey carried out by Keith Goffin in 1988 suggested that the scope of areas covered at the design stage varied dramatically and was often limited to improving product reliability. Unfortunately, much design for serviceability takes place at a relatively late stage in the process, and since the Pareto effect applies here such that 80 percent of the design is generally fixed after 20 percent of the design lead time, much so-called design for service and support is little more than a limited veto rather than a major element in the design philosophy.

The Caterpillar Tractor Company is one of the best examples of an organization that endeavors to give design for serviceability its true importance. Caterpillar sets increasingly demanding targets for the time taken to maintain its equipment or to replace a wearing component. It is surprising what can be achieved by quick release fasteners and by standardization when serviceability becomes a priority for the designer.

There is a trend to keep the product running by replacing modules or subassemblies rather than by repairing on site. This structure allows rapid repair, which for the industrial customer is often more important than cost. It is our view that this practice will tend to increase.

Centralized Service Functions or "Close to Customer"?

Most organizations are under cost pressure to centralize both materials and people. Many also have the problem of needing to support an ever-increasing range of products as new lines are introduced but the old ones remain, having given an assurance to support them for years after production has ceased.

It is unlikely that every service engineer will have the necessary expertise to carry out the full range of repairs on every piece of equipment. The trade-off to be managed here is that of cost of service provision versus a customer confidence factor of having service personnel close at hand. Some companies manage this trade-off by having regional organizations which are competent to tackle the majority of service problems but provide support from a central team of product specialists if there is the need for help to resolve more difficult problems.

As communication and distribution networks become evermore effective and products become more reliable, the continuing trend will be toward fewer regional service centers and more centralized service delivery. In this case, close attention must be paid to ensuring that customer confidence is maintained, perhaps by organizing equipment checkup visits even when all is well to maintain customer contact.

MAINTAINING MAXIMUM UPTIME

Perhaps it is an obvious statement that a customer has bought equipment or a system for use rather than for it to be always under repair. A recent advertisement for Citroen cars indicated the cars loved roads and hated garages. We think that in many industries this desire for more reliable, longer lasting products has not received the emphasis that perhaps it could. Some areas for management attention are discussed below

Increasing Reliability

Reliability is measured by MTBF. In our 1987 survey, the range of reliability was very wide indeed, ranging from as little as two months to 18 years. Alternatively, MTBF may be expressed in machine running time, our data indicating a range from 100 to 15,000 hours.

Where there are few mechanical parts, MTBFs may be quite high. In the medical electronics industry sector it is quite common for MTBFs to average four years, while the economic lifetime of such equipment is typically eight years. Thus, the equipment will break down once in its life. Service becomes less of an issue in this case, though rapid repair response is still critical where a hospital may have only one piece of equipment in its intensive care ward, and the consequence of lack of availability would be serious.

The example given may not yet be typical for all industries, but there is no doubt that this trend will be followed. As customers demand more reliable equipment and cheaper service, it may become more economic to use higher specification original equipment. A burglar alarm company discovered that a small premium paid for better quality sensors used in the initial installation dramatically reduced the cost of service given under its fixed-sum service contracts. The customers were happy because the system was more reliable, and the company incurred a lower cost overall. Cost systems must be sensitive enough to indicate overall savings rather than merely record unit costs that often indicate the wrong course of action.

Preventive Maintenance

Many customers are buying peace of mind when they take out a maintenance contract. Most companies can prove that more effective maintenance work will lead to fewer unforeseen failures, though there may still be a feeling that one shouldn't interfere with something that's working.

The reality may be that, although there is a belief that maintenance is a good thing, the short-term demands of delivery schedules mean that there is seldom space for it. We have known organizations that were too busy to carry out routine contracted maintenance because they were never able to get out of the vicious circle of breakdowns occurring, because the service work represented an overload on the department. The end result is, in the first instance, lost service revenue through not being able to charge, because contractual maintenance had not been carried out, and, more seriously, deteriorated reputation with customers.

There is no substitute for making a realistic capacity plan, which allocates resources to ensuring that maintenance, particularly when it is contracted, is carried out. This plan may demand that some time is spent with customers who will only want to release equipment at times convenient to themselves.

Replace or Repair?

In situations where the customer is seriously inconvenienced by the product not being available, some options are open to the service organization. If the product is too complex for ultimate reliability to be possible at an economic price, the product can at least be designed for rapid service, with modules or printed circuit boards being replaced, and the defective unit either disposed of or taken back for repair.

A variation on this theme may be to provide a loan machine for the duration of the repair. Obviously, it will not be economical for all organizations to have capital tied up in this way, though it could be justified as a marketing expense sometimes. The use of courtesy cars by garages is an example of this approach.

Another alternative may be to carry out the function of the equipment under repair without providing a short-term replacement as such. Toyota, for example, is investigating the possibility of providing fax facilities at some of their dealerships so that business clients can work at home when their cars are being serviced.

Remote Diagnostics and Predictive Maintenance

For high-value capital goods it may be possible to justify installing a direct line from the equipment in the customer's facility to the service organization. Some opportunities are now opened up for the service provider:

- It may be possible for the service organization to detect failure before the customer is aware of it, improving the perception of service response.
- In some cases (as with software, for example) it may be possible to fix the problem through the remote line, cutting cost and response time. Again, it may be possible to solve problems before the customer is aware of them.
- The ability to remotely diagnose probable causes of failure should improve the likelihood of the service engineer arriving with the correct spares to complete a first-time fix. Some companies dispatch spares and engineers independently, increasing the use of service specialists.

- By using the remote link to monitor the performance of the equipment to predict that failure will occur within a given time, the service and support organization can schedule maintenance at the right time to cut downtime and inconvenience to the customer.

It is apparent, particularly for capital goods where the cost of downtime to the customer is prohibitive, that the cost of installing and maintaining a remote link may be a small price to pay. Applications of remote monitoring are growing rapidly and already include computers, lifts, and other products with microprocessor control. The problem for thc service provider is how to demonstrate the value of the service given to justify the prices charged. If customers don't see the rapid response to problems, they may think that nothing is being done, so the service contract is now unnecessary.

SUPPORTING CUSTOMERS

As products and systems become more reliable, the emphasis of the organization moves away from the ability to fix problems, that is, reactive service, through to ensuring maximum availability, perhaps through planned maintenance. This general move in recent years to more consistent product quality and more reliable products has coincided with a new understanding that the customer doesn't just buy a product, but judges what is received by everything that the organization does.

This shift in emphasis has meant that companies have developed broader customer support activities for the following reasons:

- Revenue earning activities are developed to replace lost service and repair income.
- Actions that are more visible to the customer are emphasized in order to demonstrate the value of the service and support organization.
- Close customer contact has allowed the organization to identify broader business opportunities not necessarily directly related to the core business.

- Extra service and support activities are developed to enhance or support an upmarket product image.

Much of this new understanding springs from realizing that the organization may not be solely "processing material" in the sense of turning metal and plastics into washing machines, but also "processing customers." In the same way that material flows through a manufacturing process, customers flow through a process as their needs are addressed. If the organization can understand this customer process better, particularly understanding how the customer is feeling at each stage, some potential improvements may be identified.

Can the Customer Use the Product Effectively?

Most support activities are directed toward the goal of ensuring that the customer derives maximum benefit from the purchase. A customer who has paid a significant amount of money and who then uses perhaps 10 percent of the power of the product is less likely to be satisfied with the purchase in the long run. This problem may be generated at the selling stage, where the customer was oversold a product that was not required. He was sold a computer suite when all that was required was a calculator.

It may be, of course, that some overselling is a good move, as applications may be found as the customer grows in expertise. Customer support clearly starts sometimes long before the sale by providing applications advice. This approach has long been the practice for certain capital goods manufacturers and is spreading to the more expensive consumer goods such as sound systems and DIY equipment. Good advice, readily available, may be a powerful marketing tool.

Does the Customer Need Training?

Some customer training is needed for all but the most basic of products. In fact, all products need some documentation or instruction leaflet to inform the customer about how the product should and should not be used. Product liability legislation now puts the onus on the manufacturer to ensure safety in use, and not to assume, for example, that the customer will know that electric toasters shouldn't be used in the bathroom.

Some products, of course, will be either so new or complex that customer training may well be offered as part of the original purchase price. There may well be continuing business here as new employees require training. We visited an engineering company who bought some manufacturing control software. Included in the purchase price was both training on how to use the software and also management education on the principles on which the package was based. After the software had been working for two years, the vendor reminded the company that included in the original purchase price were some "maintenance" days, education, or training to be used as the customer decided. The customer was very impressed partly because they had forgotten about these days, but found the opportunity to revisit the basic philosophy behind the software a useful refresher that increased the effectiveness of the system.

Again, there is a caveat to customer training. Eventually, customers will not want to pay the equivalent of the product price over again in courses to enable people to use the product effectively. Computer companies are slowly recognizing that it should be easier to use their products without having a degree in computer science to enable the customer to understand their manuals. So, there is a growing trend to design the product for ease of use. In the medical electronics industry, even the most complex products must be easy to use, given the rapid turnover of nursing staff in some hospitals.

There may be a benefit to the service provider in giving effective customer training. Improper use by the customer may increase the service call out rate that will be unwelcome particularly if the customer has a comprehensive service contract. Good customer training will also reduce damage in use and, therefore, warranty costs.

Is the Customer Happy?

For some industries, at least, service income is now decreasing. There may be some commercial opportunity in selling extended guarantees, giving the customer some peace of mind in return for what is effectively a maintenance contract.

Organizations are increasingly seeing this area as worthy of attention for marketing product. There are a few companies that are giving broader guarantees with fewer conditions. There is nothing worse than having to employ a lawyer to go through the small print only to find that this particular circumstance is excluded. Automobile warranties are a good example of paper guarantees that often appear to be worthless for most customers because so many items are effectively excluded. The warranty is an area that will repay attention given to it as customers become more aware of what they are really getting. Indeed, a guarantee or warranty that clearly limits the risk to the seller may be worse than no guarantee at all in the customer's eyes.

Also, included under this heading should be the activity of customer audits, finding out whether customers are satisfied with products and service. This customer focus is fundamental for the business as a whole and is referred to in the chapters on marketing and quality. Now, it is sufficient to say that customers are often impressed that the organization has taken the trouble to find out what they think. This dedication to quality improvement also raises customer confidence levels.

Does the Customer Need Anything Else?

As suppliers move closer to their customers it may be that further business opportunities may be identified. An example of this approach would be that of the fastener company that instead of merely supplying nuts and bolts, provides a full stock control and storage service for some of its major customers. An often quoted example is the Hartford boiler inspection service that over time built up more information about the products than the customers possessed and was able to move into a broader consultancy role as a result.

Computer companies have been quick to make a shift from selling hardware to selling "solutions," being a mixture of hardware, software, and consultancy. We know of a software supplier that now makes more money from management education. The recent move of the retailer Marks and Spencer into financial services is, perhaps, another example of an opportunity identified when thinking about customers' broader requirements.

Of course, perhaps it should go without saying that it is very dangerous to move into areas where you have no expertise or that will mean that management attention to the core business is diluted. The old adage that one should "stick to the knitting" is worth remembering.

MONEY MATTERS

It should be understood that adding dimensions to the service and support package has a price, and, therefore, enhancements must largely be limited by what the customer is willing to pay for. This decision is always difficult because customers often want service for nothing.

There are three basic approaches to this issue:

1. Value to customer: the customer may be prepared to pay more if the inconvenience of breakdown is high.

2. Relation to product price: service is included in the original product purchase price, perhaps in the form of a warranty.

3. Cost plus: the customer is charged the cost of the service plus an acceptable margin.

Consumer goods manufacturers will tend to hide the service cost element, whereas expensive capital goods manufacturers may be able to command premium rates. If the customer is very knowledgeable about service content and industry standards, the cost plus approach must be used.

SETTING CUSTOMER SERVICE AND SUPPORT PRIORITIES

The type of product to be supported will often determine both the structure and priorities for customer support. Figure 3–2 illustrates the variety of the Customer Support task. The customer service and support organization must be aware of current and future priorities as products move from sector to sector.

Computers, fax machines, and power tools are just three examples of products that have moved from a medium/high value, low volume profile to become relatively low value, high volume

FIGURE 3–2
Customer Support Priorities

Product Description	Customer Support Priorities	Customer Support Structure
Capital goods (high value, low volume)	Increasing MTBF) Predictive maintenance Customer training Applications advice Installation and commissioning Comprehensive service support	SAS to support relatively few regulars or territorials
Industrial goods (medium value, medium volume)	Rapid response Serviceability Installation Customer documentation Ease of use Location Dealer expertise	Regulars with some Mercenaries
Consumer goods (medium value, medium volume)		
Consumer goods (low value, high volume)	Warranties Access Customer care Spares availability Distribution network	Mercenaries (Enemies)

products. The attendant changes in customer service and support priorities have not always been so effectively managed as the product development.

KEY ACTIONS

1. List assumptions you make about what your customers require in service and support. Are they right?
2. Write down any changes in priorities for customer service and support that result from product design or market changes. What have been the implications of the changes?

3. Think about elements of customer service and support you could exploit more.

4. Write down the targets for each element of customer service and support. Is it still appropriate? What changes are needed?

Chapter Four

Marketing and Market Research

Introduction

In this chapter we look at marketing strategy, the marketing proccss for customer support, pricing mechanisms, and marketing research. We see the close link hetween the marketing process and the competitive strategy for the firm that we have talked about in Chapter 2, and the operational delivery of service. We see the importance of the marketing process in creating an image for customer service and support.

ARE WE A MARKETING ORIENTED ORGANIZATION?

Traditionally, customer service and support has been seen as a necessary evil after the sale of the product. Companies often have well-developed marketing approaches to the sale of the product. Those firms selling consumer products like cars, televisions, and washing machines spend large amounts on marketing. On the other hand, companies making capital goods, like machine tools and power generation plants have perhaps not given the same amount of effort to marketing their products. In both cases though, the marketing of the customer service and support has usually been lacking.

Why should this be? Such an approach misses an opportunity to focus on the associated needs of the customer in the use of the product and to build customer loyalty. How often in surveys of your products do you find that your customers are essentially satisfied with the product but dissatisfied with the way in which they are dealt with, if they require information, or during any service activity? It is easy to blame the service personnel for this failing, but the fault more often lies with not really understanding the needs of the customers and users. What we are seeing is the absence of a true marketing orientation.

We think there are two main reasons why firms find themselves in this position. First there are those who really do see any after sales offerings as an evil that only adds costs. While many companies would deny this is their view we see many examples of the way they treat their customers. Engineers do not arrive, spares are not available, contact cannot be made with the company when things go wrong. Second are those firms who do provide customer service and support and see it as being important for profits. However, they make the provision on their terms rather than according to what the customers want. How many times are customers offered appointments at times that are most convenient to them rather than the service engineers? For example most utility companies still do not offer customers evening or weekend visits so customers who work have to take time off to get appliances repaired.

It must be clear that what needs to happen is first to understand the needs of the customers and second to make sure that those needs are satisfied. Those companies who have realized the benefits to be gained from focusing on their customers can be recognized by five traits:

1. Customer satisfaction.
2. Product quality.
3. Listening to the customers.
4. Understanding the key factors for customer service.
5. Trying to do things better.

Can we possibly acquire these traits if we are only concerned with the initial sale of the product or the installation of equipment? The answer must be no. We must use marketing as part of the process to becoming a customer focused organization. A strong indication that an organization has a marketing orientation is when they can say: "We make our profits by creating opportunities to satisfy our customers needs more effectively within the constraints of our resources and skills limitations". This is a very different orientation to one that focuses on the products alone. If we take a product focus, we are making assumptions: either the quality of performance of the product is good enough to make the customers continue to purchase them (this may be all right for cheap products like irons and toasters that are simple to use and can be thrown away when they fail); or the costs of producing the products will always mean we can compete on price; or we need to offer only a limited customer service and support to satisfy any safety or regulatory requirements. So if you think you are still not customer focused and do not have a marketing oriented firm how can you make the change?

MARKETING FOR CUSTOMER FOCUS

At its simplest level marketing is "finding what the customer wants and providing it." A marketing strategy is closely linked to the competitive strategy we talked about in Chapter 2. It requires an understanding of the markets, the needs of customers, what competitors are doing, and the key features that make the service offering attractive to customers. This last point is very important because if customers do not want what is on offer, no matter how good we may feel it is, the firm will fail. The steps to achieving good marketing for customer service and support are:

1. Understanding the market in relation to the customers and users and the competition. This approach is really the formulation of service strategy that we looked at in detail in Chapter 2.
2. Defining the critical customer service dimensions in different segments of the market.
3. Specifying the marketing mix, which is the way in which the whole package is delivered to the customers. The marketing mix includes six components:
    a. The product/service/support combination or mix.
    b. The availability of the product/service/support mix in time and place.
    c. The price charged.

    d. The communication through advertising and promotion.
    e. The service people.
    f. The process of delivery.
4. Monitoring performance over time to pick up changes that will inevitably lead to changes in the marketing mix.

Marketing in a customer focused organization is not just an isolated functional activity but one that includes everyone in the business and some outsiders. This concept is called relationship marketing. There are internal markets concerning the people who deliver the customer service and support and there are external markets, including the customers, suppliers, employment markets, and those who influence purchases. We must recognize the relationship between them all and try to ensure that everyone has a shared view of what is needed.

The process of marketing is closely allied to the formulation of a service strategy as can be seen from Figure 4–1. We need to decide on the different types of customers who need to be served, whether we want to serve them, and whether we have the capability. Let us start the process by first looking at what customers are buying and how their needs may differ before examining the marketing mix in more detail.

WHAT IS THE CUSTOMER BUYING?

What is being offered to the customer? If we are simply selling a product, the most important consideration is will the product give value. Customer loyalty will be built on the selling process and the performance of the product during its lifetime. However, as the amount of customer service and support that is needed over the lifetime of the product increases the customer is buying a mix of tangible and intangible elements associated with the product, the service and support. Included in this complex mix are things associated with the product itself, the service for the equipment, the support for customers in the use of the product, and finally the way in which the whole process is carried out. These factors include:

FIGURE 4–1
The Marketing Process

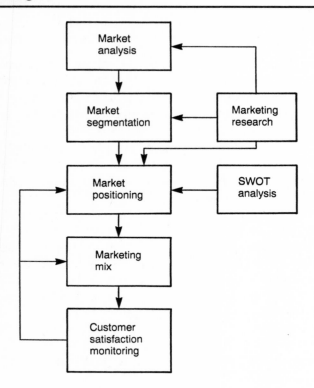

1. The product.
   a. Installed price.
   b. Ease of installation.
   c. Reliability (MTBF).
   d. Ease of servicing.
   e. Mean uptime in operation.

2. Service.
   a. Service price.
   b. Time to fix.
   c. Spares availability.
   d. Maintenance contracts.
   e. Flexibility of response.

3. Support.
   a. Customer training.
   b. Documentation.
   c. Consultancy.
   d. Advice/problem solving.
4. Process.
   a. Ease of contact with the service/support people.
   b. Control over the process by the individual customer.
   c. Attitudes of service people.
   d. Appearance of the service people and equipment.
   e. Safety/trust/confidence in the service and support organization.

The customer service and support product mix will vary from firm to firm and type of product or installation. When we were considering the formulation of service strategy we saw that competitive advantage could be gained by recognizing the critical parts of the product/service/support mix. We also recognized that competitiveness could be lost if we failed to deliver on the sensitive features of the hygiene factors. We can visualize this in another way that helps us in the marketing process.

The product/service/support mix can be seen as a core encircled by a surround of other features. The core may be the product or installation and the surround the service and support and the delivery process. Alternatively, we may see the core as being the product and the maintenance service. In consequence, the core is made up of the more tangible aspects of the mix and the surround less easy to define. This concept has implications for the marketing of the surround as part of the package and for setting quality levels. The mix between core and surround will differ for different products and customers, and this difference leads to the segmentation of the market.

ARE ALL OUR CUSTOMERS THE SAME?

A company that installs security alarms has as customers major retailers, local authorities, corner shops, and residential home owners. Would we expect them to have different needs? A first guess would be yes. Would we expect the company to deliver a different service to them all? Again we might answer yes. Do they deliver a different service to their various customers? Alas the answer is for the most part no. Unfortunately what we see with this example is repeated for many service organizations. It reflects a lack of any clear attempt to understand the needs of different customers and to tailor the customer service and support to match them.

We might ask why it is necessary to recognize differences between groups of customers. First, if we do not we may provide a service that fails really to meet the needs of any customers in the total market. Second, we might be increasing our costs by offering too high service levels for what most of the market wants. Third, we will probably never really understand what our customers value and, hence, find it difficult to retain customers over a long time. Finally we may be wasting marketing resources by not concentrating on our best customers who generate either current or potential profits.

The way forward is to segment the market and to position our offerings in different markets we have identified.

SEGMENTING THE MARKET

What approaches are there to help us decide which are the best ways to separate our total customers into groups? The work we have already done to formulate a service strategy is closely linked to market segmentation and positioning. We essentially have to look for answers to the following questions:

1. In what ways can we divide the total market?
2. What are the needs of the different segments?
3. Which of the groups do we want to serve?

In dividing the market into segments we are looking for characteristics that give some clear and meaningful differences. It is not an exact science, so the more we already know about the market the easier the process is likely to be. However there are some factors that we might want to take into consideration as the basis for segmentation. These fall into two categories: customer characteristics and customer responses.

By customer characteristics we mean any factors that give a clear statement about the customer which are independent of their use of the service. Customer characteristics would include:

- *Geography*. The location of customers and their coverage, urban or rural, national or regional, national or international.
- *Demography*. Age and sex.
- *Psychography*. Lifestyle, social class, personality.

Customer responses are dependent on how the customers buy and use the product/service/support package. They include both objective and subjective measures:

- *User type*. The type of user of the service (well informed and expert or needing hand holding).
- *Purchasing power*. The larger the user the greater may be the ability of the customer to influence the price and level of service.
- *Size*. A commonly used split on size is between major accounts and smaller customers.
- *Nature of the relationship*. Long standing as against new customers.
- *Reasons for purchasing*. Imposed by regulation as compared with a valued offering.
- *Importance of the service*. Quick response rather than tolerating an acceptable delay.
- *Industry sector*. Manufacturing, retail, or commercial.
- *Knowledge*. How much the customer recognizes the benefits of the service and support.
- *Growth potential*. Groups of customers or potential customers who may provide rapid growth in business.
- *Price*. The sensitivity of the customer to the price of the service and the support.

Once we have the factors that seem most appropriate in our markets for grouping present and potential customers, we need to identify the most important features for each of the groups by developing independent customer profiles for each segment. A

FIGURE 4-2
Market Segmentation

	International	*National*	*Small Companies*
Main Requirements	Coverage/Expertise	Reputation/Price	Price
Critical Factors* (5 = Important, 0 = Not important)			
Product	4	4	5
Service	5	5	3
Support	5	3	2
Process	4	4	3
Price	2	3	5

* Assessed on a scale 1–5

simplified example of the process is given in Figure 4–2 for a customer service and support operation for a company supplying electric motors.

The market for the product/service/support package has been segmented by the size and coverage of the customers as international, national, or small independents. The company is also able to identify some of the factors that influence the buying behavior for the various segments. The customer service and support profiles for each segment using our customer service and support profile have been carried out for each segment to identify the critical factors. We can see that there are clear differences in the attitudes of the three segments to the product, the service, the support, the process of delivery, and the price charged.

Having segmented the market for customer service and support, we now need to decide whether we want to be involved in all segments of the market, and, more importantly, whether we have the capabilities to deliver to a chosen sector. There is always the danger of coming up with wish statements at this stage. It may seem attractive to be involved in the highest quality, high-margin market, but if our resources are not up to it, we will undoubtedly fail. We may make a more rational judgment by recognizing the potential of the market but realize we are not able to finance the improvement in resources to make an entry possible, at least now.

DO WE WANT TO BE PART OF A MARKET?

Deciding whether to enter a particular market sector for customer service and support depends on a number of factors. These are linked to the sale of the original product and may in consequence limit the degree of choice we have. Often the decision is linked to the overall strategy of the organization on the products and markets it is to serve. In reaching a decision on our markets we might be addressing the following questions:

1. How important is it for us to service and support the product? There may be laws, regulations, or safety requirements that make this necessary.

2. Do customers for the product expect that we will offer service and support rather than leave it to third parties? Does this influence future sales?

3. If we have a choice will the customer service and support activity give us sufficient returns for it to be profitable?

4. Can we afford to provide the resources to provide service and support in a particular segment of the market?

5. Are we good enough to operate in a particular market segment? A route to answering this question is by way of a SWOT Analysis, where we try to identify for each segment our strengths and weaknesses in comparison to the competition, and the opportunities and threats that result from the strengths and weaknesses.

It is clear that answering these questions must involve not only a marketing activity as it is part of the formulation of strategy we examined in Chapter 2. It is part of the marketing process, however, to establish how our products may be positioned in the market sectors relative to our competitors.

POSITIONING CUSTOMER SERVICE AND SUPPORT

Positioning of our customer service and support in each of the market segments we have identified requires a knowledge of what is wanted by customers in that segment; what the competition is offering (here we are interested in both the composition of the customer service and support mix and also the quality levels); and our own performance (here we may use the results of our SWOT Analysis and an assessment of performance on the customer service dimensions relative to our competitors – see Chapter 2, on strategy formulation).

Our aim is to position our customer service and support in the market in a way that helps our customer recognize our position clearly. This idea is behind the concept of branding. We may reinforce our positioning of our brand through advertising, and we may include it in our mission statement. British Airways ("The world's favorite airline") and Avis car rental ("We try harder") are examples of this type of explicit positioning. If we do not consciously position a product, the customers are likely to do it for us—"The service company which never turns up on time," "The most authoritarian service company."

We need to be clear on the market positioning because it then allows us to make sure that our marketing mix of product/service/ support, availability, price, communication, people, and process are correct to meet the position. So if we are to position ourselves in the "high quality" position, it is going to be necessary to charge higher prices, spend more on advertising, and have well-trained service people, well supported by equipment and systems.

Positioning maps are a useful tool for presenting our position in one market relative to other competitors. Figure 4–3 shows a positioning map for the international company's market segments we created earlier for our customer service and support company. We have taken the two most important criteria in that market segment, servicing of the product and support for the customer, and placed ourselves on the map against the axes of high and low service, and high and low support. Our competitors in this market have been positioned in a similar way, based on the research we have done. We can see that if we are to be among the best in the market we need to move more in the direction presently occupied by Elecspeed by improving or increasing our level of customer support.

We would want to make positioning maps for all of the market segments. Then look at the marketing mix we are using to see if it is right for each segment or whether it needs changing.

FIGURE 4–3
Service and Support Positioning Map

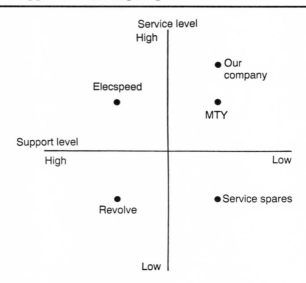

REVIEWING THE MARKETING MIX

The marketing mix is simply the combination of elements that enables us to reach our targeted customer with the offering they want. The elements are not independent but interact. This interaction increases the complexity of our task. Altering one may change another; for example, if we reduce the price we may be unable to spend the same amount on Advertising. The goal is to make the marketing mix match as closely as possible the position we wish to achieve in a market. So we must look at what is included within each of the elements.

THE PRODUCT/SERVICE/SUPPORT COMBINATION

In our earlier discussion of what the customer is buying and market segmentation we saw that for different markets we need to design the product/service/support package to match the needs of the market sector and the position we want to occupy in the sector. This goal is clearly a complex issue and involves not only marketing in its resolution, but also should illustrate to customer service and support managers the importance of using marketing knowledge in the design of all aspects of the product/ service/ support mix. For example, the importance of product design in determining ease of installation and servicing is becoming more widely recognized, even if it is not always implemented. This approach needs to be extended to consideration of the critical elements of support, for instance documentation, advice, and spares provision.

GETTING TO THE CUSTOMERS

The second part of the marketing mix is concerned with getting the customer service and support to the customers. Where and how is it made available? Deciding on how we achieve this requires both a strategic consideration of the choices between doing it ourselves, using agents or dealers, or leaving it to third parties. The Military Model (Chapter 2) shows how our decision is often influenced by how much in-house control we want to keep in the face of growing service intensity. From a marketing standpoint the question is, how do we influence the distribution channels that are created by the different choices?

Let us look at some typical distribution channels as shown in Figure 4–4. These show the number of intermediaries between the original manufacturers of equipment and the customer/user when the equipment/product is first bought. It also shows the typical ways in which service and support is delivered. Clearly, the longer the distribution channel from the original manufacturer, the lower the possibility of influencing what is happening for the end user. This factor has real implications for the use of marketing tools to position the service and support. It will affect advertising and promotion and with a long chain may mean that the customers of the end product are not even known to the manufacturing company. For instance, a manufacturer of electric showers, installed either by specialists who are not controlled by the company or DIY by the users, finds it very difficult to identify who the end users of their showers really are.

FIGURE 4-4
Marketing Distribution Channels

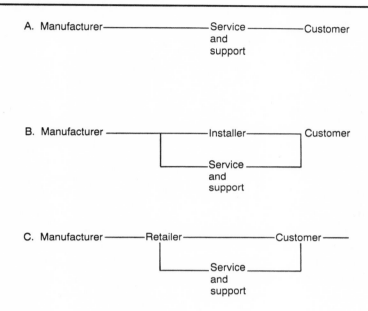

For our purposes, it is important to see the influence of product distribution channels on our ability to market customer service and support. Even if we are not manufacturers, the question still applies because we need to be able to influence through marketing what customers can expect from our customer service and support.

HOW MUCH DO WE CHARGE?

An important marketing decision is deciding what to charge for customer service and support. The price must be related in some way to the benefits that the customers perceive they gain. We have already seen this with the Strategy Compass when we set a strategic direction based on the interaction between perceived added value and price.

In considering pricing, we need to take three things into account:

1. The value of the customer service and support.
2. The cost of providing the service and support.
3. Actions taken by competitors to change either the price they charge or their offering.

Value of Customer Service and Support

The value to the customer is not easy to set; it may be linked to low price, or to the quality of the service as delivered, or relieving customers of the psychological effects of worrying about failure of equipment. The last point is important for customer service and support operations where one of the benefits is customers' peace of mind. It may also be an insurance against the customer having to expend resources if the product fails in the future. We may try to bring out the critical things that make up value, but ultimately we have to rely on the net value to the customer as being "all the perceived benefits from customer service and support less the perceived costs of not having it or the costs for the customers of doing all or part of the process themselves."

Costs

The prices that are charged need to be related to the costs of providing the service and support if profit margins for service and support are to be maintained. This relationship may not apply if the cost of the service and support is taken as part of the overall cost of sales of the products. Sometimes, customer service and support is being offered as a loss leader. We will assume that the prices charged for customer service and support determine our profit margins, so reducing prices for customer service and support without reducing costs will lead to failure in the long term. Margins will become too lean, therefore, there will be insufficient contribution to cover overheads.

One main problem is in determining true costs for the provision of the customer service and support when there are a range of offerings. For example, the cost of a two-hour response is going to be higher than for a 24-hour response, but by how much? If it is delivered as part of the same operation using the same response center and engineers, it may be difficult to separate accurately. It is possible to make some estimate of the volume of service and support that is needed to be covered by a break-even analysis, taking into account fixed costs, variable costs, and total costs.

The fixed costs include the costs of equipment, transport, salaries, and information systems. Variable costs are related to the service intensity and include fuel costs, overtime, hiring sub-contractors, and spares (if they are not charged separately). The total costs are the sum of the variable and the fixed costs. The point at which the return from charges to the customers becomes more than the total costs is the break-even point above which a profit is being generated.

The break-even analysis is useful for determining whether a particular market segment is profitable. While it may be difficult to assign the correct proportion of fixed costs to one segment, it is possible to establish the contribution from customers in that segment to cover fixed costs and other overheads.

Setting the Price

A knowledge of the costs and the value to the customers allows prices to be set on the basis of:

- A common amount to charge for an isolated event where time and materials can be easily measured is the costs plus a margin.
- The value to the customer of the customer service and support. The implication is that the offering is highly differentiated, so price is not an issue for the customer.
- The newness of what is being offered.
- The prices being charged by our competitors for their services.
- Linking the service price to the price of the original product. How much this is possible may depend on the customers' expectation of the performance of the product. If the expectation is for high reliability, it may be more difficult to charge high prices for customer service and support, unless the benefits of support can be emphasized in the selling process.
- Taking into account the sensitivity to price in a particular market. If prices are openly quoted by all competitors, it may

reduce the flexibility for changing our prices. If the customer requires a detailed quotation of work done or to be carried out, it may have a similar effect of limiting flexibility.

- The most common approach for setting the basic price charged for customer service and support is the cost plus approach. This approach places great reliance on the accuracy of costing systems if the contribution to fixed costs and profits from a service and support mix is to be a true representation of reality.

PEOPLE AND DELIVERY PROCESS

The reason we include people and delivery processes as part of the marketing mix for customer service and support is their visibility to the customers. Generally in services, unlike manufacturing, the customers form part of the process, so they know what is going on, or they see what is happening. In consequence, what happens in the operational delivery of the customer service and support needs to match the other parts of thc marketing mix. Otherwise, customers may be told to expect one thing from advertising and experience something different and worse in practice.

At one time field service operations considered it was only necessary to turn up and complete the job as though the customers were, at best, a burden to be tolerated. There is now greater recognition of the behavior of service personnel and of their appearance. We have dealt in more detail with these and other aspects when we looked at managing the service encounter and service quality.

TECHNIQUES FOR UNDERSTANDING CUSTOMERS

Now we want to review the techniques that can be used to gain knowledge of present or potential customers. These techniques come under the heading of marketing research. We have already made extensive use of marketing information in our discussions so far of segmentation, positioning, and marketing mix. The techniques that can be used to gain this information fall into two groups: information gained externally through approaches to customers or from publicly available information like trade surveys; and information that is available internally from the result of business activity or from service personnel.

The Use of Questionnaires

Questionnaires are a powerful method of gathering information on customer service and support from customers and from service personnel. There are three basic ways of administering questionnaires:

1. Face-to-face using an interviewer. This way is costly and limits the number of people, but it has the advantage that the interviewer can explain questions.

2. By phone. This is cheaper than face-to-face but does not allow detailed questions to be asked.

3. By mail. This method has the lowest unit cost, and there may be problems persuading a large enough number of people to reply. It also needs careful attention to the design of the questionnaire to avoid ambiguity in the questions.

All questionnaires require a degree of skill in their design to make the questions clear to their audience so that the result from the analysis is reliable. A pilot study, using a small number of customers, is a way of reducing the risk of poor design.

Interviews

An extension of the questionnaire process is for us to ask customers to talk about their experiences of our service and support either individually or in groups. This allows us to ask more open-ended questions and to allow the unexpected reaction to emerge. For example, they may be asked to describe their experiences of good and bad service; this process helps to identify with whom our customers are comparing us.

Secondary Information

In research terms, questionnaires and interviews result in primary data that we have collected ourselves. We often want to combine these results with other secondary information that can be gained from trade associations, newspapers, consultants' reports and any other material that gives a view on the markets we are serving. Here we are often looking for changes that may affect the need for our services. For example, a security company makes use of published crime statistics and police reports to predict likely volume of demand in different market sectors.

EXTENDING THE MARKETING ROLE: ENHANCING THE IMAGE

Increasingly, organizations are seeing the benefit of the role of marketing being extended to a wider audience than customers. The reasons for this are evident; the provision of good service and support requires relations with not only customers, but also suppliers, users, public bodies, and distributors. Relationship marketing attempts to reach all parties who have an interest in a service whether as customers or users, service personnel, or other stakeholders. Consequently, a number of markets can be identified:

- *Customer markets.* Clearly we know we need to keep existing customers and to gain new ones through the marketing process.
- *Supplier markets.* We need to have suppliers either of materials or services who are committed over a long period to supporting our levels of quality for service and support.
- *Employee markets.* Staff within a service organization often complain they are unclear about what is required of them. Internal marketing through training, procedures, and the use of videos forms a powerful way of increasing shared values and goals.
- *Influencer/referral markets.* We need to maintain contact and communication with those individuals and institutions who can either influence the purchases or refer business. For instance, being on approved lists of service and support providers can be critical in some sectors.

The most important step is to recognize those who fall into different categories and to review just how they are being included in market research and in the marketing communication processes.

KEY ACTIONS

1. Segment your customers into different groups that make sense to you.
2. Identify the key factors of the product/service/support mix your customers want in the various segments.
3. Position where you want to be in a market segment relative to the competition.
4. Do you know the products and prices and cost structures of your main competitors?
5. Review if you could set prices for customer service and support in a more proactive manner.
6. List the ways in which you communicate differently to your various market segments.
7. List the information you gather and give in all the relationship markets.
8. Create a customer satisfaction index to measure the results of any marketing actions you take.

Chapter Five

Customer Service and Support Delivery— Managing the Contact with Customers

Introduction

Each customer transaction, whether it be a major training program, routine maintenance, or "minor" telephone inquiry, is an opportunity for the organization's reputation to be enhanced or destroyed. Richard Normann and Jan Carlzon have used the term *Moments of Truth* to encapsulate the principle that customers judge the whole of the operation by the parts that they can see and understand.

Carlzon says that for the airline SAS there may be 50,000 Moments of Truth each day. A customer may wonder how the airline can maintain a complex aircraft and keep it flying safely if it cannot ensure that a passenger's luggage gets to the right place at the right time. This opinion may seem unfair when viewed objectively because the airline may be superb technically, but what the customers perceive to be good or bad is all that matters. Customers form their own judgment about whether or not they have received value for money.

The 1980s saw a large number of customer care programs that were, for the most part, unsuccessful or at best short-lived. The least effective were the "smile" campaigns, ineffective because you can't make silk purses out of sows' ears. Some staff should never be given jobs that entail a significant degree of customer contact because their personality is such that no amount of training will make them appear friendly and sympathetic. If the service delivery design is

FIGURE 5–1
Service Delivery Triangle

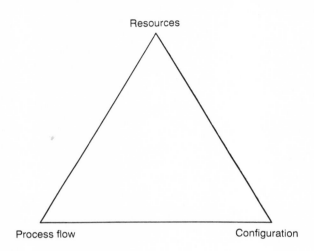

flawed, smile campaigns add insult to injury. The question "Is everything all right?" can be the final straw.

W. Edwards Deming, along with other Quality Management gurus, asserts that the people involved in the process are not the root cause of quality problems. For the most part, people prefer to do a good job rather than a poor one. He rightly states that attention must be paid to improving the systems and processes rather than exhorting people to do better. This recipe results in disillusionment if failure is built into the system anyway.

In this chapter we examine the three main aspects of service delivery that make up the Service Delivery Triangle (Figure 5–1). We discuss the main categories of resources employed in the service system, the organization or configuration of these resources, and the flow of people, information, and material through the organization. In this chapter we concentrate on the direct impact these decisions have on the way that the customer views the service organization as a whole.

One final word. Customers are like a well-known lager, they get to places in companies they are not expected to reach. It is not sufficient to legislate that they will be dealt with only by those staff designated as "customer service." Customers will get everywhere, and the organization must be able to cope with this. Furthermore,

those staff not in front-line roles must be conscious of the impact of
their activities on how service is delivered and therefore perceived
by customers.

CONFIGURATION: IDENTIFYING THE CONTACT POINTS

In this section we introduce three broad issues:

1. How much the organization's operation is "visible" to the
customer. Is the bulk of the resource cost and therefore value of the
service vested in the customer contact area, or is it predominantly
in a "support" or backroom area?
2. The need to identify all customer contact points and to ensure
that the required service is delivered effectively at these points.
3. The choice of location of service facilities and its effect on
customer perception of the organization.

The Front Office – Back Room Framework

To assist in analyzing the situation it will be helpful to think of a
simple model, where the operation is divided into two parts, Front
Office and Back Room, the first being those areas that act as the
interface between the organization and its customers and the
second, areas behind the scenes where "production" often takes
place. So, for a Customer Service and Support organization, the
Front Office will include telephone response center staff and
service engineers, while the Back Room might include repair staff
and the Information Systems used to control the service activity.

An important design decision relates to how much the Front
Office is used mainly as a contact point rather than the place where
the bulk of the work is carried out. An illustration from computer
service will help. In the early years of mainframe computers much
service work was carried out in the Front Office with repairs
effected on the customer's premises. Largely, this contact was
unexploited, the attention being almost exclusively focused on
repairing the equipment rather than on creating a good impression
with the customer. Today, the Front Office activities are much

reduced, components and assemblies being rapidly replaced rather than repaired. Repair of modules or portable equipment takes place in a Back Room workshop and is no longer visible to the customer. The opportunities to make a good impression on the customer are proportionately diminished. Of course, the equipment itself is far more reliable and the customer is not inconvenienced, which is probably more important than delivering a high-quality repair service.

It may be possible to choose between carrying out work in the Front Office or the Back Room. If the customer is present when the bulk of the work is done, the potential for disruption and, therefore, inefficiency is greater. On the other hand, the service may be carried out predominantly in the Back Room, which will be more efficient but possibly less effective in terms of enhancing the customers' perception of the quality of the service. Figure 5–2 indicates the implications of the choice of Front Office or Back Room organization.

Many high volume demand service companies have moved toward the situation where the bulk of the work is carried out in the Back Room. These companies must work very hard to make sure that the very limited customer contact is effective in conveying the impression of a competent organization that will look after the customers' needs. The use of remote diagnostics and other call avoidance techniques have moved organizations from Front Office to Back Room dominance and the implications of this move must be fully addressed.

Some organizations have made a decision to move in the opposite direction. A good example of this approach is the car repair workshop that encourages the customer to come into the workshop, to discuss any problems directly with the technician working on the car, and, if so desired, to stay and watch the work. This approach may cause some delay and the technician must be able to deal with customers as well as having product skills, but there is no doubt that it presents an opportunity to create customer confidence in the organization. Clearly, there is an element of external and internal marketing in the process. Meeting customers more regularly is more effective in creating customer focus than in stirring speeches.

FIGURE 5–2
Front Office – Back Room Organization

	Front Office Dominant	Back Room Dominant
Front Office role	Service Delivery Communication Diagnosis	Contact Communication Access to Organization
Front Office staff	Technical experts with good customer skills	Interpersonal skills with some technical knowledge
Back Room role	To provide support service to Front Office	To carry out service delivery
Back Room staff	May be perceived as inferior to Front Office staff	Technical experts with little customer contact
Challenge	To maintain consistent service standards Quality at acceptable cost To communicate effectively with Back Room To involve Back Room staff where possible	To make standard service appear special to individual customers For Back Room staff to understand problems of Front Office To ensure timely communication with Front Office

Face-to-Face Customer Contact

Most services contain an element of face-to-face customer contact. Even if remote diagnostics are employed and products become ever more reliable, the customer will still occasionally meet a representative of the company. Service Engineers may still carry out some repairs on site or perform routine maintenance tasks. Creating such opportunities so that the customer can see that the support organization still exists and has a valuable role to play can be a good strategy. A reduction in breakdown calls should allow the Customer Service and Support Manager the opportunity to schedule goodwill calls to make sure that customers are satisfied with product and service.

In managing face-to-face customer contact, the following points should be considered:

- People who regularly deal with customers should be recruited for their interpersonal skills. The "excellent" service organizations are spending more money on recruitment, recognizing that training only enhances talent that already exists. We have all seen the face above the "At Your Service" badge that says at a glance that too much should not be expected.

- Even those who are not designated as front-line contact staff meet customers sometimes. We should not expect them to know instinctively the right thing to say or to understand the impact of their actions on customer perception. Some basic customer awareness training will be worthwhile, particularly if this includes some controlled exposure to real customer demands.

- A reliance on restrictive rules and procedures is unlikely to produce a "golden moment." Customers are aware of the attitude behind the action. Positive service attitudes are more likely to be produced by positive motivation and management example than by sets of commands.

- Prolonged contact with customers can lead to deterioration in service performance or *burnout*. The effects of burnout can be decreased by consciously restricting the time spent in customer contact without respite, developing the service team to provide support, and ensuring that sufficient training and resources are available to perform the task.

Telephone contact

Telephone contact is the prime customer contact for many service and support organizations. The voice at the end of the telephone line is likely to be the initial contact at a bad time (the customer's equipment has just failed at the worst possible time), and, thus, any perceived lack of care or professionalism will be magnified many times over. A specific problem is that neither speaker can see the reaction of the other. The service provider must put in extra words or acknowledgements to emphasize that the customer is being attended to.

As with face-to-face contact, some people have a rather better telephone manner than do others, though even the worst can be improved somewhat. Again, the excellent service providers have worked hard to ensure that their telephone response is an asset and not a barrier to service.

Some examples of the approach to managing telephone contact include:

- Monitoring the time customers wait for their call to be answered against a specified target (typically three rings).
- Provision of a single, easily remembered phone number for all customer transactions.
- Effective capacity management of the telephone network to allow call switching from center to center to smooth load.
- Thorough training of telephone contact staff in both interpersonal skills and product knowledge. The technical knowledge allows some initial advice to be given. This advice may be in the form of simple equipment checks to go through or safety advice as, for example, to open all windows in the event of a suspected gas leak. The fact that these people know something about the product increases customer confidence and also increases the likelihood that accurate information will be gained from the customer to start the right service response.
- Design of working environment to help teamwork and to enable rapid access to information when needed. We visited a medical equipment manufacturer's response center that is designed around a central console equipped with screens for the service provider to call up prompts for each product in the range. Some product specialists are positioned at desks behind the console ready to give advice or take over the call if necessary.
- Some callers will have to wait because capacity to ensure immediate response at all times would be extremely expensive. The software company in America, Microsoft, has recently incorporated a live disc jockey in its telephone center. In addition to music and sales promotions, information is given as to the current average wait: "If you have been waiting five minutes, your call is about to be answered." Callers have been known to ask to be put back on hold to continue listening!

Many organizations undertake telephone training spasmodically. There is no doubt that training using role-play and recordings of how you react on the phone can be very powerful, but the lessons learned must be regularly reinforced if regression is to be avoided. A very powerful force for good or ill is peer pressure. Once good habits are accepted as the group norm there is a reduced need for policing tactics.

Some general points about the telephone contact:

- The person answering the telephone must work very hard to communicate their interest in solving the customer's problem as the visual dimension is lacking. It must be clear that the customer is receiving their full attention. Silences appear longer when facial reactions are not visible.

- The customer wants to go through as few stages as possible before the person who can deal with the request is reached. Ideally, there should be no call transfers that carry the risk of losing the customer and building a perception of delay into the response time. To achieve this efficiency requires investment in staff and systems support.

- The customer expects the representative of the company to be fully informed about all customer account details and company policies. The customer expects that the person answering the phone will know all the details of the service such as whether or not the required spares have been ordered and what the promised delivery date is.

- The customer should not be left in any doubt about what will happen as a result of the conversation, and if for any reason the promised action is unlikely to take place, the customer should be informed as soon as possible to allow him to make any necessary changes in his plans.

Paper contact

Receiving a letter or an invoice is as much a Moment of Truth as meeting face-to-face. Organizations have spent much money to ensure that the right visual impact is made by logos, facilities, and equipment.

The availability of word processors should help the production of documents to reach a consistently high standard. With accurate information systems, invoices should be correct and timely. In our service quality seminars we are amazed at the frequency with which the issue of poor documentation is highlighted. There are several manufacturers with reputations for good product quality who are renowned for submitting invoices before the goods are delivered.

We recently had cause for complaint with a major building society. The complaint was generally resolved to our satisfaction, but the effect was spoiled because the first reply letter was unsigned and impersonal, just saying that it came from the Customer Service Department. It is tempting to use standard letters to save time, but there are occasions when a more personal approach is required.

Locating Close to Customers

The siting of service facilities is a major decision for any service business. Indeed, for some it may be one of the few differentiating factors as, for example, fast-food restaurants, which attract business largely by being in the right place.

Black and Decker realized that the location of their service facilities was neither close enough to their customers nor did it convey the impression of the company they wanted. Repair centers had been set up around the United Kingdom, largely on industrial estates, away from the high street. This decision perhaps reflected a concentration, for service at least, on the professional user of power tools. The customer base was changing because more home owners were carrying out DIY activities. As a result, Black and Decker realized that service would have to be related far more to the needs and perceptions of consumers, and this resulted in a conscious switch from industrial to high street locations. The change in location reflects the need to be close to consumers and also to ensure a consistent product/service image.

The twin issues of how close to customers and the grade of the location must be addressed. For many service companies the grade of location may not matter too much because personnel visit the customer rather than the reverse. However, the fact that there is a regional service center within 50 miles may influence the decision to purchase when the competition relies on a national service center that is 200 miles away. The influence of customer confidence must not be underestimated, and must be carefully balanced against the cost benefits of centralization.

DETERMINING THE RESOURCES

The resources employed by the service and support organization can be identified under five headings:
1. People.
2. Facilities.
3. Information systems.
4. Equipment.
5. Materials.

In this section we identify the sources to be employed in service delivery, and the impact that the choice of resource has on customer contact. The management of people, information systems, and materials are covered in later chapters.

There are interrelationships between resources: a greater investment in one area can bring cost reductions in other areas. Many organizations have found that an investment in information systems has brought about sizeable reductions in inventory costs. We have found that the value chain approach previously described is a useful tool to the identification of resource linkages to improve service at lower cost. An example of this approach is included later in this chapter.

People: The Right Service Providers

Many product-related service organizations are realizing that the customer service and support personnel have many opportunities to create a positive impression. Sales staff may make the initial sale, but the customer relationship is maintained by the service and support team, salesmen perhaps making occasional visits. More organizations are recognizing the role of customer support in keeping customers and identifying sales opportunities. As a result, support personnel tend to be selected more for their interpersonal skills than for their technical competence. Someone can be taught relatively simple diagnostic routines, but if they do not possess the right type of personality little can be done to change it.

An issue to be addressed is when the organization is represented by relatively junior service staff to senior customers. We visited a security system company where the engineers stated that they were much happier dealing with systems for small business premises—where they felt comfortable with the customer—than they were when fitting major systems; this situation made them feel uncomfortable because they had to deal with managing directors of large companies or owners of mansions.

It is very important to match the customer and service provider. In academic terms these service providers are called *boundary spanners*, forming the bridge between the organization and its customers. The customer's perception about how good the service is will be influenced greatly by how good the relationship is between customer and provider. A positive bond will mean that the customer may take a relaxed view when occasionally the service falls down. A negative view will often result in the customer finding fault with the most trivial details.

A possible danger in encouraging service personnel to take a customer-oriented view is that sometimes they may become more loyal to their customers than they are to the organization. Clearly, this may not be all bad, but service managers may have to be careful to reinforce company and service team loyalty if the service engineer spends the majority of working hours on customer's premises.

For many customer service and support organizations, people represent the biggest expense, representing as much as 60 percent of the cost of service delivery. Improving service delivery may demand further investment in the service providers:

- *Recruitment Costs.* It is important to recruit people with the right service attitudes, able to cope under pressure and sufficiently flexible to deal with situations not covered by standard procedures.

- *Training Costs.* Service providers will require continuing investment in training to update product knowledge and to hone personal skills.

- *Support Costs.* Service providers will feel more confident in the organization if properly supported with good equipment and effective information systems. Scheduling is a key task, service quality being maintained when the personnel are not continually overloaded.

People: Managing the Customers

Customers may be a valuable resource for the service organization. By this we mean that there are functions that customers carry out in addition to purchasing the product. As Johnston has pointed out, customers have a critical role in service delivery:

- They may perform some of the service tasks themselves as, for example, carrying out oil and water checks on a car, acting as Territorials in our Support Structure model (Chapter 2).

- They provide information to start the process (my computer has broken down), during the process (the screen works but the printer doesn't), and they give quality feedback on the performance of goods and services providing opportunity for the organization to improve.

- Sometimes they also provide part of the "scene setting" that may convince prospective customers that this is a good company to deal with because they already deal with some well-known people. Customers also perform some service for other customers, with the service organization merely helping. An example in the customer support area would be the organization of user groups, which as well as providing an interface between the company and its customers also gives opportunity for exchange of experience and business development.

In a sense, then, customers must be managed similarly to the organization's employees. Investment in resources and management attention will be repaid in improvements in quality and productivity.

- *Recruitment.* Many organizations use a scattergun approach to selling, believing that by hitting as many as possible potential customers, sufficient business will be generated. This approach may generate volume of business but is unlikely to be as profitable as being more selective about where the largest gains are to be made. Information systems should indicate the customer groups that are likely to be most profitable for the business as a whole. Selling a computer system and maintenance package may be profitable in an office environment, but not in a retail situation. Just as you would probably not recruit an accountant with convictions for fraud, so it is with customers.

- *Training.* Training customers may provide a range of benefits for the service organization. The photocopier manufacturers have discovered that providing simple "key operator" training has reduced the call out rate for simple problems by reducing abuse caused by ignorance as well as enabling the customers to fix small problems themselves. The turnover of staff in large retailers means that security systems installers must provide training for new people to ensure the system is correctly set at closing time, thus preventing call outs or even break-ins.

Training may also be another opportunity to impress the customer as well as generate income for the organization. Unfortunately, this opportunity may not be fully exploited. We have worked with a power equipment manufacturer who was often required to provide operator training as a part of the purchase package. There was no training facility, an area being set aside on an ad hoc basis in underused parts of the factory, and a training program devised largely to keep the trainees busy rather than to impart real knowledge.

- *Motivation.* Most people respond to positive motivation rather than restrictions. There may be possibilities to give discounts to customers who do not abuse the product or perhaps to give recognition to those who maximize their use of their product. An example of this second approach is the software supplier who organizes a seminar for present and potential customers and asks its best customer to give a presentation on the benefits of the package. Valuable publicity may be gained by both parties.
- *Dismissal.* Sometimes it will be necessary to withdraw service, perhaps because invoices have not been paid, or because the product is not being used as it was intended. Dismissal is never an easy task, but it must be carried out cleanly and definitely to ensure that any adverse publicity is minimized.

A final but critical point is that greater involvement of customers in the service process may well build commitment to the organization, and also to the maintenance of quality. Higher customer involvement may lead to greater customer loyalty.

Facilities: Setting the Scene

Our perception of the quality of an organization is influenced by many factors. We may not be aware that we are picking up information about the company, but impressions are formed by many small and not so small events. The attitude and attentiveness of service personnel clearly has a significant impact on this process, but we should not forget the influence of the facilities employed:

- The location of premises.
- Size and quality of premises.
- State of repair of buildings and signage.
- Broken furniture in the reception area.
- Cleanliness/state of service engineer's vans.
- Service personnel's appearance.
- The visual impact of logos and signage

This list of details is endless, and it therefore demands constant vigilance to pick up small problems, which will, if unresolved, lead to larger issues later. In managing customer contact so much depends on creating customer confidence in the organization. A customer who has doubts about the organization will subconsciously look for evidence of incompetence. If the facilities support the view that there are problems, the customer will demand more attention, making sure that every detail is addressed before making a commitment.

Black and Decker employed a retail consultant to advise on upgrading the layout of their service centers to help customer contact and improve the image of the company. They found that the position and style of the service counter had a significant effect on the ease with which the service staff could communicate, and, therefore, an effect on the customers' perception of quality.

Customer-Friendly Information Systems

The design of information systems is covered in more depth in Chapter 3. It is worth restating the point here that a good information system can add confidence to the Moment of Truth. We recently visited a retailer who had invested a considerable sum in implementing a sophisticated EPOS (Electronic Point of Sale) system, which, though good at tracking usage of items, was unable to answer the predictable customer inquiry of "when do you expect the next delivery?"

Some information systems need only to be fairly simple to be effective, at least, in enhancing customer contact. The insurance salesman knows the value of recording the names of spouses, children, and pets to give the impression of personal care. Many service engineers adopt the same approach with their contacts. British Gas and British Telecom have both developed some powerful systems that allow the person who answers the customer query to be able to respond with specific information, because they have full details on the screen in front of them as they speak.

The service provider represents the whole organization to the customer and may be expected to be able to give information on the full range of activities. The employee must, at the very least, be briefed about how to respond in general terms before ensuring that the needed information is forthcoming rapidly.

Equipment: The Balance between Technology and People

John Naisbitt, in his book *Megatrends*, coined the phrase "Hi-Tech, Hi-Touch" to express the idea that although we want to capitalize on the increasing power of technology, we also need the contact with people rather than disappear forever into an isolated "electronic cottage." The service provider must surely be aware of this need.

The service and support manager must make decisions about the quality of equipment used, following the same principles outlined in the previous section on facilities. If the service engineer doesn't have the tools of the trade, the customer is unlikely to be impressed and, again, an investment in a higher level of equipment, perhaps for more rapid diagnostics, may save on overall cost.

An important decision is how much the service is to be delivered through equipment/technology rather than through people. Customers may require the confidence factor that comes through meeting a person rather than being treated in a totally impersonal manner. It is worth reflecting that a person may pick up sales leads and other useful feedback whereas a machine certainly will not. The service and support organization must learn to capitalize on those moments of direct face-to-face contact.

Materials: First-Time Fix

Most customer service and support organizations must develop a clear inventory policy, knowing how much stock they must hold, in what form, and where it is to be held. They must also be aware of the impact on customer service arising from changes to this inventory profile. If the inventory is not available, the customer's product can not be fixed.

An organization must realize that 100 percent availability of everything is unlikely to be economical even if it were possible and understand the relative impact of a stockout of each item on ultimate customer satisfaction. Many support organizations have the problem that they are dependent on the supply of components or product from external suppliers. The service from these suppliers can rarely be improved by the use of sanctions, but rather by finding ways that the two organizations can work more effectively together to improve customer satisfaction at reduced cost.

This approach is often termed *supply chain management* and is discussed in more detail in another chapter. It is based on developing a partnership through sharing of information, schedules, and risk to try to become more effective as a team. A possible outcome might be for the supplier to hold more inventory at an earlier, uncommitted stage to allow the support organization to respond more consistently.

The chain from supplier to support organization to dealer to customer must be understood in more detail, so that each part is clear about how customer satisfaction at the end of the chain can be maintained. Who holds which stock at which point in the chain, along with an understanding of the length of replenishment lead times, are fundamental questions to address if the customer contact is to be managed more effectively.

Managing the Balance of Resources

We started this section by indicating that an approach to improving customer perception of the quality of service delivery is to identify possibilities for resource productivity, an incremental increase in resource investment in one area saving overall cost. Figure 5–3 develops the value chain to indicate how the intruder alarm company might be able to improve.

For the example illustrated by Intruder Alarms, the value chain indicated a change in organization to set resources aside for routine maintenance and better information systems to set inventory levels. Both combine to improve the effectiveness of service engineers, which is the most expensive resource. Thus, the customer perceives the organization to be delivering better value, with no increase in overall cost.

CUSTOMER PROCESS FLOW

It is relatively easy to organize a customer support system from one's own perspective as a manager but miss how the customer might view it. It is relatively easy to think of the process employed by the organization and to produce flowcharts of materials and information flow. These flowcharts can become extremely detailed, and though they have value, this is not the approach we are describing here.

The customer service and support organization must remember that it is not just following a set of procedures, it is processing customers. A customer with a need can be thought of as the input to the process, and a satisfied customer ought to be the outcome. We have found that it is worth charting or mapping the major stages in this process considering the customer's viewpoint, particularly identifying what the customer is doing at each point.

Figure 5–4 is an example of part of a customer process flow for the intruder alarms company. It indicates the main activities of both Front Office and Back Room. We have found it useful to identify also the critical customer service and resource dimensions to give a complete picture.

FIGURE 5-3
Resource Substitution in the Value Chain

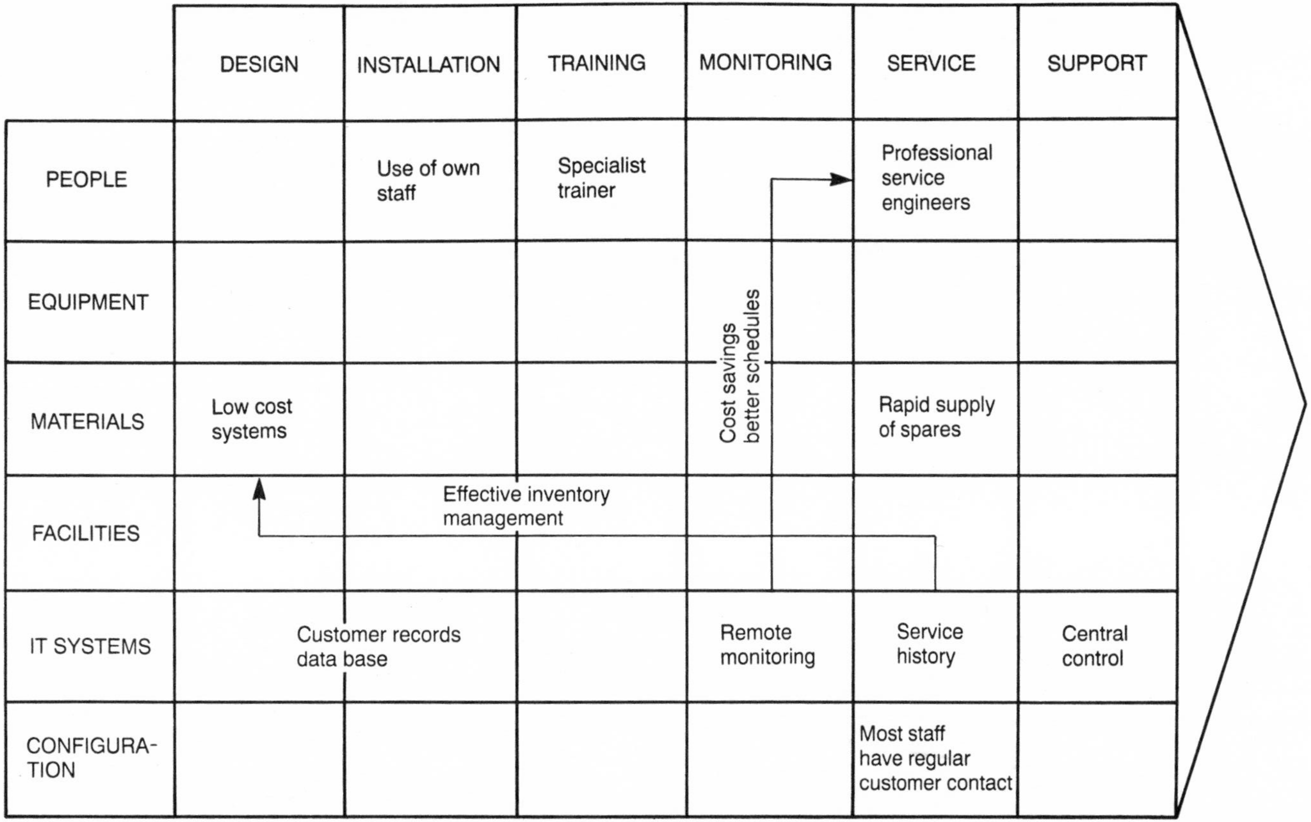

	DESIGN	INSTALLATION	TRAINING	MONITORING	SERVICE	SUPPORT
PEOPLE		Use of own staff	Specialist trainer		Professional service engineers	
EQUIPMENT						
MATERIALS	Low cost systems				Rapid supply of spares	
FACILITIES	Customer records data base	Effective inventory management				
IT SYSTEMS				Remote monitoring	Service history	Central control
CONFIGURA-TION					Most staff have regular customer contact	

Cost savings better schedules

97

FIGURE 5-4
Customer Process Flow for Intruder Alarms

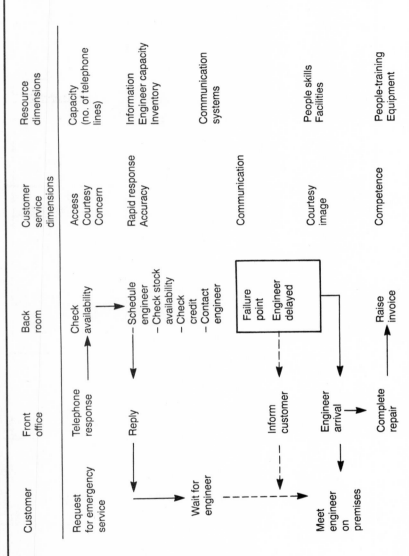

The objectives of charting process flow are:

- To identify the main stages of service delivery.
- To enhance the understanding of service personnel.
- To identify key customer contact points.
- To identify information flows between customers, Front Office, and Back Room.
- To identify support requirements.
- To identify failure points, their likelihood of occurrence, and severity of effect on customer satisfaction.

How Much Does the Customer See?

The customer process flow should identify how much of the total operation is visible to the customer. In general, the more the customer sees, the greater the chance that a degree of customization will occur as the customer intervenes or interferes. By studying the process flow it may be possible to reduce the "line of visibility," transferring more work content to the Back Room, thereby gaining some productivity benefits. Great care must be taken that the perception of customer care is not lost in this process or that the customer focus of support or Back Room staff does not deteriorate.

Where Does It Go Wrong?

Using the process flow in a staff seminar or quality action team meeting can be a useful tool to identify problem areas. It can be used as a framework to gather data as well as a communication aid to explain how the organization works. This tool is particularly valuable when the group contains staff from different departments, and they can gain insights into how the organization as a whole might function more effectively.

In Figure 5–4 an adaptation of a process flow developed during a quality workshop, the group was asked to identify the major failure points and to indicate the likely effect on the customer as well as to suggest improvements. Having identified the failure points, you can apply a simple rating system, multiplying "How likely" by "How severe" will give the basis of an agenda for improvement. A refinement of this rating scheme is to add a third factor of "How easily is a problem detected." If a problem cannot be seen, it is possible that damage to customer satisfaction will only become evident after time has elapsed, making recovery impossible.

How Does the Customer Feel?

An important issue in designing an effective customer process flow lies in gaining an understanding of the degree and type of risk that the customer feels in dealing with the organization. The customer will probably not verbalize these anxieties, and sometimes may not be fully aware of them, but the organizations that manage to address them will improve perceived service quality.

The customer may wonder if the organization is delivering value for money. It may be worth taking the customer through the service process to indicate where the costs lie. The provision of clear and comprehensive guarantees will build confidence, as will the professionalism of service personnel and the quality of facilities and equipment. Perversely, too low a price may have the effect of building a fear that the organization cannot deliver to the required standard.

The customer may be concerned about risk, either to life and limb or to expensive equipment. Garages may counteract the fear of servicing and selling dangerous cars by enforcing standards through trade associations and displaying evidence of successful completion of training courses for their staff.

The customer may also question issues such as: Can I trust the service engineer to turn up? Will my business cope with the disruption of not having this machine available? Clear guarantees and accurate estimates of engineer arrival will bolster customer confidence.

KEY ACTIONS

1. Draw a customer process flow for when and how customers come into contact with your organization.

2. List where things can go wrong in the process flow. How critical are the failures? What could you do to prevent them from happening?
3. Write down ways in which you could enhance the encounters.
4. List ways in which your Back Room staff could be given the experience of dealing with customers.
5. Write down the key linkages on your value chain. Are they working? Could they be made to work better?
6. Think how you could reduce the costs of resources in your value chain. Could some be substituted?

Chapter Six

Managing Your Human Resources

Introduction

We have seen that the customer service triangle is made up of three legs, strategy, systems, and people. In this chapter we focus on the people. We examine the role of the service and support managers and the competences they need to carry out their jobs. We also look at ways of auditing the skills needed by the service personnel and the implications for recruitment and training. Motivation of the service team is an important issue and is also a way to increase the effectiveness of the team. We see how teams can be managed within the organizational structure of the company. Finally we will look at burnout of service personnel and the ways of reducing its effect.

HOW MUCH DO YOU VALUE YOUR PEOPLE?

Whenever we bring service and support managers together to talk about their work we find that issues relating to people dominate. These include the changing role of the service engineer, the search for a service culture, changing demographic patterns limiting the recruitment of people, and increased responsibility for the service and support managers. All of these points indicate the need for staff and managers to manage change.

There has been a great deal mentioned in the recent past about the importance of people in the delivery of service, which is not surprising, given the people-intensity of the process. There have been actions, for instance, with customer care programs and total quality management initiatives designed to raise the awareness of service providers and to give some tools for involving service staff in the process of improvement. However, we know of many service organizations who have run one-day customer care programs only to find that concentration on a smile campaign fails when the service provider does not have the spares to do the job, or they are expected to carry out tasks for which they are not trained. At least the total quality movement recognizes one fundamental truth. There is no point beating people around the head if they fail to deliver or if they do not have the right skills, equipment, and environment to make it possible. In short, most of the problems come back to management failures.

So how well do you value your people? We have talked about perceived value for our customers when we are looking at strategy and marketing. We can apply the same concept to our own people. Look at the following list of statements and give each a score from 0 to 4 depending on how positive your answer is (0 = negative, 4 = most positive).

- I take as much trouble to find out what will help my people as I would my customers.
- I know the strengths and weaknesses of all the people for whom I am responsible.
- I sit down with all my people regularly to talk to them about their work.
- I keep my people informed about what the company is trying to achieve.
- I ask my people about the customers they serve.
- I know my people recommend our firm to their friends as a good employer.
- I give my people regular feedback on what customers are saying about our service.
- I know my people have a high degree of influence over the way they carry out their tasks.
- I ask my people to rate their own performance.
- I encourage and support my people to work together to solve problems.

Scoring:

- Over 36: You value your people and are doing most of the right things to support them.

- 26–35: You recognize the need to value your people, but you need to do more to support them.
- 16–25: If you claim to value your people, it is more of a wish than a reality.
- Less than 15: You probably have difficulty in retaining staff. If you have the same attitude to customers, you will probably soon be out of business, if there are alternative suppliers.

Good service providers have recognized the need to treat their service people as they would their customers. We can all think of companies who are held up as examples of good providers of service and who are also companies for whom people want to work. In the retail sector Marks and Spencer and Hewlett Packard in the high-tech sector have occupied this position for decades, while newcomers to the service philosophy like British Airways have realized the importance of caring for their staff in achieving their goal of being "The world's favorite airline." We want to look at what is involved for service managers in changing their approach to people. Just how do service and support operations introduce the sparkle into the customer service triangle through their service staff?

THE ROLE OF THE SERVICE AND SUPPORT MANAGER

The service and support manager who is responsible for either frontline service and support providers or those reinforcing the frontline staff plays a crucial role. If the person sees the job simply as allocating work or making sure spares are available, that person is missing some of the most important parts of the manager's role.

Consider the case of Kevin, who is the service manager for a retail chain. As he drives to work on Friday morning, he is turning over in his mind the events of the week and what the day holds in store for him. It has been a heavy week; some customers have called to complain that service engineers have been late for appointments, there have been problems obtaining spares from one supplier of electrical goods, and one of his supervisors has become ill and is not expected to return to work for a few weeks.

Today, Kevin knows he has a lunchtime meeting with a senior representative from one of his suppliers, who is coming to talk to him about the results of a customer satisfaction survey they have carried out. Kevin also knows he is involved in interviewing some new service engineers. On top of these immediate tasks, he knows he has to prepare over the weekend for a meeting on Monday with the regional service managers to consider changes to the structure of the service operation. Also, the next budgeting round is close. Just in time he remembers it is his wife's birthday and stops at the mall to buy a card!

You may feel Kevin's day is less full than many experienced by someone in his position. However, the range of activities illustrates some of the different roles a manager has to perform in the job at different times. One management writer, Henry Mintzberg, has identified three major managerial roles; interpersonal, informational, and decisional, which managers perform within their position in an organization (Figure 6–1). These three main roles involve:

1. *An interpersonal role* There are three activities—leading, acting as a figurehead representing the organization, and liaising with others inside and outside the organization.

2. *An informational role* There are three informational activities—monitoring, disseminating information, and acting as a spokesperson for information to other parts of the organization and outside.

3. *Decisional* There are four activities in this category—entrepreneurship, when managers look for innovation; handling disturbances that disrupt events in the flow of the service delivery, such as shortages and breakdowns; resolving conflicting demands from customers, which might entail reallocating resources; and negotiating and influencing staff and bosses.

These roles are not discrete, they overlap and interact, but managers are more commonly assessed by their performance in the decisional role.

While the role of the manager can be described in this way, we feel we can also draw out some other critical roles that are right for a customer service organization. After all, the service and support manager is in effect the frontline manager who with his staff spans the boundaries between the company and its customers and

FIGURE 6–1
Managerial Roles (after Mintzberg)

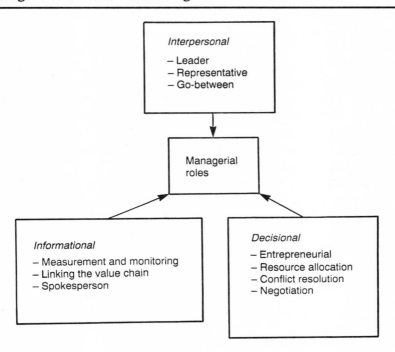

suppliers. Consequently that individual is in the best position to look critically at both the customers' needs and at the company's approaches to meeting them. How does this polarize in the makeup of the frontline manager? We see four main activities for the frontline manager: a systems architect, a role model, a psychologist, and a team builder.

The Systems Architect

There can be no better example of excellence through service delivery system design than that of Disney World. Each detail is thought through and planned down to the last detail, for instance, positioning the popcorn stands to ensure that the right smell greets the guests. This service is only achieved by having managers who have frontline mentality. Once the service delivery system is right it becomes easier to deliver good service than to deliver bad service.

For an organization to deliver good service consistently, there must be a service delivery system that is designed rather than one that just evolves. One problem we must guard against is that we often like our own design without thinking what effect it has on the customer. The maintenance scheduling that is designed to take the minimum amount of time for the engineer and give maximum use of engineers looks perfect to the manager. Unfortunately, the customers are never sure when the engineer is going to arrive and feel things could be better.

The design of systems requires managing the link between frontline staff and Back Room support. Total quality philosophy demands that everyone should have a customer or be serving someone who has. Communications from the frontline manager help to feed information on the needs of the frontline staff in the design of the internal supply chain.

The Role Model

A pub near where we work illustrates how not to give good service. Going in at midday, we were struck by how empty it was. It did not take long to discover where the problem lay. The landlord was on the phone explaining in none too sympathetic tones why a customer's request for sandwiches was totally unreasonable and impossible. There was no attempt to work out what could be done, just a flat refusal and inflexibility, an attitude copied by the rest of the staff.

The way frontline staff behave toward customers is strongly influenced by the behavior they observe from their managers, who, in turn, are influenced by the behavior of their bosses. The managing director who regularly calls customers to inquire about levels of service and who visits service depots is more likely to have frontline staff who are concerned about customer service and support.

The Psychologist

Many types of service and support contain large sections that have prolonged contact with customers. Even with relatively simple tasks, the sheer pressure of having people demanding information or advice all the time becomes exhausting. These pressures lead eventually to burnout and a loss of the service sparkle. The reaction of most people in these circumstances is to become more defensive and less willing to put themselves out. Later we look in more detail at the causes and effects of burnout. It should be apparent that we think the frontline manager should spot service decline caused by burnout and take action to limit its effect.

The frontline manager must also be a psychologist when dealing with customers and must be able to identify the unspoken needs and adapt the approach to suit. This can be a complex task when there are wide differences in the customers being dealt with, for instance, corporate customers compared to domestic, rich and poor, or young and old. One group of service engineers we saw recently said they felt more at ease dealing with ordinary people than with those they saw as being rich.

The Team Builder

The role of the frontline manager as team builder and coach is one that we see increasingly in good service providers. The benefits are in sharing of problems, more innovation in the way things are done, support to limit burnout, and a greater commitment from individuals to customer service. Peer group pressure can have a greater effect on the service people than admonishments from the manager or supervisor.

Team building also applies to customer partnerships. There are very strong indications that taking customers into the service team is a way of increasing loyalty and preventing customers from switching to another supplier.

Recognizing different roles that a service manager must perform is important, because it allows us to think about the competences that are needed to do the job.

WHAT MANAGERIAL COMPETENCES DO YOU NEED?

For a service and support manager to perform any of the roles we have introduced, they need to have a set of managerial competences that enable them to fulfill the role. By managerial competences we mean the skills, knowledge, and behavior that are appropriate to the roles.

Competences include technical, professional, and job knowledge; knowledge of the company and of its markets and customers; skills in handling interpersonal relationships, counseling, selling skills; and information gathering and problem solving. The competences set will differ in detail from organization to organization, and it is important for each service and support team to identify the managerial competences that are important for their own circumstances. Peter Norris at the Cranfield School of Management has worked with many groups of managers, assisting them to determine the set of competences that they need. As an example, one service company identified the following managerial competences.

Business Development

- *Commercial awareness.* Managers show the capacity to perceive the impact of decisions and activities of the organization on customers, competitors, and the future viability of the business. There is a focus on customers' needs. Business opportunities are identified and acted on.
- *Environmental awareness.* Managers show an awareness of changes in the political, economic, social, and technological environment that are likely to affect their jobs or the organization. Managers show a breadth and diversity of business-related knowledge about the environmental issues.
- *Initiative.* Managers have the ability to influence events. They do not passively accept what is happening, but are proactive.

Analysis

- *Problem analysis.* There is the ability to identify problems, to seek relevant data and information, and to identify possible causes of problems.

- *Numerical analysis*. Managers have the ability to analyze, to organize, and to present numerical data, be it financial, statistical, or operational.
- *Judgement*. Managers have the ability to evaluate data and information and to identify courses of action in a logical manner.

Managing

- *Planning and organizing*. Managers have the ability to set up the right course of action for themselves and for others to achieve their goals. Effective use is made of resources.
- *Management control*. Managers have the ability to maintain control over the service process and of the people. They appreciate the need for, and are willing to exercise, control.

Staff Management

- *Leadership*. Managers have the ability to develop teamwork and to maximize the use of resources in the team to meet the goals of the team. They have the ability to motivate, to influence, and to handle people, taking account of personalities, to carry out tasks effectively.
- *Team work*. Managers have the ability to make an effective contribution when the team is working on something of no direct personal interest. There is a willingness to take part fully when not necessarily the leader of the team.
- *Subordinate development*. The managers have the ability to develop the skills and competences of subordinates through training and development activities related to current and future jobs.

You may feel that anyone who matches up to the full list of competences is bound to be a paragon. The important point is to recognize the most important competences within your job and to rate your ability to meet the competences. Shortfalls in any areas indicate the need for training and development. We suggest that managers work in groups to identify the main competences needed for service and support managers in their own operation. It may well be that some of the competences are considered more important than others so a weighting can be given to each, as

TABLE 6–1
Managerial Competence

Managerial Competences	Weighting	Performance	Total
Business development			
Commercial awareness	4	0	4
Environmental awareness	3	−2	−6
Initiative	4	2	8
Analysis of problems	3	−1	−3
Numerical analysis	4	−2	−8
Judgement	3	0	3
Planning and organizing	4	0	4
Management control	5	−1	−5
Leadership	4	1	4
Teamwork	5	+1	5
Subordinate development	3	+2	6

Weighting
0= Low
5=High

Rating
scale
−3 to +3
Low   High

shown in Table 6–1. You can rate your own performance against each competence, on your own, and with your manager or personnel specialists.

DO YOU GIVE YOUR PEOPLE A CHANCE?

Many service and support managers would agree that the job of the frontline service providers is becoming more complex and demanding. While in the past reliance on technical skills was sufficient, now it is only one aspect of what is required. One writer on services, Christopher Lovelock, illustrates the change by talking about a "Service Trinity" for frontline personnel. In the minds of the customer at least, the frontline person runs the organization, sells the service, and represents what the service is worth. If this is true, then the job is more complex because it involves aspects of production in doing the technical bits and of marketing in presenting the image of the service organization.

Service managers must recognize the changing needs for their frontline people and take steps to enable them to fulfill their extended roles. We recognize that in a well-established organization this process can be long and difficult because we are managing a process of change. However, if we do nothing, or pay lip service to change, we will fail both the staff and eventually the customers.

WHAT DO OUR PEOPLE NEED TO DO THEIR JOBS?

We have already looked at managerial competences; now we turn our attention to the mix of knowledge, skills, and abilities—the KSA mix, which the service and support personnel need. Finding out what these are requires an analysis of the service delivery process. This analysis must be a systematic evaluation of what is needed to do the tasks successfully at each stage so that the quality and service levels are achieved. The evaluation leads to a detailed description for each category of work in the knowledge skills, and abilities required, including:

1. Technical skills associated with the product(s). Knowledge of the products and their use, skills associated with installation, servicing, and fault diagnosis and repair.

2. Procedures to be used in the job. Where the job is standardized, these may include the use of scripts for communication.

3. Information systems used for maintaining records of customers and equipment and for remote diagnosis.

4. Interpersonal skills for communicating information and for building relationships by taking account of the feelings, values, and needs of others. Listening skills for active listening are necessary to reduce the chances of misunderstandings.

5. Appearance of service personnel and of the equipment and other materials for which they are responsible.

6. Time management to make the most effective use of time. This use of time becomes more important when service staff are given more responsibility for organizing their own work.

7. Selling skills needed by technical specialists or call takers when they are encouraged to take part in the selling process either on the telephone or on visits to customers.

8. Team working to increase the cooperative delivery of the service and support.

9. Self-monitoring to be able to assess their own performances and behavior in response to customer demands.

Assessing the KSA mix for each job category has implications in the areas of training, recruitment, and selection for promotion. For training, we can carry out an audit of the training needs against the KSAs required for the job and identify any areas of weakness for a group or an individual. While it is easy to identify shortcomings in technical areas, it is often more difficult for the less tangible parts of the KSA mix. Here there must be a great reliance on the role of the frontline managers to be close to their people to be able to help to identify training needs.

In selection and recruitment, the KSA mix may act as a guide for those involved in the process. However, there are definite problems in making judgments about abilities in the interpersonal areas, unless psychometric testing is used as a guide to behavior. Perhaps the more important aim is to recruit those who will match the culture of the organization and who will present the values of the organization to the customer.

It perhaps goes without saying that having the right people with the right KSA mix for the job is not a guarantee for success. In a moment's reflection we can see that the KSA route is primarily from the organization's view. While this may be valuable to make sure people are equipped and suitable to do the job, it takes no account of what the individual's needs are from the job. Factors that give job satisfaction and motivation for a service person are largely ignored in the KSA process, but they are crucial to the success of the company.

IMPOSED SYSTEMS OR EMPOWERED ORGANIZATIONS

Many management thinkers talk about empowerment. While believing unconditionally that it is important to use the creativity and goodwill of all employees, empowerment in its fullest sense will not be suited for all people in all organizations.

We see two groupings, both of which may exist in the one organization because different people have different functions. Figure 6–2 shows that there is a match between an organization that is systems driven, and employees who have a relatively low perception of *discretion*. We define discretion as the ability to choose when and how I do things. This is the Compliant box. It is appropriate when consistent, low-cost, high-volume service is delivered. (Because it is called Compliant, this does not necessarily mean regimented.)

The opposite extreme is an organization that is much more skill or competence driven, where individuals have much greater discretion, and the organization is looser as a result.

The matrix in Figure 6–2 is powerful when mapping the need for change. If you are attempting to move between Compliant and Adaptive, there will be problems with groups and individuals. The most common are indicated in Figure 6–3.

We have observed a number of customer service and support organizations:

- Many service managers are promoted from the ranks of service engineers. Until this time they may have been in the Compliant box. Now they are given much more responsibility and move rapidly into Anxiety. During this transition, they must be supported carefully.
- Some service engineers, however, are used to high degrees of freedom and will perceive themselves to be in the Adaptive box. More sophisticated scheduling systems and communications devices that effectively track their progress may move them into the Frustration box.

We have found it helpful to position individuals and groups on this matrix, to decide how best to manage change.

THE DANGERS OF BURNOUT

What are the messages for service and support managers from the various motivation theories? We think they are:

1. Responsibility of the service and support manager to recognize the needs of the individual service personnel. This description fits with the frontline manager's role as a psychologist.

FIGURE 6–2

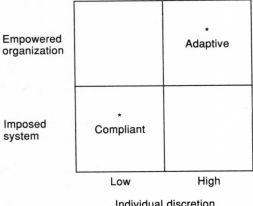

FIGURE 6–3

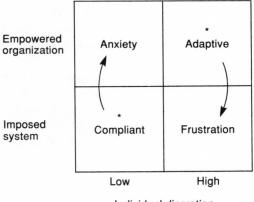

2. Managers should try to see the relationship between the rewards and the way people are assessed. A service engineer who is paid by calls achieved per day is less likely to be motivated to spend time on achieving first-time fix. Also, this behavior is going to be reinforced, if the same engineer is paid overtime for a call out.

3. When the role of service staff is changed, managers need to recognize that the new roles may be at variance with the needs set by the individual service personnel.

4. Empowerment will only be a motivator when service staff feel they are actively supported and the new role fits with their personal needs.

Failure to pay attention to these four points increases the likelihood of burnout of frontline service providers. Burnout has become recognized as one of the symptoms of stress for frontline service personnel. It was first recognized in the caring professions like social work and health care, when service providers who had previously given full caring attention to their clients or patients exhibited a lack of caring, disinterest in their jobs, and signs of stress, depression, irritability, and difficulty in sleeping and relaxing. We can see outward signs of burnout with all service people who are in continuous contact with customers. The disinterested, bored approach with robot like service is within everyone's experience.

Certainly not everyone is as prone to stress and burnout and will exhibit the symptoms to differing degrees. However, within the context of service and support operations it may become more of an issue for service managers as the role of staff changes from one of service to supporting the customer.

The points that we drew from motivation theory have an important bearing on the limitation of burnout. The clarity of service and support roles and the alignment of personal needs and the role of the job will all help to limit stress and burnout. Another factor in burnout is increased customer contact because of increased workloads. The service team approach is a powerful one of giving the support that, more than anything, helps to limit burnout.

BUILDING THE SERVICE TEAM

Why should the service team be so important? First, it gives service managers the opportunity to act as the coach to the team. Second, it gives individuals the chance to learn from others and to work toward achieving common goals. Third, it allows team members to increase their own KSAs to increase the flexibility of the team.

We perhaps need to remind ourselves of what we are trying to achieve from the service team: customer satisfaction and efficiencies in resource productivity. These will be our measures of the effectiveness of the team at the end of the day. Whether or not we achieve our goals will depend on three factors for teams: first, the clarity of what we are trying to achieve and who is involved in the process, that is, who is included in the service team; second, the motivation of the individual team members and the systems and process that allow the task to be done; and finally, the actions of the team leader.

The composition of service teams needs some thought. Do we just include frontline people in the team or should the team also contain Back Room people? Clearly, the benefit of including Back Room people is to develop a common view of the goals and what is involved in reaching them. Sometimes Back Room people are excluded because of group size or their location. Consequently, one of the main tasks of the frontline service team is to communicate with the Back Room people.

Another area where the composition of the team becomes important is when service and support is being delivered by a mix of SAS and Regulars (see Chapter 2). There is the danger of the two groups becoming isolated, especially if there is geographical separation. Here we might want to establish mixed teams of the two groups. This idea can be extended further to build service teams around product groups so that Back Room and frontline service staff are closely associated in the same product team.

The Pathway to Effectiveness for Teams

Teams do not simply come together and perform well. They go through four stages in their development to becoming an effective team. These are:

1. *Forming.* The team is simply a group of individuals without a clear idea of their task and what they are trying to achieve.

2. *Storming.* The team is often in conflict about their direction and goals, leadership, and the role of the individuals within the team. We often see strong disagreement among team members or some members not being willing to take part in the activities of the group.

3. *Norming.* the team becomes clear on tasks and goals, and individuals start to become strongly committed to other members of the team. Strong peer group pressure develops for individuals to conform to the values of the team.

4. *Performing.* At this stage the real work is done with the team members sharing and supporting one another. It would seem that the clearer the task and the greater the degree of shared values of the service team members, the more likely it is that a service team will perform well.

Some teams may never reach the performing stage, while others will reach it very quickly, especially if the outcome is very important. Developing a service team requires a very real commitment on the part of the company to devote time and effort to the process. Often firms find they need outside assistance, such as that provided by the Covedale training.

The Team Coach

The role of the service manager as a team builder depends on the ability to act as a coach to the team. Tom Peters, who has studied many organizations who deliver the best customer service in their own industries, says there are five roles for the coach:

1. *Teaching* to:
   a. Make the goals clear.
   b. Give information the team members need.
   c. Help team members to increase their skills and knowledge for the tasks.
   d. Give feedback on performance and what is required.
   e. Introduce new members to the ways of the service team.

2. *Supporting:* Supporting or sponsoring involves aspects of empowering individuals. It means encouraging individual team members to give their best and supporting them day-to-day. The support may come through giving them access to a wider range of responsibilities or skills in their work. Indications of good support are:
   a. Treating people as colleagues.
   b. Looking for opportunities to assist service and support staff.
   c. Discussing training needs and career opportunities at regular meetings and acting on the outcomes.

3. *Leading:* There are various leadership styles from authoritarian to laissez-faire. The most appropriate styles for coaching service teams include:
   a.   Setting a good example.
   b.   Challenging people to do their best.
   c.   Caring about how people are doing.
   d.   Being accessible to staff.
   e.   Being open and honest.

4. *Counseling:* Counseling involves taking measures to resolve problems that occur with the team members in a frank and open manner. For instance, there may be problems with the performance of one member or an individual may have personal problems. Characteristics of good counselors are:
   a.   Active listeners. That is to say, they concentrate on what is being said rather than make assumptions on what is being said to them.
   b.   Perceptive to the feelings of others.
   c.   Willingness to spend time helping to resolve problems.
   d.   Trustworthy with confidences.

5. *Confronting:* Confronting is about facing issues that need to be resolved rather than hiding from them. It may concern poor performance of a team member after counseling and training. It may concern confronting others outside the team who have an influence on the performance of the team—suppliers of spares or services, or members of other departments.

The role of the team coach is a complex one for service managers but without it we think it is unlikely that service and support operations will achieve their goals.

TABLE 6–2

Service Team Audit

The following are team coach attributes suggested by Tom Peters. Score yourself between 0 and 4 on each point depending on how well you consider you perform (0 = badly, 4 = well).

Teaching
- I make the goals clear to my service and support people.
- I give information to my service team members.
- I help my team members to increase their KSA levels.
- I give feedback on performance and what is required of my service people.
- I have a strong induction program for new members to the service and support team.

Supporting
- I treat all my service team as colleagues.
- I constantly look for opportunities to assist my staff.
- I discuss training needs and career development with my staff and do something about them.

Leading
- I set a good example in my approach to customers.
- I challenge people to give their best.
- I care about how my service team is doing, not only in the work environment.
- I am accessible to the members of the service and support team.
- I am open and honest with the service and support staff.

Counseling
- I am an active listener.
- I am perceptive to the feelings of others.
- I am trustworthy with confidences.

Confronting
- I am not afraid to raise issues with the team members.
- I try to resolve issues rather than letting them continue to cause disruption.

Results
Low total scores overall, indicate the need for action to correct your performance.
Low scores against some areas may indicate the need for training.

If you score highly overall you may wish to ask some members of your service team to give their assessment.

KEY ACTIONS

1. List the changes in your organization that have changed your role or the role of your staff.

2. List the management competencies need for the role now. Are there any gaps?

3. Write down the KSA mix for any new roles in customer service and support. Are there any gaps?

4. Check how well you value your service and support staff. You may wish to use the questionnaire toward the beginning of the chapter?

5. Draw out the structures of your service teams. Do they bring together frontline and Back Room personnel?

6. List the steps you have taken to build your service team. What gaps do you see from reading this chapter?

7. List the steps you have taken to motivate the service team. What gaps do you see from reading this chapter?

8. Check how well you match up as a team coach using the audit in Table 6–2 on page 121. What actions do you intend to take to rectify any gaps? Would you be able to ask your service team to complete the audit for you?

Chapter Seven

Capacity Management

Introduction

In this chapter we look at the capacity management in service and support operations. We consider the factors that affect both demand and our ability to change capacity to match demand. Also we look at the techniques that are available to plan and control the operations to get the best from the use of resources while maintaining the levels of customer service we need.

WHY IS CAPACITY MANAGEMENT IMPORTANT?

In our studies of customer service and support, we have found that a feature that differentiates good from bad is the ability to plan and control resources to match changing levels of demand. There is a strong interaction between success in this area and quality management and resource productivity or efficiency management. Getting the balance of resource capacity and demand leads to quality and efficiency targets being achieved. However, often the main problem is dealing with changing levels of demand that can occur rapidly and with some degree of uncertainty. Managers have to try to cope with these changing levels using limited resources. Consider the following story.

Uplifts Plc is a company that manufactures, installs and services elevators. It has a number of service centers to cover the United Kingdom from where engineers perform maintenance and attend failures. The aim of the company is to carry out preventive maintenance so that there are few call outs for elevator failures. Where elevators are installed to carry people, the response to failure has to be rapid for obvious reasons. The different service stations are measured on their call out performance. The perform-ance of the stations varies considerably, with some stations having double the call out rate of other stations. Also the poor performers often don't meet the published response times. The national management is concerned that the under-performing stations will bring the company a bad name, especially with their large national account customers.

At a meeting of the service managers, they considered the rea-sons for the difference in the performance between the stations. There was talk of quality control and of the mix of products in the service portfolio in different places. However, one of the clearest differences that emerged in the discussion was the approach adopted by the service managers to planning and controlling re-sources and trying to anticipate demand.

This story perhaps illustrates the problem. Some parts of the service and support are fairly predictable, like the level of pre-ventive maintenance. Others, like callout to breakdowns, are not. The only ways of controlling these activities are either to change the level of resources to meet demand or to make customers wait for attention. In many instances, making customers wait will mean that the response times specified in service contracts are not met, or customers that are generally dissatisfied with the level of service. Either case may lead to loss of business.

Managing resource levels is important because it has an effect on quality, resource productivity, and customer satisfaction. How-ever, before we can begin to think about controlling resource levels, we need to understand what we mean by capacity and demand, or service intensity, in some detail.

WHAT DO WE MEAN BY CAPACITY?

Sometimes explaining capacity is not easy in any service operation. What is the capacity of a supermarket, a bank, a bus? Is it the square footage, number of cashiers, or number of seats? Whereas these measures may indicate key resources to be managed, they are static measures. They do not take account of all the factors that affect capacity. We therefore prefer to say that capacity is the ability to work off existing demand. This measure is more dynamic. So the capacity of the supermarket, bank and bus could be expressed in customers served per day or passengers carried per day.

Once we express capacity in this way it should be clear that what we are talking about is the level of output from the use of resources. Two other features about capacity are:

1. Capacity measurement has a time dimension.
2. The amount of capacity may be affected by all resources, including staff, materials and equipment, and also customers.

We need to take things a bit further and consider how we view capacity for different parts of the service delivery. We can conveniently think about the capacity at various levels.

- *The business unit network.* The capacity of our network will depend on the extent of the network, and the number and size of the branches. This level may be national or regional and governed by our organization structure for the business units. The capacity is more likely to be expressed as the output for an accounting period or calendar year. Decisions about capacity at this level will result from the planning of resources that involve capital expenditure and major shifts in the levels of manpower.

- *The branch or service center.* The capacity of our branches or service centers will depend on the size and how much we can call on resources from centralized support. The service center is the smallest unit capable of delivering most, if not all, of the service and support. Capacity is more likely to be expressed for time scales less than one week. Decisions about capacity will be more concerned with the deployment of existing resources, although there is obviously a link with the planning at the network level for major changing in resourcing.

- *The team.* The service team's capacity will depend on the numbers in the team. One team may be capable only of delivering one part of the total service and support that is available to our customers. Decisions about capacity will concern the deployment of available resources, rather than large increases in the overall potential capacity. Capacity will be expressed in periods of less than a day.

- *The individual resource.* The individual resource may be a service person with special skills, or it may be a piece of equipment. We must be aware of the capacity of individual resources that may limit capacity of the team or service center.

HOW MUCH CAPACITY DO WE HAVE?

A service manager has 50 service engineers in an establishment, although at any particular time only 45 are available. The numbers that are actually available are what matters for getting the work done. We refer to the capacity provided by the 45 staff and other resources as the effective capacity, assuming there is constant demand to fill their time. Effective capacity is usually what interests us most. However, the service manager may also need to know the capacity that could easily be made available, at say a week's notice, by canceling training or borrowing resources from a neighboring service center. The capacity provided by these additional resources, assuming demand is there, is called the potential capacity.

Both effective and potential capacity are affected by short-term decisions because they do not involve any major change in the resource level. Also, they do not require large expenditure or increasing the size of facilities, buying equipment, holding larger inventories, or for recruiting or laying-off large numbers of staff.

When we want to assess the level of effective capacity, there are three main things that have an influence:

1. Do we have all the resources we need available all of the time? For instance, are there the numbers of staff, spares, equipment, and information about customers? Should any one of the resources not be available, then our effective capacity is zero.

2. We need to have access to customers and/or their equipment for service or repairs. Without this access, our output is zero despite having the potential to do the work.

3. The type of the service or support being offered to a particular customer will determine the capacity because the amount of work needed to complete the job may vary considerably from one service encounter to the next. So we must understand the effect on the service and support mix.

These three aspects of capacity illustrate a basic rule of capacity: variety in the resources and/or in the nature of the demand will tend to reduce effective capacity.

HOW FLEXIBLE IS OUR CAPACITY?

The movement between effective and potential capacity is a measure of our flexibility to change capacity to cater for changes in demand or service intensity. We are interested in two things about flexibility:

1. The response flexibility—how quickly can we make a change in capacity.

2. The range flexibility—how much can we change the capacity in the response time as service intensity changes.

Consideration of the response and range flexibilities allows us to understand how easy it is for us to alter capacity and the effect on the costs of making changes.

WHAT ARE OUR PATTERNS OF DEMAND?

While we may have a very good understanding of factors influencing our effective capacity at any time, we are still unlikely to match service intensity unless we understand our patterns of demand. The outcome of this failure is poor customer service or excessively high unit costs. The way forward, as in any planning process, is to try to be in a position to know precisely what we have to achieve. The better the knowledge, the better the planning process.

There are two main components to understanding demand: first, the main elements of the demand itself, and second, our ability to predict or forecast what is likely to happen in the future.

The Elements of Demand

The three components to understanding demand itself are the volume or level of demand, the variety of service packages or products we supply, and the variation in demand. We look at each in turn:

1. The volume of demand is a statement of the trends in demand over time, typically between one month and a year.

2. The variety of demand is associated with the number of different services that we are offering and the number of different tasks that are involved in making it available to our customers. Segmenting customers with different offerings increases this variety.

3. The variation in demand is associated with the changes in the volume around a general trend. The demand also changes because of major differences between groups of customers. For example, we may have business and domestic customers who place demands on us at different times.

The demand, the variety of services, and the volume are factors that we should establish at the network level rather than at the day-to-day operational level. However, variation in the nature and volume are very much the concern of day-to-day operational management.

Forecasting Demand

Our aim in forecasting demand is to separate out those things we can predict with a high degree of certainty and those that are less certain. In doing this, we must take into account volume, variety, and variation. Most forecasting methods rely on taking a mixture of information about past demand and projecting future demand. The forecast should also include known demand like service contracts for regular maintenance.

Separating the predictable and the random demand can be done by asking these questions:

- How has our overall demand changed in the past?
- Are there regular variations either throughout the day, throughout the week, throughout the month, or seasonally throughout the year? These can be found by examining past records of service intensity.
- What causes these variations? The causes may be due to buying patterns, to call out at the beginning of the week after the weekend, or longer term cycles, for instance, in the property building market.
- What causes random changes in demand? These are changes that we know are going to occur but that are difficult to determine when they will occur and how much they will affect

service intensity. Weather can be one of the main causes of random demand changes in the short term and economic business activity in the medium term.

There are some forecasting techniques that can be used to predict demand fairly accurately by past service intensity. These are available on standard software packages and can be run on PCs. The results from forecasting models should be reviewed and amended every time in light of any known future events. For example, a higher level of promotional spending on advertising may be expected to lift the level of service intensity, as would the launch of a new product range. Downturns in the economy would lead to a reduction in the short-term volume of demand but not necessarily alter the short-term variations in demand, say day-to-day.

Most customer service and support operations experience cyclical variation in service intensity by time of day, day of the week, and season of the year. The demand on Mondays in winter may well be different from Mondays in summer. However the average service intensity for one particular service branch may not change to a high degree over a year. The reason for this is the variety mix. The cyclical patterns of demand are often different for the various service products, and this tends to smooth the variations in service intensity.

CREATING THE BALANCE

If we understand the level of service intensity as driven by customer demand and also the makeup of our capacity, we are left deciding how we can create a balance between the two. There are essentially two polar opposites for managing capacity, one to hold capacity steady while influencing demand, and the other of changing our capacity to stay in line with demand. In reality we find that most operations use a mixture of the two strategies, although if there is a clear capacity constraint, there is a bias toward level capacity; this may be the case in customer service and support operations that have the SAS structure composed of specialists who take time to recruit and may be in short supply, so creating additional capacity takes time. However, it is useful for us to appreciate what each of the approaches or capacity strategies entails.

The Chase Capacity Strategy—Altering Capacity

The chase strategy is appropriate where we can alter our effective capacity to include all the expected variations in service intensity. The ways open to the service management to alter capacity to achieve this continuous balance are:

1. Personnel and Hours Changes. We may alter the number of service personnel or the hours they work. The scheduling of service personnel to correspond with the demand patterns helps to deal with daily and weekly variations in demand. Increasing the working hours of existing service people may match demand but bring with it increased costs from overtime charges. The use of flexible working hours may help us in trying to reduce the overtime burden. In one approach, we saw that an annual hours agreement for a building repair and maintenance operation gave them the flexibility to increase the working day in summer months without incurring increases in wages.

The use of part-time people to increase capacity to meet the peak demands can be useful, especially when there are peaks outside of the normal working day. An additional benefit from the use of part-timers in this way is the reduction in overtime charges.

There are dangers in using extended working hours as the means of flexing capacity in capacity-constrained service operations that use the SAS structure because of the increased strain this might put on personnel. The effect of this in the long term would be service burnout for the service personnel in the front line.

2. Customer Participation. We can also use the customers as part of our resources to provide capacity. As we have already seen, the role of the customer is to participate in some part of the service delivery process. This participation may mean that the customer: (a) provides part of the resources to carry out the work and service themselves, (b) provides information that helps the service provider to decide what is needed, to receive feedback on the quality of the service, and to make suggestions on how the service can be improved or enhanced. This information may save resources by preventing an unnecessary visit to a customer's premises. An example in the domestic appliance area occurs when customers are given instructions to carry out a simple diagnosis and repair for a blocked pump filter on a washing machine. This instruction saves the customer money in call out charges and frees resources for other activities.

When considering the contribution made by customers, it is important to distinguish between the customers always doing some part of the work and customers working as part of the chase strategy to increase capacity as we run out of resources.

If the customer provides part of the existing capacity, this involvement requires our customers to be trained in the tasks that they are required to do. A problem here may be in getting customers to accept their contribution, which is easier if DIY is part of the service concept. We see it in many day-to-day services we encounter, self-catering holidays, car rentals and supermarkets. The role of the customers is accepted. However, where changes are made to an existing system of delivery, problems may be encountered. It is interesting now to reflect that when supermarkets were first introduced in the United States, a great deal of effort had to be devoted to training customers in their new role. The shops employed staff to help shoppers find their way around the new stores.

One problem for us in using customers as a resource is that they will differ in their abilities and commitment to their task. For example, setting of intruder alarms by staff in a bank tends to be more conscientious than in a small factory.

While the use of customers may make a contribution to the overall effective capacity of the service delivery system, it is also important for us to consider whether customers could do more work at the times when demand is increasing. This approach may not be as easy as the customers providing capacity as a normal part of the service delivery. If customers are asked to participate at times when our resources are under pressure, it may lead to the customers perceiving a fall in service quality. However, this perception may be reduced or prevented if customers can see the reasons they are being asked to do something, for instance, when there is a threat to lives or the loss of use of equipment is very important.

3. *Transferring resources.* We may be able to increase our effective capacity by transferring resources from another part of our operation. Often we may be able to transfer Back Room staff to assist in the Front Office. This transfer is common in small telephone

response centers to limit the waiting time for the calls to be answered and the number of lost calls from customers not being able to get through. Transfer of staff in this way has implications for training in multiskills.

Alternatively, equipment and people may be transferred between adjacent geographical areas to help meet peak or unexpected demand. It is important to recognize that transfers of this type may lead to a drop in the service quality of the part of the service operation from which a transfer is being made because of a decrease in their ability to respond to random short-term increases in demand. A utility repair operation providing resources to a major incident in another area may not be able to give the desired level of all services in its own area, unless it is able to increase its own capacity.

4. *Using subcontractors.* Subcontractors may, of course, be used to provide capacity at all times as an alternative to maintaining that capability in-house. However, where subcontractors are used as part of a chase strategy, they may be seen as a special case of transferring resources where the capacity is provided by others at times of high demand.

The advantage of the use of subcontractors is clearly that the cost of the capacity is a variable rather than a fixed cost. The disadvantages with subcontractors stem from the uncertainty that they can perform to the standards of our service operation. Also, there may be doubts that the resources will be available precisely at the time they are needed. Forecasting of demand helps in arranging contracts for services that can be called off from subcontractors as the demand increases and laid off as demand falls.

5. *Sharing capacity.* If some resources are expensive to hold and are not used often, it may be feasible for service branches to share either discrete resources or a pool of resources. The use of specialist product teams located in one area but shared by the network may give both cost savings and increased capacity flexibility. In other cases, specialized equipment may be shared between areas.

6. *Decrease service standards.* Dropping service standards is the final way of increasing capacity in line with demand. Unfortunately, it is an all too common approach adopted by many service and support organizations. The result for the customer is, at best, an increased wait for the service or support. At worst, there

is also a fall in other parts of the service because of rushing. Jobs may not be fixed first time resulting in call backs that also exacerbate capacity problems by increasing service intensity. Sometimes organizations may get away with increased waiting if the customers see it as being unavoidable; for instance, in times of bad weather demand on utilities for call out is expected to rise.

The Level of Capacity Strategy—Altering Demand

Instead of trying to change the capacity in line with demand, we can try to influence demand to keep it in line with available capacity. This level strategy is more widely used in capacity-constrained service delivery systems. The methods used to influence demand are the following:

1. Pricing, Advertising and Promotion. Pricing has always been a method of influencing demand for the sale of products. The use of advertising and promotion and pricing to stimulate nonpeak demand is very important in capacity-constrained service delivery systems where there are high fixed costs in facilities, equipment, and staff. A service and support operation that has high seasonal costs may find it wants to stimulate demand in the quiet season by pricing and promotion. The utilities use this strategy for preventive maintenance contracts sold to domestic users to increase demand in the summer months. Using pricing to suppress demand in the winter could be more difficult. What we may do is to restrict the offering of some service and support at busy times. For instance, we may limit the amount of winter maintenance we offer and concentrate on dealing with breakdowns.

2. Customer reservation or appointments. Prebooking or reserving slots in a service activity allows some smoothing of demand and transfers demand from times when the service delivery system is incapable of matching demand. The mechanism works if the customers are willing to accept a waiting period. The use of reservation systems is often combined with price inducements to help in the process.

The advantage to the service operations management is that demand is known with some certainty in advance of delivery. This assists with the planning of resources. However, the downside of appointment systems can be when customers need to be involved in the process by giving access to buildings and equipment, and are not there at the time of the appointment. Some services penalize customers for this; for instance, some restaurants ask for a credit card number at the time of booking and charge people who do not turn up. We are not aware of this practice being employed by customer service and support organizations.

3. *Customers being made to wait.* When capacity is constrained, the most common way of dealing with the problem is to make customers wait for service. Engineers or other staff are not available to meet demand, and so there is no option but for some customers to wait. Demand prioritizes use. For instance, in the case of lift service operators a call for assistance with customers trapped in a lift will be attended to ahead of other calls.

Queueing is associated with a physical wait where the customer is in contact with the service organization. In the context of customer service and support it is a feature associated with telephone response centers. The cause is the limited number of lines available.

4. *Reducing service intensity.* If the capacity of our operation is constrained or expensive to enlarge because of the large incremental increases in capacity, an alternative is for us to look for ways to reduce service intensity. There are some ways in which we might go about this:

1. Remote diagnosis and fault fixing through the increased use of technology.
2. Increasing the reliability of equipment.
3. Reducing the time taken to carry out service and support work.
4. Increasing the access to information and in-house support teams to reduce the time to complete and close down one service event.

5. *Improving the scheduling and allocation of resources.* As we pointed out earlier, most customer service and support operations employ a mix of the chase and level strategies for creating a balance between service intensity and effective capacity. The result is that

the effective capacity is set less than the peaks in demand as shown in Figure 7–1. This strategy recognizes that at times there will be insufficient resources to meet demand. It also brings with it the third strategy for managing capacity. This is the coping strategy, by which we mean the strategy that is followed when we are unable to match capacity with the service intensity, in the short term. It is often seen in service operations in those periods when they would describe themselves as being busy or slack. In our experience, not many service and support operations have a clear policy of what to do in these circumstances. Failure to think and plan a course usually has adverse effects on customer satisfaction or resource productivity.

The Coping Strategy

As service managers become more clever at managing capacity and balancing it with demand it is at capacity break points where things start to go wrong (Figure 7–1). The break points occur in four areas:

1. When a chase strategy becomes level in the short term, because our effective capacity cannot be increased to meet demand. Usually this happens because there would be an overall underuse of resources, if we were to set resource levels near to peak demand.

2. When a chase strategy becomes level because we are not able to reduce the level of resources any lower in the short term. We cannot reduce the staff numbers anymore in the short term without dismissing people.

3. When a level strategy fails to stifle demand or overbooks appointments.

4. When a level strategy is unsuccessful in filling effective capacity because we have been unsuccessful at stimulating demand.

At these times quality of service or resource productivity will be under threat. We look at the way to minimize the potential damage from loss of quality when we consider the important aspects of recovery strategies in a later chapter.

FIGURE 7–1
Coping Capacity Strategy

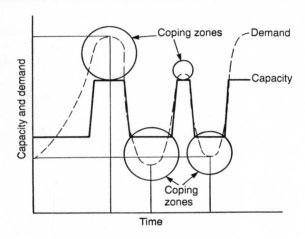

HOW DO WE PLAN AND CONTROL RESOURCES?

There are some areas in the delivery of customer service and support where resources need to be planned and controlled. These are:

- Customer response centers.
- Engineer visits for preventive maintenance.
- Engineer visits for faults and breakdowns.
- Support activities that take more than a few minutes to resolve.
- Repair and calibration of equipment in a workshop.

To be able to plan we need to know the demand in the work content for the tasks that have to be completed to deliver the service or support. The statement of work content may be in minutes to deal with a telephone call, or attendance hours, or the time taken for workshop repair. When the tasks to be performed are simple and repetitive, it is relatively easy to make the calculation. However, for more complex tasks involving diagnosis, the prediction of work content for the service or support time is more difficult to know in advance. We may deal with this difficulty by allocating some capacity, knowing that further work will be needed. However, we also know as the work proceeds we will become clear on how much resource is needed.

Customer Response Centers

The target for customer response centers is to answer customers' calls within a specified time, for example, 20 seconds. We can approach capacity management by:

- Using forecasting techniques to predict demand on a half hour daily basis allowing for weekly, monthly, and seasonal variations.
- Estimating the work content of the average call so that we can then predict the number of receptionists we need to cover the demand.
- Taking account of the short-term randomness of the call rate by using what is called queueing theory. This theory enables us to predict the number of receptionists we need to limit the wait time to our target time. At one time most service managers would have been unable to take advantage of these techniques. Now there are software packages that can be used in most situations.
- Schedule the numbers of staff at various times during the day in line with demand and the target waiting time. The use of part-time staff and flexible working hours help in this process.

Visits for Preventive Maintenance

We can schedule preventive maintenance from a knowledge of the demand from customer service contracts and the work content for each task. The certainty of the work content will be highest if any additional work over and above an allocation for unplanned work is scheduled separately for completion at another time.

Scheduling of site visits needs, of course, an allocation for traveling time. The use of route planners may help the reduction in the traveling content.

Visits for Breakdowns

Scheduling resources for breakdowns and faults is, of course, more difficult, because the level and variety of demand is more uncertain. We can use forecasting techniques to predict the service intensity so far as the number of incidents is concerned. What is less certain is the incident, the amount of resource it will consume in traveling, and work content to complete the job.

Consequently, we are left to schedule resources in anticipation of demand and to increase the response flexibility of our capacity. We may do this by arranging call out transfers from other areas. In the process we will be thinking about the trade-off between having more resources than may be needed and, hence, the cost of this redundancy and the added call out costs.

There is often a decision to be made about whether or not to keep preventive maintenance and breakdown activity separated and to use teams dedicated to one or the other. The advantages and disadvantages would seem to us to be:

1. Mixed team approach, Pros:
    a. Higher resource productivity.
    b. Greater job satisfaction through increased variety.
2. Mixed team approach, Cons:
    a. Need for multiskilling.
    b. Preventive work may be reduced because of the urgency of breakdowns.
3. Separate teams approach, Pros:
    a. Dedication brings increased learning and expertise in each activity.
    b. Preventive maintenance is completed which may reduce call back rates.
4. Separate teams approach, Cons:
    a. Higher resource productivity costs through lower use of resources.

Support Activities

Scheduling resources to deal with support activities requires us to have a knowledge of the expected level of demand and of the work content. Where we are dealing with standard problems, it is easy to estimate the work content from past experience. In more complex cases this job may not be so easy.

We have found in the support area one problem is the closing of jobs within a target time. This problem can happen for customers seeking help with a software package from a computer support activity. While the job may only require a few hours' work, the specialist may have to consult others and request additional information, all of which takes time.

In the meantime the specialist may start other jobs and return intermittently to this one. It is rather like the juggler spinning plates. Once he has started a plate spinning he must return to it to keep it on the go. There is a limit to the number of plates that can be kept spinning, and eventually one or all falls. For the customers the result of this crash is poor customer support.

A better approach is to try to progress jobs to completion once they have been started. This approach requires the support of people working more as a team rather than as a set of individuals. The results are that jobs are completed sooner, and when there are bottlenecks they become apparent early on in the process so that some action can be taken to remove them.

Workshop Repair

We can gain a lot from the new concepts of manufacturing to improve the use of resources in the workshop repair and calibration situation. The target as in the support activity above is to ensure turnaround of jobs within target times. The secret to success is to limit the number of jobs that are being worked on and to make sure they are completed once they have been started. Also, we need to ensure that equipment that cannot immediately be repaired in the workshop, perhaps because of the lack of spares, does not remain there but is brought back to a central control point.

Availability of spares is crucial to the repair activity, and, again, improvements in logistics through just-in-time supply of major parts can assist in the process.

The benefits of these approaches are seen in a tidier workshop where everyone can see what is happening, hence, contribute to better quality of work, and a more consistent turnaround time for repairs.

USING THE NETWORK?

A major way in which service and support operations can flex capacity is to use the network. We have already seen how resources can be transferred from one part to another to provide extra capacity and how we might share expensive equipment between branches. When we look at managing resource productivity we look in more detail at how the use of the network can lead to greater use of resources.

KEY ACTIONS

1. Write down how you measure your capacity.
2. List the key resources that limit your capacity.
3. Write down your capacity management strategy. Do you mainly try to chase demand or influence demand?
4. Write down the actions you take as a coping strategy.
5. List the ways in which you can flex your capacity. How far can you change, and how long does it take to make the change?
6. Think about what actions you could take to increase either your flexibility range or response that would help you to reduce the time you use the coping strategy.
7. List ways in which you could influence demand or service intensity.
8. List the steps you could take to increase the accuracy of your forecasting of demand.
9. Write down the ways you could make better use of your network to flex capacity.

Chapter Eight

Managing Service Quality

Introduction

In this chapter we briefly introduce the main principles of quality management and describe how they might apply specifically to the customer service and support organization.

Product quality and, latterly, service quality has received a great deal of attention in recent years. In the 1980s, achieving consistently good product quality levels gave some companies a strong competitive advantage. In a sense, consistently meeting specifications is only doing what customers assume we will do and the strength of advantage through consistent quality will diminish. How can you market a product by emphasizing that it really will work as it is intended? So in the 1990s and beyond the gap between industry leaders and the rest will close as organizations manage their processes more effectively.

The problem for quality management is that each management decision and each management action has an implication for quality. The saying that "The management of quality is about the quality of management" is perhaps obvious, but largely true. Time after time our work with service organizations brings us back to the fundamental operational issue of managing service demand and service capacity. The quality guru, Philip Crosby, has said, "There are no quality problems, there are only symptoms". Reflecting on what is poor quality leads us to identify the real problem as one of the following:

- Insufficient resources were available to cope with the demand for service.

- Resources were provided, but they were not of sufficiently high standard for the expectations of the customer.

- There were general communication problems, information not being passed to the required destination soon enough, if at all.
- The people involved had received insufficient training for the task.

Figure 8–1 illustrates the principal issues discussed in this chapter. The essence of service quality management lies in reaching a clear, customer-related specification of goods and services, and then designing systems that consistently deliver to that specification. Both definition and delivery must be subjected to regular review in light of the way that customers view the service and provide feedback for improvement.

It is helpful to distinguish between two activities in Quality Management. The first, quality assurance, relates to the need to instill customer confidence. The aim is to demonstrate that the systems and procedures of the service and support organization are under control and will produce the required result. Activities under this heading relate to formal quality systems, audits, and the use of statistical evidence to indicate that the processes are in control or to formulate improvement priorities.

The second activity, quality improvement, relates more to an attitude of mind or culture within the organization that refuses to accept that some problems are always with us. A culture that supports continuous improvement asserts that problems can be permanently fixed, often through the creativity and goodwill of employees who have been involved in the quality process rather than treated as if they had no contribution to make.

Both activities have evolved and have benefitted from the best of Total Quality Management. Quality Assurance has moved in emphasis away from determining "acceptable quality levels" and actions directed at preventing poor quality from being visible to the customer through to designing systems and processes that are statistically "in control" which means that the probability of failure is often far less than 1 percent. Quality improvement, likewise, has grown from "exhortation" through stirring speeches and poster campaigns through to activities aimed at solving quality problems once and for all. This quality improvement is often linked with a structure of quality teams that serves another purpose in encouraging integration across the organization.

This chapter addresses the following issues:

FIGURE 8–1
Service Quality Improvement

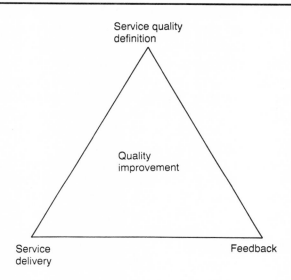

- The importance of quality management to the organization, its customers, and employees.
- Defining quality: the effect of product specification on customer support and formulating service definitions.
- Delivering quality: the role of management, quality systems, quality techniques and people involvement.

WHY IS QUALITY MANAGEMENT SO IMPORTANT?

Although maintaining consistently good quality has a lot to do with systems and procedures, quality management has much to do with people. The attitude adopted by the organization to quality will have tremendous impact on customers and employees alike.

Quality and Customers

It has become fashionable to talk of customer satisfaction in terms of being "delighted" by the goods and services received. Unfortunately, there are far too many organizations whose customers are pleasantly surprised or even amazed when things go right for a change! Organizations must know that customers have the final word. They may not be able to protest too loudly in the short term if no alternative goods or services are available, but there will come a time when customers will find a better service, and the organization will be the loser.

It can be argued that it is always better to keep the customer happy, because dissatisfied customers tend to be more disruptive and, therefore, expensive to look after. There are other sound financial reasons for keeping customers happy. If a customer spends $20,000 on purchasing a car every three years, and perhaps $600 on annual service costs, it makes no sense to lose a long-term annual revenue of nearly $8000 by paying insufficient attention to service quality. There are few businesses that can afford to lose a customer, and it must be remembered that if one is upset there is a strong probability that others will also be unhappy. In the same way that customers now calculate the lifetime cost of ownership, service providers must consider lifetime revenues.

The benefits of good quality are:

1. *Higher perceived quality commands high prices.* Market research and academic studies such as the PIMS (Profit Impact of Market Share) project at Harvard Business School have indicated that companies with a higher perceived quality level tend to be able to command higher prices than do those with poor quality reputations. Christian Gronroos has suggested that this is a function of the relationship costs, that is, the cost of doing business with the organization. An example of this cost is the time spent by managers and employees checking and rechecking work and, of course, correcting errors. Some people are employed by the organization purely because things go wrong and the cost of not discovering these problems as early as possible is great. Customers have "relationship costs" which are greater or smaller depending on the confidence they have in the organization they are dealing with. Customers pay more for products they can depend on because they cost less in the long run.

2. *Long-Term Income*. Companies should be aware of the lifetime income represented by an individual customer. A customer usually makes more than one purchase over time in addition to the service income relating to the original purchase. Good quality will secure this business and reduce the likelihood of customers switching to a competing product. It is much more expensive to generate new customers than to keep existing ones; apart from that there may not be an endless supply of new business.

3. *Quality Image*. Good quality is good marketing in the sense that satisfied customers tend to tell others. The opposite is also true. On average the unhappy customer tells 10 others about the poor service he has received.

Quality and Employees

Quality is an important element in the morale of employees. There is nothing that disillusions people as rapidly as having to perform a substandard task. Gerald Ratner gained some publicity by suggesting that the products sold in his jewelery shops were "rubbish" (edited version!), a pair of earrings being worth less than a prawn sandwich from Marks and Spencers. Some of his staff were not pleased to hear that they were working hard to sell poor quality goods.

The employee-related benefits of good quality are as follows:

1. *Improved morale*. Employee confidence is directly related to their view of the product they are dealing with. High morale will yield benefits in reduced employee turnover and absenteeism, and improved productivity.

2. *Positive customer contact*. For contact personnel, the benefits of good quality are multiplied. Being in regular contact with customers can be demanding at the best of times. Good quality will tend to make the job of the contact person that much easier; at times they may even receive compliments instead of complaints. Compliments tend to encourage service personnel to try harder, and so give better service, thereby building a positive spiral of improvement.

3. *Involvement.* Companies that encourage problem solving as part of the organization's culture have discovered a major resource in their employees. In some World-class companies, genuine suggestions are being generated at rates in excess of 100 per employee per year.

Reducing Quality Cost

Many organizations are aiming to be "Right First Time" because the total cost of quality may be in excess of 25 percent of turnover. The elements of quality cost are:

1. *Failure costs.* The costs involved in repair and rework, putting in place recovery actions, warranties, and guarantees. The greatest cost may be the loss of customer goodwill, which will result in lost sales and ultimately business failure.

2. *Appraisal costs.* These are the costs involved in inspection procedures to ensure that specifications are met. Appraisal costs are "policing" costs, as they add no value to the product.

3. *Prevention costs.* This cost is what the organization spends to improve quality before the event. This cost includes quality education and process development.

Many organizations have found that their first estimate of quality cost was much too low because the full information was not available. It is not uncommon for failure costs to be the largest component of quality cost with relatively little spent initially on prevention. As more money is spent on prevention, this balance shifts, and total quality cost reduces. This reduction in quality cost may be translated directly into increased profitability.

Organizations with a high degree of customer contact and involvement may assert that it is impossible to be "Right First Time, Every Time", because it is impossible to legislate for customers. This may be true, but most would agree that it is possible to be Right First Time rather more often, and in the Back Room there is no reason why the Right First Time standard should not apply.

DEFINING QUALITY

A working definition of quality is crucial if the customer is to receive a consistently high standard of goods and services. Without a clear description of what is to be produced, procedures about how it is to be produced, and objective measurement, service standards become matters of individual opinion and service is inconsistent. The customer also has no means of judging whether or not the service has lived up to its promise, leading to potential dissatisfaction.

Various blanket definitions of quality have been developed:

- Fitness for purpose.
- Quality that meets the customer's requirements.
- The totality of features and characteristics of a product or service that bear on its ability to meet stated or implied needs.

This last definition is particularly pertinent for customer service and support. In our surveys of the manufacturing sector we have found that many companies believe that product quality levels are now consistently high. Service quality improvement is critical to support the newly enhanced quality image of the manufactured product and to differentiate the company from the competition.

We believe that quality management is about ensuring that everything the company does adds to rather than takes away from customer confidence. A wonderful product will soon be let down by poor service and support. Customer confidence can be rapidly eroded by relatively small details. Total Quality Management should mean that everything the organization does is defined clearly and delivered consistently.

A problem arises if product quality and service quality are managed as separate entities. This separateness means that how much one impacts on the other is not understood, and a major source for improvement is lost. Clearly, an upgrade in the specification of the product ought to reduce the risk of failure and should also be directed toward improvements in the ease of product maintenance. It may be difficult for product designers to balance all requirements, but they must be aware of all the implications of their designs.

Dimensions of Product Quality

Having said that we should consider product and service together, it is useful to review a list of quality dimensions that was generated by David Garvin of the Harvard Business School, who makes an important point in looking at product quality. He says,

> Quality means pleasing consumers, not just protecting them from annoyances. Product designers should shift their attention from prices at the time of purchase to life cycle costs.

His Eight Dimensions of Strategic Quality follow. The customer service and support manager will need to be aware of the issues here as the support task is affected largely by the quality of the product and, of course, the support organization will be a valuable source of information about product quality and customer preference.

1. *Performance*. The product's primary operating characteristics, such as maximum speed or fuel consumption for an automobile, may be intangible or subjective. Garvin quotes the noise of a product as an example. A product may appear noisy when compared to a competitor's product even though the noise is within the design specification. The customer support organization must be able to cope with customers who are worried about their purchases, reassuring them without appearing offhand, and not dismissing them as a waste of time. Quality reputations lie in the perception of the customer and are strongly related to customer confidence. The noise level of the product may not be of technical concern, but that the customer is worried is all that matters.

2. *Features*. The extras that, though not vital for product performance, make up the value for money equation, such as the choice of options for product or service. There will be implications for the support manager here in spare parts inventory or skill requirements to service the product or to explain the range of options and facilities available. For complex products the purchase package will commonly contain a period of training, which must be readily available, and therefore be carefully scheduled by the customer service and support organization.

3. *Reliability.* Quality and Reliability are not synonymous. There will be a statistical chance that the product will last for a given period of time without problem or breakdown. This time will be represented by the product's MTBF and will have a significant impact on the load on the support organization. As products reach maturity, it is common for MTBFs to lengthen, and it becomes increasingly difficult to justify expensive service contracts to customers. At this stage the emphasis may move to routine maintenance.

4. *Conformance.* Garvin here means how much the organization's processes are capable of meeting the "ideal" or target dimensions that have been set by the organization. If this dimension were to be applied to a service organization, we would need to know whether the range of service engineer response time achieved is 2 hours plus or minus 5 minutes, or plus or minus 30 minutes. If the latter is the best that can be achieved, it would be wise to promise a 2½ hour response time so as not to raise customer expectations. The Japanese approach to product quality has been to steadily reduce the variability in all the organization's processes, thereby ensuring that all performance measures are well within specifications. This reduction in variability is particularly valuable when tolerances are stacked up, perhaps leading to the situation where the assembled product is out of specification even though the component parts are to drawing.

This approach has general application to the support organization in that a reduction in variability of the organization's performance will improve the customers' view of its quality. A specific application is that if spare part manufacture is subjected to this discipline, there will be few problems with interchangeability, and repair times will be minimized.

5. *Durability.* Again, this dimension of product quality has significant implications for support. Is the product capable of economic repair on failure? A cheap ballpoint pen will be thrown away, whereas a more expensive fountain pen may be repaired. The war of ever-lengthening guarantees is part of the process of increasing customer expectations. Many organizations find that a significant proportion of warranty expense arises not because the basic product has failed, but because the design does not cope with all the possible uses and misuses of the product. For example, VCRs do not cope with small children posting objects in the cassette slot.

The robustness of the product in use must also be considered, and the support organization will have useful information for the designer. Computer terminals for use in a factory workshop will be "ruggedized" to cope with adverse conditions, but they can be less sturdy in an office environment.

We had a problem with a cordless iron whose design meant that it was difficult to replace on its stand. Inevitably, the day came when it fell onto the floor and, being largely of plastic construction, part of it was broken. The only advice the customer service department could give was not to drop it! The product must be designed for every aspect of its purpose and environment.

6. *Serviceability*. Largely, the ease and speed of service is fixed at an early stage of product design. Unfortunately, most engineering departments do not address these needs until the end of the design process, by which time it is too late to make a significant change. The number of stages of disassembly and the number of fixings to be removed to replace or repair a wearing part must be considered with as much importance as the primary operating characteristics of the product. The customer service and support manager must fight to ensure that these issues are fully considered as early as possible.

7. *Aesthetics*. This dimension relates to how the product looks, feels, tastes, or smells. Not all will be relevant (it is not important how a machine tool tastes!), but it should look impressive.

8. *Perceived Quality*. We must recognize that a customer does not always view the product in the same light as its designers, and realize that a product's quality may be judged not by its technical merit but by image, whether someone treated the customer well or badly or by its general reputation.

The last dimension here is particularly important for the customer support manager, who can influence the perception of the customer to the extent of making or breaking the organization's quality reputation. The Eight Dimensions of Product Quality proposed by Garvin are an extremely useful starting point to consider all aspects of product design and how they might impact on the service task. We must now consider how the service task itself can be defined more exactly.

Dimensions of Service Quality

Garvin's Eight Dimensions of Product Quality do not give sufficient details for the customer support manager to form a thorough definition of service quality that is necessary if the organization is to be serious about managing quality. Schonberger proposed four more dimensions to aid this process:

1. *Quick response.* The need for the organization and its employees to acknowledge its customers quickly, and to carry out all tasks rapidly.

2. *Quick change.* The flexibility to produce a different product from the same system in a given time.

3. *Humanity.* Does the organization and its employees respond with understanding of an individual customer's needs?

4. *Value.* Does the product represent value for money in the customers' eyes?

This list adds to the Garvin Dimensions, but we have found the list of service attributes generated by Berry, Parasuraman, and Zeithaml to be a good starting place to generate service definition:

1. *Reliability.* Consistent performance, meeting promised dates, keeping to routine maintenance schedules. The support organization should include here making and keeping promises to return telephone calls, confirming appointments where possible in advance and rescheduling only when absolutely necessary and on very rare occasions.

2. *Responsiveness.* Prompt service, an attitude throughout the organization to respond to customers' needs rather than find ways of avoiding them. Most service organizations have stories about how employees have worked extraordinary hours or walked through snow drifts to ensure the customer received good service. The problem is that these stories are often very much the exception. The good service providers are those who anticipate most customer requests and who do not find reasons why these requests cannot be met.

3. *Competence.* Product knowledge and necessary skill to perform service and support tasks. Customer confidence may be boosted by employing experienced service staff with evidence of appropriate training courses completed.

4. *Access.* Easy telephone access through easily remembered telephone numbers to the right people to take and solve the customer's problem, hours of operation that fit the customers' needs, location of support personnel and facilities.

5. *Courtesy.* Politeness of service personnel, and Berry also suggests "consideration for the customer's property." The state in which the service engineer leaves the customer's premises may indicate the competence of the repair carried out.

6 *Communication.* Keeping customers informed about the service in terms they understand and at times that are helpful to them. Letting them know when there is a problem rather than hoping they won't find out. Giving clear and accurate cost estimates before the customer is committed.

7. *Credibility.* Reputation for honest, competent dealings, personal characteristics of customer contact personnel.

8. *Security.* Physical safety, no damage to property, confidentiality, value for money.

9. *Understanding the customer.* Distinguishing the customer's true requirements rather than what is stated, individual attention, ensuring that their needs are understood, making customers feel "in control" rather than constrained by the system.

10. *Tangibles.* Appearance and quality of facilities and equipment, quality of invoices, tenders, letters.

This last dimension leads us back to "perceived quality" in Garvin's list of product quality dimensions. The product itself clearly is a major ingredient in the customer's perception of the support organization.

In a sense, it doesn't matter which set of dimensions you follow as long as the definitions you employ fully describe the breadth of product and service quality. In Chapter 2 we described an approach we have used to determine Customer Service Dimensions and the priorities within them. We have found it useful to group them under four main headings and then to develop subheadings as appropriate for the situation under review. The headings are as follows:

- *Product.* Those attributes of product design that affect customer perception and therefore also the service task. MTBF would be included here. Garvin's Dimensions might be used here.
- *Support.* The degree and extent of customer support services provided such as availability of advice and training.
- *Service.* Activities directed at ensuring that the product is maintained or repaired to give maximum availability. This would include response times and spares availability.
- *Process.* The process of dealing with customers. Is the organization easy to deal with, and are the employees responsive? Many of the Berry, Parasuraman, and Zeithaml service determinants apply here.

How Do We Set the Right Standards?

In setting quality standards there must be an overlap with marketing because we must discover what is important to the customer to set the priorities for the organization. To manage quality the service and support manager must be able to set clear standards, combining attributes such as those listed above, and understanding which internal standards are critical in delivering service that customers perceive to be good. Figure 8–2 illustrates this relationship. A number of the major automobile manufacturers are working hard to establish the links between the elements of an overall customer satisfaction index for dealer network performance and the internal standards achieved at each stage of the service and supply chain. One company is considering internal customer satisfaction indexes, allowing the dealer to rate the parent company's performance.

We find that many organizations pay lip service to the idea of listening to customers. The excellent service providers invest significant resources in listening to customers, gathering objective data on customers' views of quality, and spending time listening to the strength of feeling behind the hard data. Methods for customer research include:

1. *General surveys.* Customers are asked to rate their overall impression of the service as well as rating specific elements of service delivery. It is important to give space to allow the

FIGURE 8–2
Quality Relationships

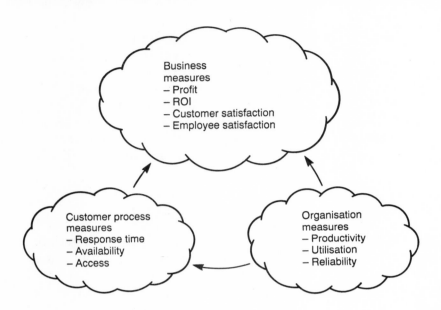

respondent to explain their rating of any of the elements as well as to give more general feedback. We have found that the questions "What did we do well?" and "What did we do badly?" are very valuable in indicating areas for improvement as well as opportunities to feed back praise to departments or individuals.

The warning that must be given is that simple rating scales, while easy to administer, yield averages that may cover a multitude of sins. If the spread of response is consistently narrow, the average reading is a sufficient guide, but a wide spread, particularly if grouped at two extremes, indicates a problem.

2. *Transaction-based surveys.* To counteract the average problem, it may be valuable to design a more specific survey to investigate specific areas of the organization. British Airways and similar organizations when surveying a particular aspect of their service now ask a number of related questions. So, if a customer says that the service was poor, they are able to link this back to operational reasons such as late flights or overloads at check-in counters.

3. *Customer focus groups.* It is often instructive to feed the results of surveys back to a cross-section of customers, asking for their reaction to the figures. It may transpire that the questions and answers have subtly different meanings to organization and customers. It is instructive for senior managers to hear the strength of feeling that may be hidden by data.

4. *Employee surveys.* The staff, and, in particular, those in regular contact with customers, know how well the service is delivered and they see the customers' reactions to it. Linking their view on customer satisfaction with a survey of attitudes can be very useful. A question such as "What would help you to deliver better service?" may help direct investment plans.

Having heard what customers and employees have to say, it should be possible both to define the relevant attributes of service delivery and to set performance levels to be achieved against each of them. It is important to measure your organization against the best in the world and many carry out "Benchmarking" programs, taking each aspect of the operation in turn and measuring performance against any similar organization. Thus, Rank Xerox, which has carried out extensive benchmarking, compared its logistics function against the best logistics networks of any type, not solely those in the photocopier market.

It must be said that there is no point in setting service standards if the system is not capable of delivering them or there are not definite plans to invest in improvement. Setting unrealistic targets will demotivate in the long term if they are seen to be unobtainable, and will thus become irrelevant.

It is a well-known saying "Without measurement there can be no control." It is also true that "With too much measurement there is confusion." The handful of key measures that drive the organization must be consistent throughout service delivery. It will be no use trying to emphasize customer responsiveness if it is known that the only thing that the organization rewards is keeping costs as low as possible. Organizations must be aware of the impact of their motivation and control systems on service quality.

How Can We Make Sure We Deliver the Right Quality?

Having discovered how customers view quality for the support organization, a customer specification can be drawn up, and systems and processes employed to deliver to this specification must be audited as to indicate where there are quality issues to be addressed.

The Quality Triangle (Figure 8–3), developed by Professor John Oakland of Bradford University, provides a useful framework for a balanced approach to quality management.

The Role of Management

It is perhaps easy to say that quality requires senior management commitment. It is too easy for senior managers to say they are committed to quality, but then for their subsequent decisions to give the lie to this statement.

There is a "tension" in quality management that must be addressed. The emphasis behind most of today's quality thinking is that continuous improvement should be a way of life, with zero defects being a theoretically attainable goal. Zero defects may be possible for a manufacturing process or a routine service and support activity where each action is under the direct control of the organization. This zero defects goal looks much more difficult when a significant part of the process, namely, customer participation, is not under the support organization's direct control. Even so, we need to press on, believing that improvement is always possible, but knowing that some imperfect short-term decisions must be made.

Having said all this, employees see the underlying attitude of their managers toward quality. They see if the fine words mean nothing at all when the crunch comes. They see and copy the example set for them. Rank Xerox claims that its organization is driven first and foremost by customer satisfaction goals rather than profit goals. That is not to say Rank Xerox is not interested in profit, rather it believes that if customer satisfaction is managed well, profits will follow.

One of our friends was appointed as managing director of a small electronics company, which is part of a larger group. It was

FIGURE 8–3
The Quality Triangle

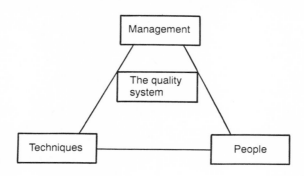

known that the company had quality problems and, after putting in place a quality recording system, it was soon identified that the main problem was that the company was unable to manage new products adequately from design into production and thence to support. The new managing director took the decision to delay the launch of the next product until these issues were properly addressed. This was not a popular decision either internally or with the group board, who saw a decline in short-term profitability. As a consequence of his actions the company retained a major customer who was on the point of dropping them as a supplier as a result of poor quality. These signals are central to quality success.

Likewise, the management team is largely responsible for what is generally termed the *culture* of the organization. Is it dynamic, innovative, paternalistic, or bureaucratic? We have worked with service and support organizations where employees have told us that suggestions were not encouraged and were met with the response, "That's not your job or concern." Clearly, this response will not cultivate an atmosphere for quality improvement. It takes time to wait for employees to make suggestions, when sometimes the solution is obvious to managers, but the time spent will be worthwhile.

Last, senior management must develop and pursue a quality strategy that sets out the targets for each business area and ensures that there are sufficient resources devoted to achieving the plan.

Too many quality programs have failed because, although the opening stages of announcement and increased quality awareness have gone well, there has been no follow through. Figure 8–4 shows Caterpillar's Quality Program, with goals and actions in each area spread over 10 years. Quality improvements will not come about without a realistic allocation of resources behind it.

Using the Quality Techniques

Some techniques have been developed, often based on collecting data for objective decision making. These fall into three main groups:

1. *Process statistics.* Statistical Process Control (SPC) charts are used by some service and support organizations, tracking performance on repair times, response for service, first-time fix, return calls, and so forth. Tally charts allow organizations to track cause and effect simply, often highlighting areas for possible improvement.

2. *Design techniques.* Service functions, who by definition have a high degree of contact with customers, may provide useful information as input into the design process. A technique that is becoming more common is Quality Function Deployment (QFD), which is effectively a quality planning matrix, translating the "Whats" of customer requirements into the "Hows" of product and process design parameters.

3. *Techniques for involving people.* There is not space for detail here, but the quality circle literature contains description of techniques for encouraging creativity through brainstorming.

Involving the People

Many organizations have tried quality circles or other forms of voluntary improvement group activities and declare they don't work. The reason for these failures often lies firmly with management who have not resourced these programs sufficiently or thought how their efforts can be effectively coordinated.

Unguided quality groups may solve the trivial many rather than the critical few problems, but this undervalues the role of such groups in communication and involvement. Organizations that

FIGURE 8–4
Eight Point Quality Program – Milestones

1 Setting Standards — A quality standard setting process based on customer needs and competitive levels which incorporates product quality requirements into functional, reliability and durability terms.

	'82	'83	'84	'85	'86	'87	'88	'89	'90	'91/'92
Setting Standards	OGO/SEGO setting reliability standards	PRM 200 Hr DRF Stds set	Field follow standard reduced 50%	PRM 201-1000 hr targets set DRF lowered 20%	•Apportments developed •Response targets lowered	90% of targets set for Expansion Line Products	Reliability apportment installed in production PRM			Product & process targets represent high customer preference

2 New Product — A product design, testing/evaluation and manufacturing readiness program which results in meeting quality requirements at first production

	'82	'83	'84	'85	'86	'87	'88	'89	'90	'91/'92
New Product	Reliability Growth installed	New Product Strategy initiated	Quality Strategy reviews begun	NPI Checklist used at production readiness	Quality guide book for NPI published	Reliability apportment used for new designs	80% products meet targets			All products meet targets throughout life cycle

3 Manufacturing — A manufacturing conformance program to plan and achieve conformance to design requirements

	'82	'83	'84	'85	'86	'87	'88	'89	'90	'91/'92
Manufacturing	Qual indicator NOPS includes DLY loss scrap & rework	Piece part conformance at 50%, all characteristics	Conformance measure changed to Defects 1000	Worldwide plant conformance audits	Processes evaluated at 50% capability	CPK introduced as process improvement indicator	Internal Quality Certification established			All processes – 15 CPK major commodities certified

4 Supplier — A supplier quality assurance-certification program to supply parts and components which confirm to the design requirements

	'82	'83	'84	'85	'86	'87	'88	'89	'90	'91/'92
Supplier	Certification discipline reinforced	Quality Plan guide in use	Certification video & brochure	Quality Evaluation Profile	60% of volume Certified	AQI video & brochure for suppliers	80% Certified SPC AQI required			– 5% Rejections – 15% CPK AQI Manufacturability Consolidation JIT

5 Product Support — A product service to the customer from factory and dealer which maximises the return on his investment in Caterpillar product

	'82	'83	'84	'85	'86	'87	'88	'89	'90	'91/'92
Product Support				Dealer service quality survey started	Measures of CAT support to dealers defined	Dealer service surveys growing	Surveys introduced at subsidiaries			Dealers & customers acknowledge product support as superior

6 Field intelligence — A field intelligence and response system which causes rapid and complete correction of product problems

	'82	'83	'84	85	'86	'87	'88	'89	'90	'91/'92
Field intelligence	SIMS providing field data	Field follow feedback strengthened	Product problem system reviewed	Operations Grp reviewing past due impact problems	Problem response time improving	Dealer inquiry system in place	Apportment used to identify problems of sub impact			Field intelligence & response cause high customer satisfaction

7 Education — An annual quality improvement program using quality education to improve the knowledge, skills and attitudes of all personnel which impacts all corporate processes

	'82	'83	'84	'85	'86	'87	'88	'89	'90	'91/'92
Education	Quality Education begun	•Juran training •SPC Course	•QUEST newsletter •Juran met w officers	•Diagnostic Tools Course •Officers met w media on Quality	•AQI Matrix •Taguchi •CFD	Quality Institute initiated	Keynote at IMPRO 88 by CAT officer			Process improvement rate exceeds competitors

8 Non-quality costs — An accounting and evaluation system for quality improvement to help management direct resources to their most effective use by quantifying the cost of product defects and process waste

	'82	'83	'84	'85	'86	'87	'88	'89	'90	'91/'92
Non-quality costs			Product related cost elements identified	Costs estimated at $400 Mil/Yr		Corporate ADI team established				Costs reduced to < $80 Mil/Yr

Source: Eight Point Quality Program (reprinted from The TQM Magazine, November, 1988. © IFS Ltd., Kempston, Bedford, UK, 1988)

have persisted with small group activity have usually evolved some sort of structure to coordinate voluntary departmental groups, groups with product focus, groups with a specific customer focus, and task forces formed to solve specific problems and then disband. A critical issue for ensuring the commitment to quality from the people is that of motivation through rewards. The measures used to assess the success of customer service and support have a major contribution here. Some service organizations measure the effectiveness of their engineers on a mixture of repair time, numbers of quality failures, journey management, and customer satisfaction. A balance of quality and productivity measures is essential to create the right motivation.

Within a service organization there is much untapped information about quality because many people are frequently meeting customers, seeing where the organization fails, and seeing where customer needs could be met more effectively. Management must work hard to create the right environment for quality improvement, encouraging suggestions for improvement. Sometimes, this will mean waiting for employees to make suggestions to gain their ownership of change rather than simply implementing management directives.

Developing the Quality System

In the center of the Quality Triangle is the *Quality System*. This term may bring to mind negative images of thick and boring quality manuals gathering dust on the shelf or quality auditors joyfully pointing out your shortcomings and explaining why you cannot get on with the business of making money until the correct procedure has been followed.

We think of the Quality System as giving the structure to Quality Management that it requires. It should describe the key processes employed to ease consistency of operation, provide the necessary checks and audits to allow review of the operation, and generally act as the organization's quality conscience.

Writing a Quality System requires some expertise, particularly where it relates to customer contact roles. Procedures must allow for some discretion where customer preferences must be acknowledged or accommodated. Flexibility is important here, while procedures must ensure that the core of the operation is maintained.

Putting the Quality Triangle Together

Successful Quality Management requires consideration of many things at once. Management must review its attitudes to quality, systems must be put in place, and reward structures changed. Of course, it is unlikely that everything can be done on day one. In putting together a quality strategy, the organization must revisit the points raised by the Quality Triangle to decide what needs to be done and which must be addressed first.

For example:

- The Ford Motor company started with an SPC program to improve supplier quality before incorporating other techniques and developing a more integrated quality strategy for the whole business. Ford's culture is such that systems govern much of the company's activities, and therefore an SPC approach was not alien to its employees.
- Many companies have started quality improvement campaigns with a major management announcement that they were now in a new era of excellence. Many of these programs have failed because the necessary follow-up activities were not put in place.
- Many companies have commenced a quality circle program and have then developed broader actions as a result of lessons learned, building a structure for quality.
- Some companies have sought and achieved quality recognition and have then realized that the attitude of those employed in the company has not changed for the better. They are aware that poor quality is still "policed" rather than prevented.

The point about these scenarios is that it doesn't matter where you begin. Start somewhere, but be very clear where you have not yet been and make sure you go there!

A key quality principle is that systems and processes must be capable of meeting the specifications laid down for them. If your system has an average customer response time of four hours, you will not achieve this every time. Sometimes you will beat it and sometimes you will be late. Let us say that 99.99 percent of all service calls fall within a response time of four hours ± ten minutes. If response time is a key element of customer satisfaction, you must decide if this level of performance is satisfactory. If not, resources must be assigned to improving the system. Capable systems, in effect, equate to not making promises you cannot keep.

Many quality problems boil down to having insufficient resources some or all of the time. As the organization moves closer to full use, quality problems become more frequent. The organization copes, but at the risk of poor technical quality or poor customer care.

It is useful to address all the quality principles contained in this chapter but also to ask two final questions:

1. What happens when you run out of capacity? Which quality dimensions suffer as resource use approaches 100 percent?

2. How can you tell? What indicators or measures are in place to give you rapid feedback for recovery?

In Chapter 7 (describing capacity management), we indicated that organizations and individuals within them employ coping strategies to deal with the problems of short-term overloads. It would be better if we could address these inevitable overloads to minimize the loss of customer satisfaction by deciding what should be done rather than leaving it to people to cope in the way they think fit. The organization's ability to recover effectively from mistakes is critical.

Measurement is one of the tools of management. We believe that three measures should be used together to balance the needs of the organization. These measures are:

1. Customer perceived quality measures.

2. Internal productivity measures.

3. Use of key resources.

Moving the organization from 90 percent to 95 percent use may improve productivity but may have a disastrous effect on customer satisfaction and long-term profitability.

There are many benefits for the customer support organization in pursuing quality. Quality Management is a mixture of major strategic actions demonstrating genuine management commitment, and also many detailed actions aimed at ensuring that nothing is left to chance.

KEY ACTIONS

1. Write down the definition for quality for your customer service and support function.
2. Draw out your structure for quality. Are you satisfied with it?
3. Think about your quality costs. Write down the causes and try to quantify them.
4. List the steps you take to try to ensure that designs take customer service and support into account.
5. List the actions you take to continuously improve quality. Are there others you should be taking?

Chapter Nine

Improving Productivity

Introduction

Along with capacity and quality management, the management of resource productivity is one of the trinity of operational controls that affect performance of customer service and support. In this chapter we look at what we mean by resource productivity, the ways it can be measured, and the techniques that are available to improve resource productivity. We examine the role of technology in both the measurement of and improvement in resource productivity.

WHAT ARE YOUR TRADE-OFFS?

Operations management in any form is concerned with managing trade-offs that affect resource productivity and quality. Common trade-offs are between capacity use and customer waiting, between absolute perceived quality of the service and support and costs, and between labor costs and capital equipment costs, including information systems. All the trade-offs point to there being no one system of service and support delivery able to do everything. We cannot deliver the highest perceived service and support in our sector, immediately available to all our customers, all at the lowest cost.

Our thinking about the trade-offs affects the quality of service and sets the parameters for resource productivity. What we are always seeking to do though is to reduce the effects of the trade-offs. For instance, the Total Quality Management movement has been very successful at ending the traditional trade-off between consistency of service delivery and cost; an explanation for the "quality is free" philosophy. We have also seen that the better we are at managing the match between service intensity and capacity, the higher the use of the resources while keeping the minimum waiting time for customers. So we want to reduce the effects of trade-offs. Our aim always will be to look for ways in which we can get more from the resources we use, while delivering the same or somewhat higher levels of service quality.

WHY IS MANAGING RESOURCE PRODUCTIVITY SO DIFFICULT?

Various reasons are put forward to explain the problems of managing productivity in services: the involvement of customers, the intangible part of the customer service and support mix, the complexity of the task, and the diversity of branch networks. All of these relate in the first instance to problems associated with measurement.

So if we are to get better at using resources, we need to improve measurement. However, this is only part of the issue. We also need to understand how our use of resources is influenced by the demand for the service and support. This understanding will give us clues to the best routes for understanding the barriers to productivity improvement.

UNDERSTANDING PRODUCTIVITY

At its simplest, productivity is defined as the ratio of outputs to inputs. The more we can produce from a set of resources that includes people, materials, equipment, facilities, and systems, the higher our resource productivity will be. However, we soon realize that while this definition of resource productivity may seem convenient because of its simplicity, when it comes to making measurements, things are more difficult. As with any arithmetical ratio we need to have all the denominators in one set of common units and the numerators in another common set. Let us look at the problem this raises.

Measuring Outputs

The outputs from customer service and support operations could be described as the number of service and support incidents that are dealt with. If each event were the same, this would give us an acceptable measure of the output. If there is great variety, then things are not so easy. So how much each incident is standard or customized for each customer will influence the variety.

Where incidents are standard we might get an aggregate for the service intensity simply by counting incidents. However, if each incident is highly customized, it is not possible to get an aggregate number for all incidents. So when variety is high and changing, we might relate the total output to a monetary value, such as the revenue generated by the total customer service and support operation over time.

A second problem in measuring outputs relates to quality. It is easy to increase the number of service incidents we deal with by reducing the quality. Perhaps we spend less time resolving a problem or we rush a standard maintenance, even though we run the risks of making mistakes. It is apparent that in making any measurement of the outputs, we need to ensure that quality standards are kept. We can easily increase productivity by reducing service levels.

A third factor in measuring outputs is associated with a general characteristic of service delivery. Many types of service and support cannot be delivered until the customers request them. The service and support is then needed at short notice. Also, sometimes the customer takes part in the process. Usually, setting resource levels is done by forecast demand, as we saw when discussing capacity management. If the rate at which customers want to use the service is fairly constant and we are close with our forecasts, then measuring output will be realistic for that level of resource capacity. If, however, the rate at which customers use the service is erratic, then the time at which measurements of output are made could affect the result. If the customer demand is lower than expected for the resources deployed, the output would be low, and, hence, the resource productivity seems low. So in measuring outputs we have to ask the question, are we working at our effective capacity? This is in line with the argument that productivity measures are only valuable when they are a true reflection of managerial skill. This happens when outputs are not constrained through lack of resources and when input resources are at the level set by the managers.

So in measuring outputs we have to be aware of:

- The mix of service offerings and their variety.
- The quality service levels.
- Whether output is constrained through lack of customer demand or other resources.

Measuring Inputs

If we were to make a measure of total productivity, including all outputs and all inputs, we would have to find a way to get these into common units. The only way to do this for the mix of resources, including people, materials, and equipment, is to express them in monetary terms as the total input costs; otherwise, we must rely on what are called *partial measures of productivity*. Here we take one of the main inputs and use this in the productivity calculation. The commonest resource taken for the partial measure is people. In services where the labor cost is the highest proportion of total cost this measure is reasonable. If the labor cost is reduced considerably through the deployment of technology, then the labor cost becomes a very small proportion of the total cost; this measure then could be misleading. This situation is perhaps not the case in most services yet, but a pointer to the future comes from the manufacturing environment where labor costs are now often less than 10 percent of the total costs.

So in making measurement of input resources:

- Total resource input measures can only be in monetary terms.
- Selecting resources for partial measures should take account of the contribution of the resource to the total costs.

Deciding on the Level for Measurement

When thinking about resource productivity, there are some levels at which we need to have information. The levels correspond to:

- The business as a whole, which is usually the network of branches for the delivery of service and support.
- The service branch.
- A section of activity within the branch.
- An individual resource.

In managing and improving productivity, we need to have measurements that give information on productivity at each level. At the lower levels we will be wanting to find methods of measurement that can be used to compare the performance of different service branches, service teams, or individual resources such as people or equipment or materials.

HOW CAN WE APPROACH THE COMPLEXITY OF MEASUREMENT?

As a general comment from our work we could say that the measurement of resource productivity is not well developed. Often, this results from a failure to grasp the nettle surrounding the inherent difficulties of measurement, people give up. However, there are approaches that yield valuable information for monitoring and planning improvement. It is our contention that there can be no effective improvement in resource productivity unless there are appropriate measurements. This raises the questions:

1. What is measured?
2. Who is responsible for carrying out measurement?
3. What use is being made of the information on resource productivity that is generated?

The most general approaches to productivity measurement are ones that look for partial or surrogate measures of productivity. These can be summarized as:

- *Output/input measures*. These are true productivity measures and include revenue, generated/employee or profit/employee, both cost-based measures. Alternatively, the number of service calls handled per employee that are a volume-based measure can be included.

- *Input/output measures.* These are the reciprocal of productivity and are commonly unit costs for each service incident, or costs per customers.
- *Input costs.* These are usually staff costs, rather than total resource costs.
- *Use.* This is a measure of the proportion of time resources being used in the service delivery on activities that add value. The measures may apply to people as individuals or teams, or equipment, or facilities.
- *Efficiency.* Here we are making an assessment of the use of resources against a standard of performance. Standard times for the completion of activities can be set up by work measurement techniques to give a target for performance. For instance, efficiency can be measured as a ratio of service calls to the target standard. Another common measurement is the service time compared to a standard, for example, actual times to fix, and actual response times compared to standard times for the two tasks.
- *Effectiveness.* Here we are trying to make an assessment of the way in which resources are used without wasting them. An example would be the number of times we achieve first-time fix, as a percentage of the total incidents.

It is apparent that only the first two of the above measurements are in any way true productivity measures. However, the rest do help the service manager to know how well the resources are being used. Use is a very good way of checking the performance of an expensive resource. The linking of quality and productivity measures in effectiveness measures and achieving time targets also shows that one measurement can be used to indicate the performance on both dimensions of quality and productivity.

WHICH MEASUREMENT AT WHICH LEVEL?

Another question arises: Which measurement is right for the different levels of the service and support operation? All are not suitable or applicable at all the levels: the network, the branch, the section, and the individual resource.

Measurements like revenue or profit per employee that aggregate all the complexity of the customer service and support mix in monetary terms are most suitable at the level of the network and the individual branch. However, care needs to be taken in making comparisons at the level of the performance between branches. If the revenue generated per employee in one branch is $4,000/month and in another $2,800/month, can we draw any worthwhile conclusions about the performance of the service managers of the two branches? To do so, we need to know something about the mix of service and support activities each is engaged in and also any other features of their resources that might have a strong influence on the productivity. These may be physical space, different information systems, or different levels of skills of the staff.

Efficiency measures based on work measurement or historically based estimates of times are more appropriate at the team and individual resource level. They work best when the work is standard and repetitive so that the setting up of standards is worth the cost of doing so. Preventive maintenance activities lend themselves to work content and time-based efficiency measures.

Measures of use for a resource being used for tasks that add value are again more suitable at the team and individual resource level. They are particularly useful for separating traveling time from productive work time. However, we need to know that resources are being used in similar ways if comparisons are being made. For example, measurements of the use of engineers on service work in different regions are only feasible if the regions are similar.

It should be clear that if we are to gain a full understanding of resource productivity, we need to be able to make measurements at all levels. At the higher levels we want to use the results to make decisions about the overall performance of the business network and the relative performance of the branches. At the branch levels we want information for setting targets and monitoring the performance of teams and individuals. So we now look in more detail at issues related to measurement of costs, the mix of measures to be used, and the measurement of relative performance of branches.

How Accurate is Our Costing

In our work with manufacturing and service organizations, we find a common theme. Most will control costs relatively well at an aggregate level. Most will admit that they are not as sure about the relative contribution and resource absorption of individual products.

To give a simple example, we worked with a systems installer whose philosophy was to discount the installation cost to gain the long-term maintenance contract. A review of the cost structure revealed that installation, even at a discount, was profitable, whereas maintenance often ran at a loss. They were effectively discounting to lose more money!

We believe that approaches such as Activity-Based Costing (ABC) that identify the relative impact of the various cost drivers are necessary to manage the business effectively.

HOW MANY MEASURES?

The question that is often raised in considering productivity measurements is "How many different measurements are needed?" A supplementary question is "Should we try to combine measurements into a total index of performance?" The answers to these questions are not easy without the context of a specific operation; however, the experience of Data General's Customer Service Group provides an example of choosing the measures and combining them into an index for total service and support profitability.

Seven productivity measures were identified as being important:

1. *Product liability.* A function of product MTBF and the mix of products for service and support.

2. *Material efficiency.* A function of changes in the costs of materials and the rates of usage of materials.

3. *Incident repair productivity.* A function of MTTR and labor costs.

4. *Off-site and support productivity.* A function of the numbers and use of support resources and labor rates for support staff.

5. *Logistics productivity.* A function of costs of materials as spares and the costs of distribution.

6. *Revenue yield.* A function of contract rates and the product mix being supported.

7. *Staff productivity.* A function of staff effectiveness and use on service contract tasks.

Numerical quantities are calculated for each of the seven indexes and these are combined into a total service productivity measurement.

HOW CAN WE COMPARE BRANCH PERFORMANCE?

Making a comparison of the performance of branch units across a network has always presented problems because of the multiplicity of different inputs and outputs. Service branch units may differ in numbers of staff, costs of facilities, traveling costs, and may have a different mix and volume of service and support activity. Trying to make a comparison by traditional methods of allocating cost is almost impossible. A new technique, Data Envelopment Analysis (DEA), takes a different approach.

DEA examines the relative efficiency of use of resources in each branch in a way that discounts the mix of service and support activities and ends the need to develop standard costs for each service. It can be used to identify branch units that are relatively inefficient and give indicators about why this might be true. However, the technique will not indicate whether the performance of the best branches is an optimum performance that cannot be improved. The results are always relative within the branch network, so if competitors were more efficient, DEA would be no better than other techniques for identifying an optimum.

The use of DEA requires the identification of the main outputs from the operation. This output could be a mix of installation of equipment, preventive service, and repair and fix in response to breakdown. Similarly, the input resources needed to produce the outputs are identified as people, materials, equipment, and the facilities from which they work. The outputs and inputs are measured over time for each branch. Sometimes the information is available within existing information systems, or it might have to be gathered separately.

The results from DEA can be used to identify inefficient branches as against the most efficient branches. It is up to the service management team to find the underlying causes and to look for ways to remedy them.

Let us look at how DEA can be applied in practice by way of a simple example. Our network consists of six branches, and we wish to monitor which of the branches are less efficient in their use of resources than the others. For simplicity we will take the outputs from the service and support operation to be preventive maintenance and the inputs engineer hours and the cost of spares.

The DEA "black box" takes the data and compares each branch against all of the others to establish which are the inefficient ones. The results of the process are shown diagrammatically in Figure 9–1. The branches that on comparison, are equally efficient and rated at 10 percent efficient are B1, B2, B4, and B6. These are joined by the solid line. The other two service branches are found to be less efficient, B3 when compared to B1 and B2, and B5 when compared to B2 and B4. Both B3 and B5 are inefficient by an amount proportional to the distance from the efficient line joining the points B1, B2, B4, B6.

DEA does not say why the service branches 3 and 5 are less efficient, but allows managers to look for the reason in the way that resources are used in the inefficient and the efficient branches.

The use of DEA requires the identification of the main outputs and inputs from each of the service units in the network and a system for watching these for a fixed time. Sometimes the information will already be gathered, but in others, new systems will have to be set up.

HOW CAN WE IMPROVE OUR RESOURCE PRODUCTIVITY?

When we consider improving productivity we mean both getting the level of costs down and using resources more effectively. Improvements in quality often in themselves lead to improvements in resource productivity through the elimination of waste.

FIGURE 9–1
DEA Curve

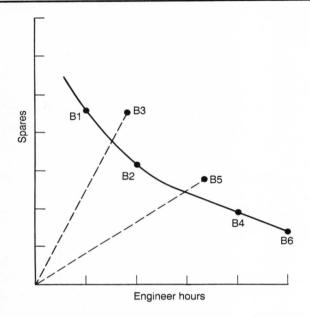

Engineer hours

What though is likely to frustrate our attempts to improve productivity? The answers lie in part with the service operations task. This takes us back to the elements that constitute the demand for our customer service and support, the trends in volume, the variations in volume in the shorter term and the service and support mix. Let us look at each of the demand factors and see their effect on resource productivity.

Volume

If we were just delivering one service, this would give us the opportunity to:

- Gain from economies of scale.
- Get better volume from the increased learning because of the specialization and frequency.
- Get high use from the resources because they are devoted to the one activity.

Variation in Demand

Variation in demand tends to take away from the high constant volume situation by:

- Increasing costs from having to increase the flexibility of the effective capacity. These costs include labor charges for overtime or the use of subcontractors and additional systems costs for planning work. Additional costs come from underuse of capacity through not being able to match effective capacity and demand all of the time.
- The differing pace of work from busy to slack times, which may mean that people do not work efficiently all of the time.

Variety of the Service and Support Mix

The variety of the service and support mix tends to reduce the effects of high volume through:

- Increased costs because of the need for a greater skills mix and increased costs because of the loss of any volume economies of scale.
- Loss of specialization in the work tasks that decreases the tendency to get things right first, which leads to increases in waste.
- The increased amount of managerial and supervisory effort that must be put into managing the increased complexity.

All of these factors point us toward understanding our service and support and trying to reduce the inherent effects of the demand elements. It also reinforces the benefits that can be gained from specialization, and standardization, and limiting the effects of growing variety.

WHAT ARE THE BARRIERS TO IMPROVING RESOURCE PRODUCTIVITY?

What might we describe as the main barriers to improving resource productivity? We have seen that the demand mix can make improvement difficult. There are also the following factors that we have found from our own investigations:

1. Not having good measurements. The absence of measurements for resource productivity makes it difficult to set targets and monitor progress.

2. Changes in demand. We have already seen that variation in demand tends to lower resource productivity, and the effect is exacerbated if we are poor at flexing capacity.

3. Organization of service delivery. If we do not understand and evaluate what happens in the process of delivering our service and support, we will not be able to identify constraints, where waste is occurring, and inefficient stages in the service and support delivery. A lack of understanding what the organization is trying to do is another barrier.

4. Cost of gathering data. Organizations often don't gather data on resource productivity because of the cost of the systems and people to do the job. There is a link here with the perceived appropriateness of measures. If measurements are not seen to be useful, there will be little incentive to meet the costs of gathering data and producing information on productivity.

5. Frequent changes in staff. It is not surprising that if a customer service and support operation finds itself with a high staff turnover, the need for induction and training will tend to reduce the potential productivity from resources. It takes time for new starters to come up to speed in their tasks.

6. Variety of service and support. We have discussed the aspect of variety above, and we can see a link with the complaint about the barrier caused by the way we do things. Increased variety will make the process more complex and difficult to understand what is happening.

HOW CAN WE BREAK THE BARRIERS AND IMPROVE RESOURCE PRODUCTIVITY?

There are three approaches that we think are useful to break the barriers and improve resource productivity:
1. Understanding the process of service and delivery.
2. Measurement.
3. Trade-off resources.

Understanding the Process

We have discussed the importance of understanding the process flow for service and support delivery when we discussed aspects of quality and the service encounter. When we examine resource productivity, we are looking to identify those stages that impede the process and cause bottlenecks. If we can eliminate the effect of bottlenecks, it may allow us to increase some service incidents we handle or to increase the use of one resource that is causing the bottleneck. For example, a review of engineer activity may lead to the scheduling of a better mix of service activities that increases the proportion of time an engineer is either working on a product or interfacing with a customer.

If we are forever changing the methods by which tasks are carried out, it will make the job of improving productivity more difficult. Anything that can be done to focus groups on particular tasks will increase the level of learning, which will have benefits for effectiveness, including elimination of waste—for example, higher levels of first-time fix to reduce the number of callbacks.

The motivation of service teams with which we dealt earlier is integral to realizing productivity gains only when the service delivery system is capable of achieving the results.

A final part of the process of achieving capable systems for the delivery of service and support is capture of data while it is used in the design of new products to increase their serviceability. Any improvements in this direction will decrease the amount of resource that is needed to deal with any service incident with that product.

Measurement

We already have looked at some of the options that are available for making productivity measurements at the different levels in a service and support operation. In summary, we would say that measurements should be:

- Linked to the most important resources that affect productivity appropriate to the level at which measurement is made.
- Taken as a series of measurements that may be combined into a productivity index.

- Examined for trends in performance rather than striving for an absolute measurement. It may be time consuming and costly to gather data with great accuracy, and so we decide not to make any measurement. Good indications of the use of the resources can be gained by looking for trends in measurement, which, in themselves, may not be particularly accurate because they are only partial measures of resource productivity.
- Linked to targets for improvement in productivity that are associated with the quality levels set for customer service and support.
- Made visible to frontline staff as well as other service managers. The message is the same as for quality measures; make them visible to those who can make a difference.

Trade-Off Resources

We may be able to improve the overall productivity of resource by trading off one resource for another. For instance, an increased spending on managing spares may increase the labor productivity of engineers because it increases the proportion of time they are working on value-added tasks.

The installation of technology like remote monitoring and other information and communication systems are a similar trade-off. Spending on technology may increase the labor productivity while reducing what is called the *capital productivity* because there is now more money invested in technology. As most firms do not measure the capital productivity, spending on technology is often measured as a labor productivity gain if fewer people are needed.

The use of remote diagnostics brings with it gains in the use of resources as well as aspects of improved customer satisfaction. We see these including:

- Reduction in warranty costs.
- Maintenance increased and repair at breakdown reduced.
- Reduced time on site because of improved diagnosis and accuracy of spares specification. The reduction will be increased where there is the capability for remote testing or repair.
- More complete data on the performance of equipment.

KEY ACTIONS

1. List your main measurements for resource productivity. Do the measurements cover aspects of costs, use and effectiveness?
2. Write down any gaps in the measures currently being used.
3. List the barriers to improving productivity in your delivery of customer service and support. How could they be removed?
4. Write down the ways in which your ability to improve resource productivity is affected by the volume, variation, and variety of demand for customer service and support. What could you do to remove the barriers?

Chapter Ten

Managing the Information

Introduction

Information is a critical asset for any service business. Information is necessary not only to make decisions about the direction of the organization, but also to control its regular activities. The information possessed by the service organization about its customers often provides a major barrier against its competitors.

In managing information systems two questions must be addressed:

1. What information is needed to run the service and support organization?

2. How will the way information is presented affect those involved?

Information is required for strategic decision making and for tactical control, but it must be remembered that the mere fact that information exists will tend to affect actions of the members of the organization.

A chain of restaurants marketed "quick service with good quality food" as its main attraction. Unfortunately, its management information system did not reflect this priority. Instead, the major emphasis was placed on the management of cost. Performance against cost budgets was reported weekly, whereas customer service and satisfaction feedback was compiled annually. Which set of targets would you perceive to be most important? It is not surprising that the majority of actions were taken to reduce cost rather than to improve service and the reputation of the chain suffered as a result.

DO WE NEED A NEW INFORMATION SYSTEM?

It will be critical to match the system to the state of the business. This may be best analyzed by reference to the product life cycle (Figure 10–1).

FIGURE 10–1

Changes in Information Priorities through the Product Life Cycle

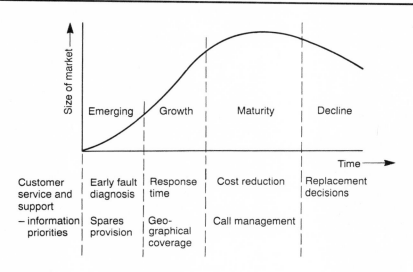

With an emerging product the demand for product and service will be uncertain. The emphasis of the information system is therefore placed on market and customer research. For the service manager, it will be particularly important to gather a comprehensive service history, tracking fault diagnosis and reliability data for feedback into product development, and to assist in scheduling resources. With a mature product, on the other hand, the emphasis is more likely to be on cost and volume, and the design of information systems will be toward cost and efficiency targets.

The service and support manager must be aware of changes in the way that product and service compete and ensure that systems are changed to reflect this. There are a number of examples of systems that are appropriate for part of the product range being "forced" to cover the whole task and, of course, not to do so. Given that information is central to the service manager's task, systems development must receive more than a passing interest.

DEVELOPING STRATEGIC INFORMATION SYSTEMS

How much information can be used to create a competitive advantage can be analyzed by using Porter's five force model, set out here.

Combating the Threat of New Entrants

Service or maintenance companies are often under threat from new organizations, sometimes started by people who were previously employed by them. There are two barriers here that may be erected by the service company using information systems. While former employees may be able to cope with those products with which they are familiar, they will no longer have access to the support needed to service the full product range, and, of course, this product knowledge will become increasingly out of date as new products are introduced.

It may be that a potential new entrant may not have sufficient data about the customers' installations to give an adequate service level. The organization must market its own capability in this area, emphasizing the full range of support available.

The second barrier will lie in those information systems that are visible to the customer. There may be a confidence factor in being able to demonstrate that the service organization has a full service history readily available, sometimes even knowing more about the customer's equipment than the customer does.

Good service may well depend on rapid supply and distribution channels, which again will be helped by the rapid interchange of information. If the organization has control of these channels, it will be difficult for a new entrant to compete.

Quality information fed back to product designers will provide the basis for development, which will ensure that the organization stays ahead of the competition, keeping its customers satisfied.

The Threat of Substitute Products or Services

A specific threat for the service and support organization may be the desire of the customer with a complex network of products and services to hand over service management to a single service provider, who offers the reduced administrative cost of one-stop shopping. Building customer databases that include details by customer site of related equipment that might be included in one service agreement may provide a capability to offer total system service management.

In many organizations, much information is held informally by customer contact staff. They may be able to assess how customer tastes and needs are changing. If the products and services do not change with them, the customer may switch to new providers. An information system may be provided to "formalize" this customer intelligence.

If substitute products or services have already come onto the market, this arrival will probably mean that the organization's own market will reach the mature/decline phase of its life cycle rapidly, if it is not already there. Then competition will be price dominated, and information systems to manage this new emphasis of low cost and efficiency will be needed.

The Effect of Industry Rivalry

Fierce industry rivalry may be good for the customer in the short term if competition results in price cutting. Prolonged rivalry will be detrimental to the company's profitability, and may restrict choice in the longer term. If the service organization has to cut prices to compete, clearly, timely information about profitability will be a top priority. This will enable the customer service and support manager to find the right service levels to give value for money to the customer. This will be particularly critical if differential service levels are to be offered. Tight control is all-important.

The strategy of raising service levels may have a disastrous effect on short-term profitability, particularly if the wrong market segments are chosen for service improvement. In mature industries, there may be little that can be done to differentiate the basic product by design or price, so many companies offer extra services, many of which may be delivered at marginal cost if the information is available to make clear decisions.

The Threat of Strong Buyers and Suppliers

If the purchasing power of the organization is relatively weak, or it is supplying a dominant customer, the organization may find that it can not manage its business as it wishes. For the service organization, this may mean not being able to purchase replacement items to meet service commitments. Strong arm tactics are unlikely to work in this situation. The organization is most likely to succeed by persuasion and clear communication of its needs. Getting its needs into the suppliers' schedules as early as possible may not be a cast-iron guarantee, but it is surprisingly effective. If early reliable information about needs is followed up by regular feedback on supplier performance, the battle may be won.

The strong customer, likewise, needs to be managed. The strong customer without confidence in the organization's ability to deliver will tend to make increasingly stringent demands. Any loss of customer confidence that may arise if the customer does not feel the situation is under control will result in more demand for faster response and higher levels of service. If the service organization can demonstrate competence, supported by good information on its own business, the strong customer's demands may be contained.

Opportunities for Advantage through Information

Information systems may be used to create time advantage. If the service engineer can respond more quickly through better scheduling or faster communications, this speed will be reflected in higher customer satisfaction. The move to remote linkages giving early warning of failure or possible failure is a good example. Many service organizations are equipping their staff with handheld terminals that allow 24-hour communication with central information systems.

Many of the systems that create time advantage also create cost advantage. Predictive systems that give rapid response also allow better resource management. Sometimes problems may be solved over the telephone. This approach is known as call avoidance, which may also be effected by analyzing service demands. For example, analysis that 40 percent of service demands result from customer ignorance rather than product failure might justify investment in clearer documentation or free customer training. Other savings are likely to be generated through better control of the two major costs represented by inventory and people. These might include bar codes, engineer data, and quality costs.

Again, linked to time and cost, are the systems that help better decision making. Service organizations may develop models to indicate locations for service points, capacity scheduling programs, or systems for financial analysis. There is much to be said for giving employees at all levels business data rather than solely operational data to enable them to carry out their function. A view of the impact of what they do on the success of the business may promote more commitment to improvement.

It is worth separating out market intelligence systems. Feedback from customers on quality or changing needs is vital for product development. Tom Peters, in Thriving on Chaos, identifies one of the attributes of excellent companies as being "obsessed with listening to customers." Such listening may allow the organization to identify further business opportunities. Rank Xerox created an early advantage by identifying when a customer's copier was overloaded and feeding this information through to the sales department, which was often able to sell a bigger copier at an attractive price. Rank Xerox was happy to do this because overloaded copiers mean higher service demands. Hewlett-Packard likewise has developed a combined sales-service database that helps the development of qualified sales leads.

Finally, it may be possible to give enhanced customer service through customer-oriented systems. Jan Carlzon of the airline SAS recognized this advantage when he stated that they were in the information business, not the transport business. He recognized that the customer basically wants to find out quickly which is the best way to travel from A to B. The fact that it is by air may be incidental.

Examples of this approach are the garage that sends reminders to its customers for regular tune-ups (thus giving an impression of better customer care) or companies that provide support for complex products by having the ability to produce equipment "health checks" that allow the customer to manage the installation more effectively.

Customers expect contact staff to be fully informed about all areas of the business. It is important that managers consider what questions are likely to be asked of service providers and ensure that such information is given in the form of briefings, manuals, or training, at the very least, so that contact people know where to go to get the information with minimum delay.

Everything must be done to give a professional image to the customer. One bank gained a small competitive edge because it featured on-line terminals that allowed the customer to see at a glance the state of the account with its debits, credits, and standing orders. The competitor that still operated a microfiche system with information that was at least 24-hours old was at a serious disadvantage.

WHAT INFORMATION CAN BE PROVIDED?

In this section we indicate the breadth of information used by organizations.

Financial Systems

Many service and support organizations are run as a business or a profit center; therefore, they require all the normal financial systems to indicate profitability, variance analysis, cash flow, asset management, and capital budgeting.

Customer Management Systems

Under this heading come all the market intelligence systems. What is current and projected demand? What is our current market share? What trends can we identify? Can we identify any segments in the market that must be managed in different ways? Is there any reason why service demands are lower per installation in region A?

We must also consider the way in which individual customers are handled. There should be information about maintenance contracts, sales order processing, invoice details, credit rating, and so on.

Perhaps it should go without saying that there should be one integrated database where possible. We visited one service center where the staff couldn't tell whether the person calling in was a bona fide customer or someone who had called the wrong organization because there was no link between the service file and sales ordering process. Sometimes the mistakes were not discovered until the engineer arrived at site.

Quality Systems

Data should be collected on product reliability (MTBF), faults, warranty claims, Dead On Arrivals (DOA), and other pertinent factors to allow trends to be identified as early as possible for product development. Information about service quality should also be logged, in particular, the key dimensions of response time, time to first-time fix, and areas of customer perception.

Systems should be set up to monitor customer complaints. It is vital for the organization to know how many complaints there are and to what they refer. Equally important is tracking the resolution of complaints. The best organizations have clear procedures about how complaints should be handled, with standards such as callbacks within 4 hours, a letter within 24 hours, resolution within one week. There is no point in such standards if they are not checked. The monitoring will emphasize the importance of the issue.

More positively, there should be information available to customers about product upgrades. For computer software, it may be part of the service contract that upgrades are offered to existing customers. In other situations, there will be possible business in retrofitting modifications.

Resource Management

Included under this category will be information about resource use. What equipment is overloaded and what is no longer needed? The provision of inventory management systems is part of resource management. A key system will be scheduling of equipment and materials as well as service personnel.

People Management

In a sense, people are just another resource, but they probably deserve their own category. The point has been made in other places that you get what you measure, so the design and emphasis of people measurement systems needs careful thought.

A system commonly used by customer support organizations is call management, which gives the present status of all current requests for service and the organization the capability to track and measure the effectiveness of its resource management and individual service personnel. Individuals may be monitored on a range of issues, including repair times, callbacks, journey time, and customer care.

The organization should also have more general measures such as labor cost, absenteeism, and turnover. If the second two are rising, it is likely that excessive demands are being made on the staff, and they are voting with their feet.

As the product range increases, it will become necessary to match skills and product knowledge to service demands. Hewlett-Packard has clear job specifications for its service and support staff, itemizing the product knowledge needed and the training to be given to a new appointee.

Other companies have the ability to match service providers to specific customers, taking into account both skill and personality. They have identified those engineers who deal most effectively with each customer.

THE TRIGGER-INPUT—PROCESS-OUTPUT MODEL

Ives and Vitale have developed a useful way of analyzing the service activity. In considering the elements of inputs, maintenance, triggers, and outputs, in turn, a specification for an information system for day-to-day control of the service activity can be drawn up.

Ives and Vitale have gone on to develop this simple model to reflect different aspects of the service task. Triggers for service requests, they say, fall into three categories: repair because failure has occurred, actions to prevent failure, and enhancement to equipment as developments become available. Figure 10–2 demonstrates the way that these triggers can be structured to indicate valuable information requirements.

Figure 10–2 also demonstrates a powerful way of dividing information requirements into customer concerns and repairer's concerns. The mere activity of thinking through each category may yield insight about how customers could be served better.

TWO ORGANIZATIONS THAT HAVE RECOGNIZED THE VALUE OF INFORMATION

Otis Elevator

Otis provides low- and high-rise elevators in all parts of the world. They see themselves as manufacturers and maintainers of elevators. It is important to them to reduce the number of unscheduled callbacks.

In 1981, North American Operations made the first step into investigating the use of information technology to accept customer requests for maintenance outside working hours. At this time they were using an independent answering service used by other maintainers to deal with this. By 1985, Otis had established a service center to deal with all customer requests 24 hours a day. This center with its information systems is called OTISLINE.

Otis says that the system has dramatically improved the quality of products and service. Customers obviously prefer to be able to deal directly with Otis at all times rather than through an intermediary. The system provides good information to senior management on performance, particularly highlighting any installation that is generating a higher than average number of callbacks. This knowledge allows better customer service and, again, possible product improvement. The system was designed to cope with 100,000 calls per day, about a third of which would be customer requests for service, and the others were communication to and from service personnel.

OTISLINE, used to market the company to customers, gives them confidence that excellent service will be provided. OTISLINE

FIGURE 10–2
The TIPO Model—Developing Information (Ives and Vitale)

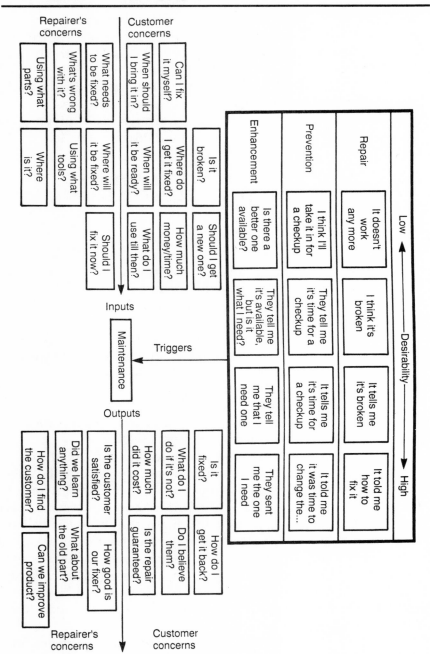

has provided the basis for the company to make future developments in information systems, notably Remote Elevator Monitoring (REM), which identifies problems before the elevator breaks down, hopefully avoiding the worst situation with customers trapped until the service engineer arrives.

The system dramatically improved response times through better call management, improved diagnostic capability by building up repair histories, strengthened the service team by better communication, and increased customer satisfaction levels.

Caterpillar

Perhaps the major component of Caterpillar's competitive strategy is the development of comprehensive information systems. Part of this system is responsible for inventory and logistics to support the claim that Caterpillar can deliver any spare part needed anywhere in the world within 48 hours.

Apart from Logistics, though, there is a massive database set up to watch product performance in the field. Caterpillar's marketing function has a department known as Service Engineering to deal with administering this set of systems.

Service Engineering operates a worldwide reporting system for dealers or the company's own service personnel to log failures by product area, part number, and type of failure. On a weekly basis over 30,000 entries are processed. From this volume of data Caterpillar can identify when products are reaching an age where more defects will occur and take action to reduce their use. Warranty information can be analyzed to indicate design or manufacturing problems.

They have an ability to attach a signal to a potential failure code, so that at each new occurrence the responsible designer will be notified to analyze if some pattern is emerging. Over 6,000 projects are "live" at any one time. Once a problem has been identified as needing a solution, the progress of the remedial action is tracked, with full documentation once the design change is finalized, and tracking after to ensure that the solution is effective.

The information system is particularly important in maintaining communication with the dealer network. Once a dealer reports a potential problem, the progress of any investigation is reported back to him until the solution is implemented. Information about failures is available to the dealer through the system, as are the full range of dealer performance statistics.

Caterpillar has devoted many man-years to its systems and is continually enhancing them and to making them easier to use.

KEY ACTIONS

1. List your main information systems that have any affect on customer service and support.
2. Indicate if the system was designed for efficiency or customer service. What should it be?
3. Could information systems be developed to improve the linkages across the value chain?

Chapter Eleven

Managing the Materials

Introduction

Inventories of spare parts or replacement products are the lifeblood of many service and support organizations. If the spares are not available, there is little point in the service engineer turning up to repair the equipment. All the customer care and smile campaigns will be to no avail if the basic product is not forthcoming.

For manufacturers of complex products there will probably be significant profits to be made from the supply of spares. Some have found to their cost that the spares business is sufficiently attractive to encourage pirate manufacturers to enter the market, possibly with spares that do not meet the original specification. Managing inventories to provide good availability levels at a reasonable cost may be a defense against these competitors, who may damage the safety reputation of the business as well as take profits.

For the average service and support organization, inventory will be the largest element of operating cost after the cost of employees. There are often opportunities to make savings in inventory cost that allow the organization to make improvements elsewhere. Black and Decker financed part of its service enhancement program through a review of its inventory policies.

This chapter is in three main sections:

1. *Why do we need inventory?* This section outlines the role of inventory for the service and support organization in providing the appropriate level of customer service. In this section we discuss the various reasons for holding inventory, which will enable the customer service and support manager to formulate an inventory policy.

2. *How do we manage inventory?* What philosophies and techniques of inventory management are valuable for the customer service and support manager?

3. *Managing the service supply chain.* Many companies are finding benefits in working in closer partnerships with other organizations involved in supporting the final customer. By working closely it may be possible to reduce the inventory held by the chain as a whole, with benefits shared by all.

THE COST OF INVENTORY

With the advent of the Just-in-Time (JIT) philosophy with its emphasis on ending waste, the pressure for inventory reduction has increased still further. The reasons are well known to service managers and broadly come under the following categories:

- The carrying cost of inventory is enormous, comprising cost of capital tied up, storage and system costs, shrinkage, and obsolescence costs. It is not uncommon for companies to fix the inventory holding charge at 40 percent or more.
- Inventory represents waste, largely because processes, suppliers, or demand forecasts are unreliable. We hold stock because we expect things to go wrong.
- Inventory is present to act as a buffer, which may be necessary to some degree, but its very presence reduces the need to solve problems permanently. It may dampen motivation to improve products and processes to the extent that the inventory is no longer needed or needed in much smaller amounts.

The JIT approach may help, and we will return later to the place of JIT in service and support. In looking at the role of inventory we should always be questioning whether it is still needed. A problem with inventory is that it tends to grow through many small routine decisions made by many people in quite separate functions. In this sense inventory is unlike a purchase of capital equipment or company vehicles. These capital decisions are large, visible, and nonroutine, receiving a high degree of senior management attention. The aim of this section is to describe the role of inventory so that managers will be able to develop a rationale to justify the level of investment in inventory, rather than to merely say "we need an inventory of $10 million to manage effectively."

WHY DO WE NEED INVENTORY?

In thinking about inventory it is useful to make the following distinctions:

1. There is inventory that must be held given the current systems and processes employed, even if they work perfectly. So, if a service depot's stock is replenished once a week and the weekly demand is 50 units, the inventory holding will average 25 units if no safety stock is held and demand remains constant.

2. The second portion of inventory is that which must be held because systems and processes do not work perfectly. Suppliers don't deliver on time, manufacturing processes may produce more scrap than anticipated, and customers don't order to a predictable pattern. This inventory is a reflection of the variability in the system.

This broad distinction may already point up some areas for investigation and improvement. A traditional plea for inventory has been that demand forecasts are always inaccurate. Though forecasts can often be improved, they will never be perfect, but in our work with companies, we find that the majority of inventory is put into the system because of supply side problems, and demand side inventory is relatively small.

We can illustrate this concept in our example above. The weekly delivery cycle itself results in an inventory holding of 25 units, whereas the extra inventory held because demand is variable is likely to be limited to 1 or 2 units. On the other hand, if the reliability of suppliers is such that only 90 percent of what is ordered is received on the next shipment, a further five units may be held to ensure that availability levels are maintained.

This section describes four broad categories of inventory. The service and support manager should be able to identify how much stock is held for each of the categories; this knowledge will indicate priorities for improvement activity. The four headings are:

- Fluctuation stocks. These are stocks held because a stated level of service or availability is to be kept despite fluctuations in demand or supply.
- Anticipation stocks. This inventory is held because providing capacity to cover peak demand is believed to be too expensive. Spares are therefore manufactured ahead of the peak.
- Lot-size stocks. These are stocks held because there are discounts available for bulk purchase, or there are minimum economical batch sizes for manufacture.
- Pipeline stocks. These are materials that are in transit through the distribution network and may include both raw materials en route from suppliers and finished goods in despatch to customers or service depots.

Fluctuation, Safety, or Buffer Stocks

These stocks are held because there is variability in the system, but service levels to customers must be maintained. Typical reasons include:

- Suppliers do not deliver on time. Of course, internal suppliers such as the internal manufacturing function are included here, and they may be rather worse than external suppliers at meeting production schedules for service requirements.
- The quantity of supplied items may not be to the required specification. It is not uncommon for orders to be received with quantities less than expected, often because of quality problems at an earlier stage, but the company has not been notified in sufficient time to take remedial action.
- Inventory may be scrapped or damaged during the service or installation process itself. For example, carbon gland seals for pumps are extremely fragile and easily damaged during dismantling or reassembly.
- The demand for items may vary considerably and be difficult to predict. Demand may vary between customers. For example, a garage may have difficulty in predicting demand for brake pads as wear is a function of driving style.

Many supply issues can be addressed through supplier development or improved customer–supplier partnerships. This "Supply Chain" approach is discussed in more detail later in this chapter.

How Can We Improve Our Inventory Service Level?

The demand side inventory level must be set in consideration with the required level of customer service. This relationship is illustrated in Figure 11–1. The basic principle behind this curve is simple. If you want to increase customer service levels in availability of inventory to meet a greater percentage of demand from stock there is an exponential increase in cost involved, because the extra stock is effectively held longer than stock for lower availability levels.

The first question that arises from consideration of this relationship is "What is meant by service level?" Retail organizations, perhaps selling spares to the general public, will measure first pick

FIGURE 11–1
The Service Level Problem

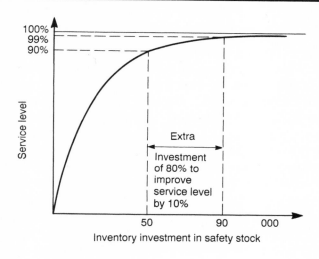

Inventory investment in safety stock

availability. Thus a 95 percent first pick availability will mean that 95 customers out of 100 will be able to purchase and take away the required items in one visit. In fact, retail consumers will probably expect availability levels in excess of 99 percent, particularly when equivalent products can be purchased from a variety of sources.

Service level may be defined in other ways. For example, a manufacturer supplying spares to a dealer network may measure the percentage of orders shipped to dealers within the agreed 48-hour turn-around. A typical target would be between 90 and 95 percent, with a complementary target of order completion within seven days.

It must be said that service levels are notorious for being "adjusted" to look better than they are. It is possible to quote items or value shipped to meet a theoretical 95 percent service level, which hides that a significant number of critical items have not been delivered, and customer satisfaction is falling rapidly.

Service levels must be managed alongside customer satisfaction monitoring. There are examples of companies that have consciously reduced their service level to contain cost. Unfortunately, few of these also carefully monitor customer satisfaction at the same time to ensure that the savings in inventory cost are not overshadowed by potential loss of business.

There are some actions that an organization can take to increase the overall service level without increasing cost. Better forecasting will enable the inventory to be matched more effectively to demand. More accurate stock control will reduce the panic actions brought about by selling something that the system said was there but didn't exist in practice. These actions inevitably increase unit costs, as premium charges are incurred in meeting impossible deadlines.

A useful approach for the customer service and support manager lies in reviewing the number of locations at which stock is held. There is a well-known relationship in inventory management: Inventory is directly proportional to the square root of the number of locations. There is a continuing trend toward centralized stock holding for this reason. Managers of field service departments will recognize the problem of controlling van stocks. Every service engineer likes to have a private store of goodies in an emergency. The way to reduce stock holding is not by sanction, but by ensuring that the service given by the central stores is excellent, perhaps tying part of the bonus scheme to overall inventory reduction. Information systems that are able to monitor these stocks to coordinate transfers where feasible will pay for themselves through inventory reduction.

Finally, service levels should be reviewed so that critical items have a higher availability than those that are relatively unimportant. We visited the central stores of a large company whose system made no discrimination between nonessential items such as erasers and forms that are essential for the company's business. The same service level and the same degree of inventory review were applied to both groups of items.

Two dimensions must be considered. The first dimension is criticality. The question is "Which parts must I hold to ensure that key customers are not inconvenienced?" We worked with a manufacturer of marine propulsion engines who decided that crankshafts of all units currently in service must be held as spares to ensure that bad publicity resulting from a ship laid up for months would be avoided. The direct cost of this decision could be justified for engines in current production but not for semi-obsolete models. It was, however, the right decision in overall quality cost.

The second dimension is cost, usually calculated by Annual Requirement Value (Unit Cost × Annual Demand). Here, the Pareto or 80–20 rule applies, with 80 percent of the value represented by 20 + percent of the parts. In ABC analysis, high value or A items receive more management attention to decrease the inventory investment.

Anticipation or Seasonal Stocks

This category applies largely to a manufacturing process and relates to manufacturing capacity and peak demand. It is rarely economical for the organization to provide capacity to meet peak demand. Therefore it will build up stocks prior to the peak to cope with it without increasing delivery times to customers.

The Service and Support Manager must be aware of this situation if the internal manufacturing unit allocates a fixed amount of capacity to production of spares. Within the service organization this type of inventory may be built up in the form of service packs or assemblies that reduce the degree of work to be carried out on the customer's premises.

Lot-Size Stocks

An organization may hold this type of inventory for two reasons: first, because the process demands a certain batch size as, for example, in brewing a vat full of beer; or second, because the supplier offers discounts for larger quantities.

Some organizations will be able to use the EOQ (Economic Order Quantity), and, indeed, sometimes the EOQ will give a useful guide to setting batch sizes. Figure 11–2 shows the relationship between order costs and inventory carrying costs. The EOQ does not work well when demand fluctuates dramatically, and implicit in the calculation is the belief that it isn't possible to improve the processes involved so that they become flexible enough to allow smaller batch sizes at lower costs.

FIGURE 11–2
Economic Order Quantity

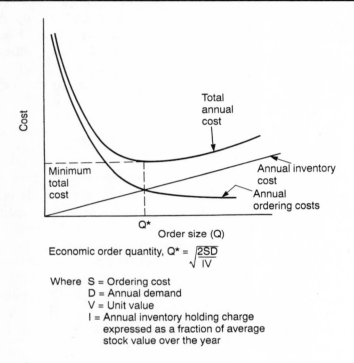

Economic order quantity, $Q^* = \sqrt{\dfrac{2SD}{IV}}$

Where S = Ordering cost
       D = Annual demand
       V = Unit value
       I = Annual inventory holding charge
           expressed as a fraction of average
           stock value over the year

Increasing the frequency of deliveries to service depots may reduce the average inventory held throughout the system. A move from a monthly delivery to a weekly delivery will result in lower stock levels in the depots and an increase in service level, because it is easier to forecast one week ahead rather than four. There will, of course, be an increase in transportation and handling costs, but these may be reduced with the use of specialist carriers who have established complex networks to speed delivery and reduce costs.

Transportation or Pipeline Stocks

If the total network is geographically dispersed, inevitably there will be inventory in transit. Japanese companies manufacturing in the United Kingdom initially found it difficult to source some items locally. For these materials there was, therefore, some six weeks of inventory on ships between Japan and the United Kingdom.

Does this matter to the customer (surely the goods are not paid for until they arrive)? The fact is, of course, that all costs are ultimately borne by the consumer. The cost of transportation and extra inventory owned by suppliers will eventually become part of the final product cost. This is why Marks and Spencer have worked so hard at developing suppliers in the United Kingdom who can rapidly deliver direct to the store.

There is a second benefit arising from reducing pipeline stocks. If inventory is taking six weeks to travel from the Far East to the United Kingdom the feedback loop in the event of quality problems becomes rather lengthy. Reducing the time for feedback increases the possibility of problems being traced to the source and then solved.

HOW DO WE MANAGE INVENTORY?

There are numerous textbooks on inventory management that describe the various techniques in more detail than is feasible to do here. In this next section we indicate the approaches that are most relevant to the service and support manager.

How Much Inventory Have We Got?

In a typical inventory profile, the organization should be able to identify how much inventory is being held for each of the reasons described in the last section. This profile will be divided into two parts. There will be inventory that can be identified as that which was planned, perhaps to meet customer service level targets. There will also be unplanned inventory that arises because of failures in the materials system. The relative size of each component will indicate where attention must be directed.

Can the Task be Simplified?

It is an obvious statement to say that all management tasks are easier if levels of complexity can be removed. However, before embarking on a massive investment in inventory and inventory control systems, it is well worth reviewing product structures to see if some rationalization can reduce the total need for inventory.

For example, the marine propulsion engine manufacturer discussed earlier discovered it was possible to hold one crankshaft forging that would cover several semi-obsolete engine types. Extra machining would be needed sometimes as the forging would be bigger than necessary, but the saving that resulted from holding one forging rather than many far outweighed the extra unit costs involved. Of course, much of the responsibility for this activity lies with the product designers, but the business issues must be discussed by all, including the service and support function.

This move to simplification may be impeded by costing systems that apportion overheads to direct labor alone, taking no account of the extra costs that arise from low volumes or more complex products. If the designer is working by inaccurate unit costs, there will be no motivation to simplify. Many organizations are now applying Activity-Based Costing (ABC), and this approach is discussed in more detail in Chapter 9.

Managing the Manufacturing–Service Interface

When inventory is within the control of the manager who needs it, problems may be manageable, but when stock must be ordered and therefore becomes part of another person's production plan, problems seem to multiply as differing priorities, second-guessing, and poor communication each contribute to complexity and confusion.

We conducted some inventory management workshops for a manufacturer of consumer goods. During a discussion about how good they were at meeting schedules, a materials manager said that they had recently met the full requirements of the service department only to find parts shipped back because they couldn't cope with the amount of inventory. This was the first time for many months that the service schedule had been met in full, and in this situation second-guessing and overordering becomes a way of life. Disciplines must be applied across the organization for this practice to be ended and inventory managed more effectively.

All manufacturing units should have a formal master schedule, detailing what must be produced and when it is needed. The master schedule must be based on what can be produced rather than it being a wish list of what we would like. It should be put together with full knowledge of material and capacity availability.

Many companies employ a form of MRP II (Manufacturing Resource Planning) to help both business planning and manufacturing scheduling. MRP II is driven by a master production schedule, put together on the basis that sufficient resource is available on the known capacity constraints. Businesses that succeed with this approach consider the Master Production Schedule (MPS) to be the company plan rather than merely a means of scheduling production. This means the composition of the MPS and any major changes to it must be subject to senior management review.

The service and support manager must be part of the master production schedule formulation and review process. The MPS is the manufacturing plan, and it therefore must reflect all demands for production and contain all service requirements. The MPS review meeting has often proved to be a useful means of integrating all business functions and is one that can be used by the service and support manager to raise the visibility of the service function.

Some common sense must be applied here about how the MPS is composed. A tractor company may operate its MPS at the level of major subassemblies, such as cabs, chassis, and options. It would be unrealistic to create a new master schedule entry for nuts and bolts for service, but it may be possible to draw together useful "Service kits" that could be included in the MPS. An example of this approach would be to create a subassembly for a cylinder head overhaul, including all the gaskets and fastenings required. Otherwise, such details would be included in a standard reorder point stock control system.

Good MPS management results in high strike rates (in excess of 95 percent schedule adherence, period on period). Once this level of performance has been achieved it becomes relatively easy to maintain, because the benefits of better control and lower inventory cost are then visible to all. Some actions that build successful MPS management are:

1. The MPS should be fully "owned" by the business as a whole and should not be viewed merely as a manufacturing plan.

2. Senior management must be disciplined to work within the plan. This may cause frustration on some occasions but will yield benefits overall.

3. The business must be able to identify those areas or resources that constrain output. These constraints must be fully considered in the formulation of the plan.

4. Good MPS management depends on honesty from all concerned. Overordering or pretending that requirement dates are earlier than needed increase the chance that a realistic plan will not be formulated or achieved.

Maintaining a Service Focus in the Manufacturing Function

Complaints that service requirements receive too low a priority in the manufacturing schedule are common. Indeed, there may be a strong case for creating a separate spares manufacturing unit, particularly when there is need to make customized spares rapidly to respond to a breakdown situation.

There is likely to be a difference in the criteria by which original equipment manufacture and production of spares are judged. In manufacturing a component for original equipment built, it is likely that the key task is to have it available for assembly in six months time while reducing unit cost. In the breakdown situation, speed is all, the inconvenience to the customer meaning that unit cost is comparatively unimportant. It is unlikely that the same operating systems will cope effectively with such opposing requirements. It is quite common to create a "Plant within a Plant" for service needs.

Those spares that relate to current production can be scheduled into the main manufacturing plan, particularly if there are significant quantities involved. Once the product supported moves to semiobsolete status, however, this becomes increasingly difficult. It will be uneconomical to break down current production setups to make small quantities for spares, and original equipment built will probably take priority leading to lower availability levels for service.

Organizations deal with this by making a closing batch of components for service at the end of the main production run, by estimating total needs for the next 10 years, or by subcontracting these components to a supplier who will have the flexibility to provide the necessary items at reasonable cost without the overheads of main production.

Material Requirements Planning

In essence MRP II is directed at creating a master production schedule that considers all the capacity and material constraints in the system. Having formulated this top level schedule, MRP II then uses Material Requirements Planning (MRP) to schedule all the detail activities of production and procurement that are required to meet the plan.

A form of MRP may be very useful for the service and support manager. It allows items to be tied together to ensure that imbalances in stock do not occur. Thus Figure 11–3 shows a bill of material (BOM) for the parts needed for a routine repair. By ordering at the top level, all the other parts are also ordered in the correct quantities.

There are many MRP and MRP II software packages available that range from the immensely powerful which run on mainframe computers and which are designed for complex manufacturing situations through to relatively cheap personal computer applications. Implementation of these systems will take some effort, but the systems will reduce inventory cost and give better control in the long run.

The MRP approach is particularly valuable when kits of parts must be marshalled for specific jobs. The installation department, for example, may need to be sure that all necessary components will be available to meet a commissioning date. An MRP approach may prevent last minute "borrowing" and provide much needed visibility to see when parts are currently promised.

Managing the Bits and Pieces

For many items, fasteners and other consumables, a major inventory control system will be overkill, or just impractical. Figure 11–4 shows the two most common forms of simple inventory control, Reorder Point and Periodic Review.

FIGURE 11–3
Bill of Material for Cylinder Head Repair Kit

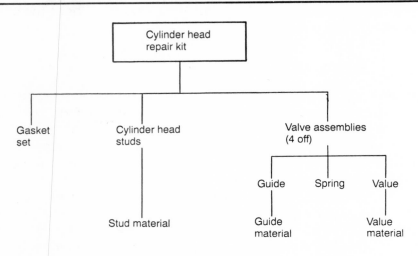

The Reorder Point system can be operated by using a simple card system, or, frequently, the two-bin system will be used, where the item is reordered when the first bin is empty, with the second bin acting as the reserve that covers the order replenishment lead time. There are some simple computer packages available.

The Periodic Review system is useful where a number of stock items are ordered from the same supplier. The system is set up to ensure that these items are reviewed at the same time, by allowing one purchase order to be raised to cover a range of stock items, rather than by raising many smaller ones at frequent intervals. Although the administration of the Periodic Review is simpler than Reorder Point, the safety stocks employed tend to be greater, and the system is less responsive to sudden increases in demand. There is a higher chance of a stock-out in this case, which may be counteracted by higher buffer stocks.

Safety stocks will be relatively high when:

FIGURE 11–4
Fixed Order Quantity and Periodic Review Stock Control

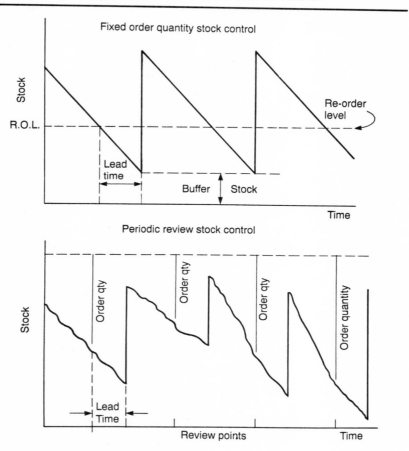

- The pattern of demand is variable and relatively unpredictable.
- Large numbers of the stock item are used on each installation or service call.
- There is a long lead time for replacement of the item. Long lead times tend also to mean that delivery reliability is reduced, increasing the pressure for high safety stocks.

Forecasting Demand

Some stock control computer packages include a simple fore-casting capability. We are surprised that so few companies use any forecasting techniques at all, given that inventory is such a significant cost (and the cost of not having it when you need it may be even greater). Forecasting may be difficult for the service organization where demand is lumpy, but with effort some progress can usually be made.

The service and support manager can employ some relatively simple methods of forecasting to take account of seasonal patterns and growth trends. The most simple form of forecasting is to use a simple moving average, perhaps weighted to take greater account of recent periods' results. With sufficient data, seasonal factors can be built in to give quite useful results for relatively little effort and would be suitable for use with many of the high-usage stock items.

Exponential smoothing is perhaps the most popular forecasting method, and it is available with many stock control packages. The forecast for the current period, F_t, is calculated using the following formula:

$$F_t = a (D_t) + (1 - a) F_t - 1$$

The forecasting constant, a, reflects the weight that is given to the most recent actual demand figure, D_t. Previous demand data has been incorporated in the calculation of last period's forecast, $F_t - 1$. High values of a will respond rapidly to most recent data and should be used if the situation is changing rapidly. It will be more common to use a smaller value of a, perhaps 0.1 or 0.2, to ensure that due account is taken of earlier demand. As with moving averages, exponential smoothing can also incorporate a seasonal adjustment.

The trick with forecasting is not so much in generating the forecast, but in recognizing when the forecast is no longer accurate. There are some error-tracking techniques that indicate when the forecast accuracy has deteriorated. One that is commonly used, Trigg's Tracking Signal, may be incorporated in the forecast, giving an element of self-correction.

A useful technique for the service and support manager will be the linking of outside indicators to service demand. Thus, there should be some relationship between published figures of activity in the construction industry and the number of excavators used by contractors, and, therefore, also the number of service calls generated. This relationship can be explored using regression analysis. Regression models can be simple, using one independent variable, or they can be more complicated, known as multiple regression, where the relative value of each variable can be established.

A common application of regression analysis is to link the number of units operating in the field to service demand. This plan is particularly useful in comparing performance when the department is regionally organized. One might expect a region that services 100 customers to generate more business than one that serves 50. Exercise care to ensure that comparisons are made under similar conditions. A tractor company discovered that their European market, which contained relatively new tractors, generated a quite different service profile from its African market, where the tractors were considerably older.

A final issue in forecasting relates to supporting the launch of new products. There will be no demand history to base usage on, and stock levels can only be estimated by the demand profile of similar products, so remember it will be very important for the product's reputation that spares are available when needed. In this case higher safety stocks may be justified initially. Unfortunately, often manufacturing is struggling to meet the demands of original equipment programs and spares inventory is slow in reaching target levels.

Commit the Inventory As Late As Possible

Inventory savings can be made by holding the material in a state such that it can be made into several finished items. The earlier example of the marine propulsion crankshaft forging that could be used for several applications illustrates this point. There may be a unit cost increase in the item held, but since the higher specification allows use on a wider range of applications, the total inventory cost will be reduced.

There are two approaches here. The first is to see whether a more expensive item can cover more applications, and the second is to improve manufacturing or assembly lead times to give greater flexibility to respond to the latest requirement.

Stock items should also be committed as late as possible in their position. A spare part once delivered to a warehouse in Scotland is unlikely to be immediately available in France. Where possible, stock should be held centrally, and this philosophy must be supported by an efficient distribution system.

Can the Just-In-Time Philosophy Be Used?

Just-in-Time is aimed at reducing inventory in the total system by eliminating waste and involving people more effectively in the process. So, the straightforward answer is yes to some extent for any organization. The heart of the JIT philosophy lies in providing a flexible and reliable system that provides the foundation for reducing inventory, cutting replacement lead times, and giving impetus to improve the quality of products and processes still further.

Hewlett-Packard has made widespread use of this approach not only in manufacturing, but also in its repair facilities. Prior to JIT their repair workshops, in common with many others, were littered with returned units in various states of assembly. Ensuring that units were not allowed into the workshop area until all parts were available has brought the work in progress down dramatically, cutting lead times sometimes from months to days.

JIT brings visibility to the process as Hewlett-Packard has discovered. As they pursued this policy, they realized that considerable disruption was being caused to the process by customers ringing in to discuss the state of their units with the engineer responsible. If the engineer was in midoperation, this lengthened the time spent by the unit in the repair area and increased the possibility of making errors as the number of interruptions increased. HP reviewed its customer handling policy and they restricted the access of customers to engineers outside their core repair working hours. The improvement in repair turnaround far outweighed any relationship problems brought about by lack of access, and it often ends the need for the customer to call because the unit is returned faster.

MANAGING THE SERVICE SUPPLY CHAIN

There has been a shift in thinking over the last few years. Previously, there was a desire to trade "at arm's length," but today there are many examples of companies forging partnerships, believing that there is significant mutual advantage in working together closely. Effectively, this move is a return to vertical integration, with the advantage that one company isn't responsible for every activity; instead, it can join forces with another and they can complement each other's strengths and weaknesses.

Figure 11–5 shows a supply chain for a manufacturer selling its product through a network of dealers who carry out service work for their customers. If the different parts of the chain work independently, each will be working on less information than could be available and therefore will be less effective. Sometimes there will be more inventory than is needed, and at others, insufficient inventory. This is known as the Forrester Effect, which observes that the swings in over- and undersupply become more dramatic the further you are from the point of initial demand (Figure 11–6).

Supply Chain Management attempts to take out the unknowns in the chain, tie the constituent parts closer together, and by removing excess inventory, reduce the lead time from start to finish. As a result the total chain will be far more responsive to changes in customer demand. In fact, the ideal is for the constituents of the chain to be "making to order" rather than "making to stock," thus removing inventory and excess cost from the system. These benefits must be shared across the chain.

What Must the Supply Chain Produce?

Customers are looking for ever-increasing levels of customer service. This impatience is a reflection the of modern life and can be summed up in the cry "I want it now!" In some markets, at least, immediate availability is becoming a given or order qualifier, and customers assume it. Thus, the aims of the supply chain are as follows:

- At the very least, a significant improvement in response times. For example, Caterpillar spares can be sent anywhere in the world within 48 hours.

FIGURE 11–5
Service Supply Chain

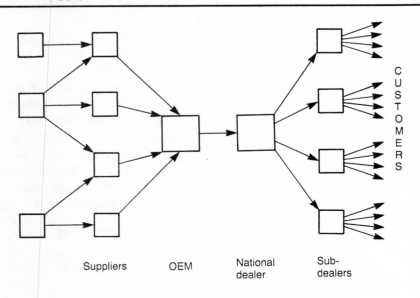

Suppliers   OEM   National   Sub-
                                 dealer   dealers

- High availability levels. Inventory service levels of 95 percent and above and increasing.
- An increase in service level, but at reduced distribution cost and with reduced inventory levels
- High levels of management control and visibility of materials through the pipeline.

Clearly, the demands outlined above will not be met by traditional incremental improvement programs. Service supply chain management needs a major change in attitude to dealing with both customers and suppliers.

What Is Needed to Make the Supply Chain Work?

At the risk of using too much jargon, an integrated approach is needed to solve the problem of providing improved service at lower cost. All the components of the chain must be coordinated to

FIGURE 11–6
The Forrester Effect

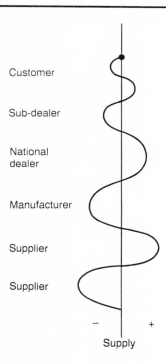

remove the excess inventory and ineffective management effort from it.

Each stage must be as flexible as possible, able to respond to changes in demand rapidly. For members of the chain to invest in systems, people, and processes to make this possible, there must be an apparent long-term benefit. Hence, the move toward developing long-term partnerships with some confidence of sustained business, which should yield both improved flexibility and lower cost through time.

A key element in managing the chain is the development of schedules that are realistic and give sufficient time to react at each customer/supplier link. The ultimate aim is to move from suppliers making to stock to a situation where they can make to order. There is an element of continuous improvement here, a fixed schedule 12 weeks ahead that is necessary today may be reduced to 8 weeks after 12 months' cooperative action to develop more flexible and reliable processes.

Some key requirements for supply chain success are:

- Effort to generate realistic schedules and the discipline to keep them.
- Investment in rapid information processing systems such as EDI links.
- Action to build teamwork both internally and externally. Many organizations are forming product-based teams that cut across traditional functional barriers.
- Joint projects to build channels that are more responsive to changes in demand. The emphasis is on creating planned flexibility, the ability to respond within defined limits.

Is Supply Chain Management Worth It?

Companies that have pursued this route have reported some benefits. A key measure is total supply chain inventory turns. If the inventory is merely shifted to a different place, typically back to a supplier, in the end no one wins. Companies that have developed partnerships are reporting a reduction in inventory across the chain, a representation of true cost savings.

Lower inventory levels mean faster output times, shorter lead times and therefore greater responsiveness. This, in turn, means that schedules are achieved more often, with the positive benefit that much of the second-guessing disappears and a further reduction of inventory. Schedules that are not continually changing are good news for manufacturing efficiency and also for quality, again yielding the possibility of further improvement.

What Can the Service and Support Manager Do?

There is much work to be done by all members of the chain to build relationships along the chain. For service and support, this means work with:

- Designers to improve the product.
- All members of the chain must promote a customer focus, and show understanding of the customer's needs and problems.

- All suppliers, whether internal or external, must give accurate, timely information about future needs.
- All members must work with customers to understand their needs and to explain more fully how the support organization works. This approach may promote joint improvement activities.

KEY ACTIONS

1. Write down your service level targets for inventory and the inventory levels you hold.
2. List ways you could reduce your inventory.
3. Think about actions you could take to influence manufacturing to give a high priority to customer service and support.
4. Write down ways in which you could improve your relationships with external suppliers. Who should take action?

Chapter Twelve

Managing Through Intermediaries

Introduction

Earlier we discussed the structure of customer service and support and related it to the dimension of how much "In-house control" the original producer must retain of this activity. It is always desirable to maintain control of the service activity for quality reasons to build customer relationships, and of course because revenue can possibly result.

However, for some reasons it may be deemed impractical, uneconomical or ineffectual for an organization to attempt to deliver service and support to all customers everywhere in the world. When this happens, there will be one and sometimes more organizations between us, as the Original Equipment Manufacturer (OEM), and the end consumer. We shall consider this issue primarily from the viewpoint of the OEM, with a final section from the viewpoint of a service provider who is not a manufacturer.

The decision to use an intermediary is not usually that of the customer service and support manager alone. Often, the marketing of the original product demands that there should be a local selling point, close to customers. If the primary motivation to appoint dealers is to increase sales turnover, the task of the Customer Service and Support Manager may become more difficult. In this case the intermediary may have been chosen for sales expertise, not for service proficiency, and will need considerable control and support.

Capital goods manufacturers do not face this issue to the same extent. Sales are often the responsibility of the OEM's own personnel, and the decision to appoint an intermediary is likely to rest largely in the customer service and support function. A typical reason for appointment would be to ensure rapid response when there might be few installations in the geographical area. Here the problem for the customer service and support manager would lie in imparting sufficient product knowledge to the agent.

In this chapter we discuss the issues involved in operating a dealer or agent network and give some guidelines about how they can be managed more effectively. The chapter concludes with a case study that illustrates one company's approach to managing intermediaries.

WHY USE INTERMEDIARIES?

Close to Customer

The most common reason for choosing to use dealers or agents rather than an in-house organization is geographical coverage. The ability to get close to customers both geographically and in understanding their particular operating conditions may be critical both for original sale and for continuing support. Customers may feel more confident if there is a local presence. The organization may desire to increase customer service and support coverage worldwide rapidly to meet higher sales targets and, as with franchising, building an independent dealer network may accomplish this by using finance supplied by other people.

Local Knowledge

The organization may have insufficient knowledge of local trading conditions. This knowledge may be particularly pertinent for relatively small companies who want to expand internationally. This option will be attractive if initial sales volumes are likely to be small, making the commitment of opening a new sales and service branch economically unattractive.

Apart from the loss of control and the loss of potential revenue, a further drawback in using agents or dealers to expand internationally is that it reduces the opportunity for the organization to move down the learning curve in working in that region and delays any proposed move to set up its own organization.

Skill Shortage

A third reason for using intermediaries is that of expertise. The manufacturer may feel that its strengths lie in design and production and doesn't want the organizational overhead of developing other skills. The intermediary may supply local selling skills as indicated above, or develop a specialist application of the equipment. For example, the vast majority of electronic products for security systems are installed and serviced by independent companies who combine products from various manufacturers to provide the most effective solution for the customer. The manufacturers at present have no expertise in designing, installing, and maintaining the systems.

Another example is typified by the total solution approach much favored by computer companies. A common scenario is for computer manufacturers to sell hardware and operations software directly to customers and also to Value-Added Resellers (VARs) who have a particular expertise in applications software. The VARs are able to supply a solution rather than a toolkit to those customers who have no wish to become computer experts. In this case the OEM and the intermediary may be dealing with the same customer.

A service and support organization may find that it is not able to support every technical aspect of its products. For example, many products that have traditionally needed most mechanical expertise are now incorporating an ever-increasing content of microprocessors. In the short term, these skills may have to be supplied by subcontractors. The security systems company may have to subcontract the support of closed-circuit television equipment that needs specialist knowledge.

Low Service Income

Some manufacturers will use intermediaries because the service revenue is negligible. An example, again from the computer industry, would be that of peripherals that are likely to be replaced rather than repaired. In the event of failure the manufacturer must ensure that warranty claims are handled properly to decrease any irritation experienced by the customer. The customer must have ready access to operating advice either through the intermediary having sufficient resources or by provision of a help desk by the manufacturer.

Demand Exceeds Supply

The final reason for using intermediaries is lack of service capacity. A strategy employed for dealing with peak demand may be to use subcontractors rather than have excess capacity underuse. This approach needs much policing to ensure that the customer does not see any deterioration in quality of service. Some service organizations adopt a "top and tail" approach, starting off the service activity by ensuring that the subcontractor has the right expertise and information, and by inspecting the completed work before invoicing the customer. This may be possible where subcontractors are used sparingly, but it still does not control what happens between start and finish.

WHAT APPROACH SHOULD BE ADOPTED TO CONTROLLING INTERMEDIARIES?

This section outlines broad philosophies that may be used to manage the relationship between manufacturer and those organizations used to sell, service, and support its products.

Economic Rewards

Manufacturers of consumer products use distributor margins and allowances as an incentive to intermediaries to promote their product in preference to the competition. This approach may be particularly appropriate when the intermediary sells and services the products of more than one manufacturer. If the volume of business generated by any one product is relatively low, a dealer may handle a range of products, and sometimes these may be competing offerings.

Manufacturers of more expensive products, such as trucks or cars, also employ financial incentives. It must be remembered that the intermediary exists to make profits for its owner rather than to service a particular product. Additional discounts for increased business, improved margin on spares, or payments to improve equipment or facilities are all examples of this approach. This incentive may ensure that adequate effort is applied to the product at the expense of the competing offerings.

A possible drawback of this approach is that it needs considerable administration, setting and reviewing targets, and checking the total scheme to ensure that the returns are worth it, and to ensure that quality standards are maintained to levels that justify the bonus payment. The car manufacturers make wide use of this tactic, though it can become devalued if the targets to qualify for payment are easily attained.

It is worth making a general point here. Managing a dealer network can be described as an art form. Dealers may be rather temperamental, and therefore measures and rewards must be seen to be equitable if goodwill is not to be lost.

Strong Arm Tactics

Some organizations adopt the tactic of punishing poor dealers through reduction of rewards or, in extreme cases, total withdrawal of their franchise. This approach has not generally proved to be effective in improving network performance in the long term. Organizations have found that frequent threats tend to lead to general discontent among dealers, even though those penalized were widely known to be below standard. Penalizing one dealer sends ripples through the rest of the network with the others wondering if it will be their turn next. There may be a general loss of confidence in the parent organization.

However, there may be a good argument for applying sanctions sparingly. Some automobile companies have taken franchises away for poor performance, and in the case of Nissan, the entire United Kingdom chain has been discarded. This tactic has its place "to encourage the others," but it is not recommended as a general management style. Customers may be impressed that the parent has dealt decisively with poor performance but, in general, more positive forms of motivation are more effective.

Providing Expertise to Support Intermediaries

The intermediary chosen may not have the full range of management and technical skills available to the large organization. The sales and service dealer has possibly been founded by a local entrepreneur who is excellent at building up businesses in the area, possibly an excellent salesperson, but likely to be weak in sustaining the systems needed to maintain business control as volume grows. The subcontractors used to cover gaps in technical expertise will be able to deal with the product but may be weak on customer management.

Identifying weaknesses is an opportunity to build the relationships in the network. Not only will the end customer see a better service if these weaknesses are addressed, but also the intermediary should gain confidence in dealing with a professional organization that is prepared to give support where needed. Caterpillar has succeeded in building a network of competent, committed dealers through good support in such areas as inventory management, marketing assistance, and general management training.

The Quality Reputation—Building a Relationship

There is a general belief that some organizations are better to work with than the rest. They are perceived by customer and industry alike to "have got it right." Knowing that intermediaries have profited from the relationship consistently over the long term may motivate the intermediaries to provide high levels of service without the need for other inducements. This result may arise from fear of losing good business or from knowing the product that they support is genuinely the best in the market.

A manufacturer of household goods dealt harshly with its agents in the days when demand far outstripped supply. When business conditions became more difficult and the manufacturer tried to become more effective through developing more cooperative relationships, the attempt was hindered because its earlier aggressive stance was remembered. As with any culture change, it may take several years for people to believe and accept a fundamentally different approach.

Most companies believe that good communication and open dealing are fundamental to effective network management. This applies at the level of the organization as a whole as the intermediary deals with different business functions, but specifically with those individuals in the parent organization who are appointed to control and liaise with the intermediary. Since relationships are a function of people, those employees who have specific responsibility for dealing with intermediaries must be chosen with care. Once personal relationships are established, they should not be changed without good cause. Managing these contact people effectively will mean that some specific issues such as career progression must be carefully addressed.

Manufacturer's Rights to Realistic Controls

Some controls that the parent imposes on the intermediary may be seen as legitimate demands on the part of the manufacturer and therefore are not a matter for negotiation. For example, it may be a reasonable demand that the dealer employs staff who have received a given level of product training before they are allowed to service customers' equipment.

Standards and controls may be accepted as part of the requirements of the job or the conditions of being appointed as an approved agent of the company. Such standards should be regularly reviewed to ensure that they are giving the right result or are indeed reasonable.

An example of such a control might be some measure of stock cover. Current practice seems to vary tremendously from company to company with some imposing no requirement for stock cover to others insisting that at least one unit of each stock number must be held. This control could be put positively in a recommendation, and then monitored by the requests for replacement stock. If the dealer is always making emergency requests for stock, inventory levels are too low.

Quality of service from intermediaries is difficult to watch. Some companies with relatively small service subcontractor networks are able to make sure that all service requests pass through the central service department so that completion and quality may be checked. Larger service organizations must rely on customer surveys or incidence of customer complaints to monitor quality. Most dealers or agents would accept the right of the producer to impose some quality standards and to expect therefore to be audited regularly against them. This doesn't have to be an "end of term examination," but a more positive review of what works and what doesn't work with the aim of identifying joint action for improvement.

It is becoming common for the parent company to watch overall customer satisfaction levels, linking these with more specific quality standards. The parent company may publish league tables of customer satisfaction performance, allowing the individual dealer to see his position in relation to the others. It may be wise to publish these figures anonymously so that the individual sees his score but is not able to identify other dealers. This practice allows the below standard dealer to generate self-motivation to improve rather than be ridiculed by those with better scores.

HOW CAN THE NETWORK BE IMPROVED?

A degree of conflict will occur in all relationships as goals differ or there are breakdowns in communication. The aim of the service and support manager is to ensure that these remain infrequent and minor, solved as they occur, rather than allowing them to escalate into long-term bitter disputes. Some actions can be taken to prevent disputes occurring and to raise the performance of the network.

Establish Clear Performance Expectations

As has already been stated, setting up and managing a dealer network demands a great deal of administration. A key task in the early stages of relationships will be setting proper goals for both parties. Inevitably, there will be continuing debates over margins and discounts, which will be handled more effectively if the basis for negotiation is clear from the outset. The dealer will want to know how profitable the business will be in volume and margin, whereas the manufacturer must be satisfied that service levels will be maintained. Key issues to be resolved, apart from the obvious financial targets, will include the number and competence of personnel employed, quality of service and facilities, and range and level of inventory to be held.

Minimize Network Disputes by Design

Those managing networks of intermediaries talk of two issues. The first issue is channel density, which relates to the conflict which may arise because two dealers are trying to serve overlapping populations of customers. By giving exclusive rights to sell and service specific products in a geographical area the company will help to resolve this issue, provided the distribution of territories is seen to be equitable and sufficient to sustain profitability.

Computer companies have faced this problem where in one territory they may be competing with mini- and mainframe offerings against their independent dealer network who are largely selling and supporting personal computers. A major computer manufacturer belatedly imposed restrictions on the total number of dealers to be appointed after encountering severe problems of administration and overlaps that, in turn, led to a deterioration in service quality.

Car companies have faced problems of channel density as they have launched initiatives to increase market share. If the initiative works and the number of dealers has not increased, the new customers will be dissatisfied. On the other hand, if new dealers are appointed in advance of the new demand, the existing dealers may find that their revenues are reduced in the short term at least as territories are reallocated.

The second major issue of network design is that of channel length. The greater the number of stages in delivering goods and services to the customer, the greater the opportunities for conflict. Some manufacturers appoint national dealers or distributors with regional dealers and even subdealers beyond them. The potential for financial disputes at each stage is multiplied as there are yet more relationships to be managed, and the performance of the chain in quality of service and level of inventory held is likely to deteriorate. Of course, it may seem attractive to deal solely with one national contact, but the loss of control may far outweigh the savings in administrative effort.

Select the Right Intermediaries

As with most management issues, time spent upfront in evaluation and planning will pay off many times over. It will be important to check the general health of the agent's business rather than concentrate on the specific requirements. So, an automobile dealer must have marketing and customer service skills as well as the ability to sell cars, and a subcontractor installer must be financially sound as well as technically competent.

Some areas for review in selecting intermediaries include:

- Financial standing, credit rating, gearing.
- Labor profile, skills, knowledge, and industrial relations record.
- Degree of market understanding.
- Local market knowledge.
- Whether or not competitors' products are sold or serviced.
- Implementation of control systems: cost, quality, scheduling, inventory.
- Percentage of total business that a new contract would represent.
- Assessment of overall desire to carry out the business to a satisfactory level.

Most manufacturers make progress carefully in appointing agents. Studies on the choice of dealers indicate that most organizations try to draw up a reasonable shortlist of candidates to be visited by the management to audit the competence of the applicant before the final decision is made. This process is still adhered to even if an overseas dealer is to be appointed, though government advice may also be sought in this case.

Positive Motivation

As indicated earlier, management by threat is rarely an effective tactic. A study carried out by Shipley et al. indicated that territory rights, keeping the dealer up to date with developments and plans, and regular contact were the actions felt to be the most effective in improving the performance of the network and the individual dealer.

Actions that were felt to be useful also included giving general appreciation for good performance, financial incentives, giving commitments to long-term relationships, and ensuring that the intermediaries are included in policy making. Some automobile companies keep a percentage of allowances against good performance. If the dealership meets its targets, this money can be used to upgrade its facilities.

Actions used less frequently were threats, sharing market research information, and training of staff across all functions in the intermediary's organization.

Train the People

Although the survey mentioned in the previous section indicated that relatively few manufacturers see training as a way of motivating their dealer network, our view is that it represents a good opportunity to build relationships and commitment on both parts. The survey indicated that 73 percent of companies gave product training, whereas only 17 percent gave any form of interpersonal skills training. Since the customer doesn't see that the dealer or subcontractor is an independent company, but rather thinks of them as the parent company, there is no doubt that poor customer service will not only damage the intermediary's reputation, but also that of the parent company.

The case study at the end of this chapter describes one company's belief that its intermediaries should be trained across a wide range of areas as a means of increasing commitment and improving overall quality levels.

Regular Evaluation

Many manufacturers check their dealers on a formal basis at least once a year, using the opportunity to discuss the business as a whole, consider future plans, and set appropriate targets for the next period. The parent may also find it valuable to hold a dealers' conference, giving them the opportunity to meet others and to feel included in the service team. Some have shied away from this approach, perhaps fearing that the dealers may become too powerful if they take concerted action.

Regular evaluations of intermediaries will normally include:

- Volume of business.
- New business generated.
- Value of business.
- Customer service performance.
- Dealer administration costs.

This last item is worth considering. Some dealers will cost more than others to manage. For example, some will not carry as broad a range of spares, and will constantly request priority shipments over and above the normal service. Others will not have the same technical competence, needing the support and advice of the company's personnel. The review process should identify actions that will enable the intermediary to manage the business more effectively as this will represent cost savings to the network.

Many consumer goods manufacturers run continuous customer satisfaction assessments, asking their customers to rate the dealer service. Volvo, for example, was also able to relate high performance on the customer satisfaction index to dealer profitability.

Customer Complaint Management

Some customer complaints are not handled effectively by intermediaries because the parent company's policies are not clear on what is and what is not reimbursable. The procedures for dealing with customer problems and how the costs are to be apportioned should be developed with input from the dealers concerned. At least one car manufacturer operates a system of goodwill payments to smooth over customer complaints. We feel that this approach avoids the issue of improving service rather than managing in spite of poor service quality.

It is usually helpful to make it clear to the customer that there is recourse to the parent organization if the customer is unhappy with the intermediary's performance and there appears to be no desire on the part of the dealer to resolve the issue. Obviously its a sensitive issue, but better addressed head-on rather than avoided.

Meeting Deliveries from Parent to Intermediary

A common source of dispute between parent and intermediary lies in the supply of spare parts. Of course the dealer must hold a reasonable level of stock, but must also have confidence that the stated replenishment lead times will be kept. If the delivery schedules are not reliable, there is no basis for challenging the dealer's performance in inventory management.

This problem is compounded when deliveries must cross national frontiers. Even with free trade agreements, customs and immigration authorities conspire to delay shipments and introduce variability into shipping schedules.

THE RETAILER'S VIEWPOINT—GETTING CONTROL

This chapter has been written from the viewpoint of the producer who uses intermediaries to provide sales and service. Most of the principles outlined apply in reverse to the service provider who needs to ensure that the supply of product, information, and spare parts is kept at a reasonable margin.

The secret of success lies in discovering and exploiting the mutual advantages of partnership. Some electrical retailers give their own after sales service, and while this may compete to a degree with the original manufacturer, it may be that the increase in sales volume arising from increased customer confidence may make it worth supporting.

The retailer will be concerned to reduce the size of the service task. Each new product means an increase in inventory to be carried as well as new product knowledge to be gained. The way to contain this is to make sure that valuable feedback for quality improvement is given to the manufacturer so that both benefit from increased product reliability.

For this reason some sales and service providers may choose to limit the range of products dealt with to better manage those that remain. To do this, the service provider must have accurate information about which products provide the majority of contribution to revenue.

THE CASE OF EARTHMOVERS LTD.

The earthmoving equipment industry is extremely competitive. There are relatively few major competitors who each have worldwide sales coverage. The problem for service and support in this industry is that the equipment doesn't stay in the same place, being moved to wherever the latest construction project is taking place. Much of the equipment is sold to plant hire companies whose customers have a relatively low commitment to looking after it. On the other hand, the cost to the user of equipment failure may be catastrophic.

The task for Earthmovers Ltd. is to ensure that its equipment is capable of the job demanded of it, that it is as reliable as is possible, given the heavy work carried out, and to ensure that should the equipment break down, the customer is inconvenienced as little as possible.

To ensure global coverage and to capitalize on construction industry contacts, Earthmovers Ltd. chose to develop and support a network of dealers, some of whom would be owned by the company and others owned independently. Many of these independent dealers were plant hire companies and were already customers of Earthmovers Ltd.

Because this was a major strand of the company's marketing policy as well as a means to deliver service and support, the needs of the dealership network were regularly communicated throughout the company; designers in particular were aware of the implications of engineering change for the intermediary. To justify having higher product prices than its major competitors, Earthmovers Ltd. emphasized the strength of its service backup to its customers. To ensure that this move was not seen as mere publicity, Earthmovers set about training its dealers in the belief that this investment would result in improved dealer performance.

Technical training of mechanics was only one component of the program. Earthmovers felt that it was equally important for the dealer to understand the needs of the customer and to be given general business awareness briefings. Earthmovers enabled their dealers to analyze local market conditions more effectively with the result that both businesses benefited. Marketing specialists spend time in each dealership every year.

Its strong dealer network has proved to be a major barrier to the competition, whose networks are relatively dispersed and less committed to the OEM. This aspect of local strength has increased sales turnover.

Apart from the training program that dealers feel has contributed greatly to their own effectiveness in general management, sales, and service, Earthmovers Ltd. works hard at maintaining regular contact at all levels of the dealership with briefings, dealer conferences, and engineer visits. Earthmovers' approach to managing its intermediaries is widely praised, and the general approach has been copied by OEMs in other industries.

KEY ACTIONS

1. List the main ways in which you manage your intermediaries. Are you satisfied? If not what actions can you take?
2. Write down the training programs you organize for intermediaries. Are they effective? How could they be improved?
3. List the ways in which you recruit and dismiss intermediaries. Could you improve?

Chapter Thirteen

Recovery Strategies: The Key to Customer Retention

Introduction

In this chapter we look at service recovery, and the reasons it is important for service and support organizations. We give some approaches for developing strategies for dealing with service recovery, including recovery procedures, empowerment, and performance assessment related to recovery.

WHY SHOULD WE BOTHER ABOUT SERVICE RECOVERY?

Let us look at the experiences of two customer service and support organizations who supply domestic appliances, including washing machines and dishwashers. On different occasions we have had the following experiences with the two companies' service centers. The washing machine had a breakdown, and we called the service center for an engineer. The engineer came at the arranged time and appeared to have repaired the fault. Unfortunately, when the machine was next used there were still problems. On calling the service center, we were told the engineer would call again next day. Our experience with the dishwasher manufacturer was somewhat different. Again, we needed to call the service engineer to fix a fault. This was done but some problems still remained. Calling the service center we were given an apology and reassured by the receptionist that the engineer would return later the same day. The engineer returned with further apologies for the inconvenience the failure had caused.

It is clear that the second service experience was far better than the first. The dishwasher service organization was willing to accept failure and to do something to recover from it. It is inevitable that to do so would involve extra cost of overtime or rescheduling of resources. Is it worth the cost? We would say from the market research that has been carried out for service companies in a number of sectors that it is. Why? Because it has been shown that good recovery from mistakes builds customer loyalty and increased profitability. Let us look at the evidence for this.

Customer Satisfaction

Technical Assistance Research Program Inc. (TARP) is a market research company that has worked with many of the leading service companies on customer satisfaction and customer loyalty. The focus of their work has been to examine how customer satisfaction is influenced by a company's approach to customer complaints and their performance in recovering from their mistakes. TARP also relates performance to loss of revenue.

TARP takes four service scenarios and examines the willingness on the part of the customer to use the service provider again. The four are:

1. The service is delivered to meet the customers' expectations and there is full satisfaction.

2. There are faults in the service delivery, but the customer does not complain about them.

3. There are faults in the service delivery and the customer complains but feels he/she has been duped or mollified. There is still no real satisfaction with the service provider.

4. There are faults in the service delivery and the customer complains and feels fully satisfied with the resulting actions taken by the service providers.

The reactions of customers to the four experiences are very different and greatly influences whether a customer will continue to purchase from the service providers. Figure 13–1 shows some typical results from marketing research data of customers' intentions to continue to be customers of the service organization. Clearly, they show that dissatisfied customers who complain but are not happy with what happens feel worse about the service providers than if they had not bothered to complain at all. The result for the customer is to reinforce the impression of the service company being inadequate. On the other hand, good recovery from mistakes results in customers' loyalty being maintained at the level that would have been achieved from a first-time perfect delivery of the service. Obviously, the precise values for intention to repurchase will vary according to the costs involved for the customers, but the trends for the different scenarios are always the same. Also TARP is able to relate the drop in customer satisfaction to losses in revenue and profits.

The other finding that has a bearing on low customer satisfaction is word-of-mouth publicity about the service experience. It has been found from marketing research that a customer who is satisfied with a service experience will typically tell 5 others, whereas when they have not been satisfied they will tell 10 people. When they have experienced good recovery they will tell three. Word-of-mouth advertising is important because, if it is positive, it can lead to referral of business.

Profitability

Studies by the consultants Bain & Company have looked at the relationship between service, customer satisfaction, and profitability. Their results show that the key to profitability is to be found in customer retention. *Customer retention* is defined as the number of customers present at both the beginning and the end of a period divided by the numbers of those present at the beginning. For instance, if we have 200 customers at the beginning of the year and 250 at the end of the year but only 100 of these were customers at the beginning, then our customer retention rate is 50 percent.

The effect of high customer retention is to increase profitability. Why should this be so? Bain claims the following reasons from its work:

1. The cost of getting new customers is high. Retaining customers spreads these costs over time. So the longer customers stay with us, the higher the profits, because there are not the costs associated with bringing in new customers.

FIGURE 13–1
Customers' Intentions from Service Experience

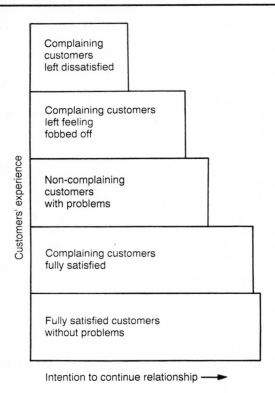

2. Customers who stay are more willing to spend more. They will buy additional services and they may be more willing to pay a premium price for the service.

3. Regular customers cost less to serve, particularly in administration costs.

The results of increased profitability from a 5 percent increase in customer retention range from 25 percent to 125 percent for a range of different types of service. These increases result from reductions in operating costs, extra profit from price premiums, profits from additional purchases, and profit from referrals because customers tell others of the good service we are providing.

What Do These Results Tell Us?

The powerful messages coming from these studies are:

1. Doing everything we can to retain customers will increase profitability.

2. Getting a service delivery system that never fails to achieve customer satisfaction may be the ideal but may lead us to ignore the consequences of some inevitable failures. TQM programs may concentrate on getting it right first time and miss the consequences of failure.

3. Getting customers to report shortfalls in service gives an opportunity to redress our mistakes and maintain loyalty.

4. Recovery must be genuine and not lip service alone. Apologies may help, but real action is what counts in the end.

WHAT'S INVOLVED IN DEVELOPING RECOVERY STRATEGIES?

Customer service and support organizations who are not good at delivering customer service will not be in a position to implement recovery strategies. Typically, their customers will not complain but go elsewhere for their service. When complaints are made they are hidden and suppressed by the service managers lest it will affect their performance ratings. Good recovery is only possible once there is a service and support system in place, which is in itself inherently capable of delivering good service quality and high customer satisfaction.

Avis, who has their mission statement in the three words "We try harder" see the achievement of customer satisfaction as being made up of the two components of "Doing the job right first time" and "Effective complaint management." Therefore, the starting point for recovery is in getting the system right to start with. We have talked about quality programs and the techniques to identify failure points in service delivery and ways to rectify them earlier. We have to be careful that this approach is not so inflexible as to prevent us dealing with the unexpected and being able to act quickly.

Developing recovery strategies will involve us in a number of actions:

1. Getting better at the basics of service and support delivery.

2. Recognizing when things are most likely to go wrong and developing coping strategies.

3. Getting the full potential from the network through escalation procedures.

4. Measuring what is happening with customer complaints and our ability to satisfy them.

5. Giving our service providers the means and power to act quickly to redress faults.

6. Recognizing what customers value when things go wrong.

Getting Better at the Basics?

The first stage on the road to recovery is to make sure the basics of our customer service and support are working. This task involves checking the whole of the service delivery. Is it capable of doing the task the service managers are asked to do? We can gain some idea if we are moving in the right direction by looking for answers to the following questions:

1. Do we have a clear idea of the service and support we are trying to deliver?

2. Do we know who our customers are and what they value from our service and support?

3. Do we understand the patterns of demand and what they mean for managing our resources?

4. Do we know what unit costs have to be, so we can meet profitability targets?

5. Do we understand the main constraints that might affect our service delivery?

6. Do we know how well we are performing against our competitors?

7. Do we have clear targets for performance for service quality and resource productivity?

8. Do we understand our delivery system in detail, and are we aware of factors that limit the flexibility of our capacity?

9. Do we know the potential failure points in our service delivery system?

10. Do we consider that our resources are up to the challenge of meeting our performance targets?

11. Do we have a measurement system capable of giving information that enables us to meet our targets for service quality, customer satisfaction, and resource productivity?

If we can answer positively to all of these, we are probably in a position to make real gains from concentrating on recovery strategies.

What Are Coping Strategies?

We have discussed capacity management and the effect on service quality and resource productivity from not getting a balance between effective capacity from the resources we have immediately available to us and the service intensity. The two capacity strategies of chase and level may enable us to manipulate both our level of resource and the demand creating service intensity. However, there will be times when these capacity strategies fail us. It is inevitable for most service and support operations that at times they will run out of capacity, if only in the short term; however, to prevent any shortages of capacity would be costly. We would have resources underused for much of the time to be able to cover the peak loads. So we are often in the position of running out of resource capacity when our chase strategy effectively becomes level, and we are powerless to influence demand to bring it back to within our capacity limit.

The consequence is poor customer service through either the service being rushed or customers having to wait longer than they would expect to. Many service and support operations accept these times as a feature of the way in which they do business. They take the view that it is hard luck on the customers, who should realize the problems and accept them. We take a different view and suggest a solution: what is required is a coping strategy to deal with these busy times.

We see the following as the stages in developing coping strategies for customer service and support:

1. Understand what suffers for customers when things get busy. Does it mean customers cannot make contact? Do they have to wait longer than contracted times for service or support? Do they incur costs from our failure in increased machine downtime or administrative costs? Do we find that our frontline people become less attentive to the needs of customers? Do we find that customers complain more about failures associated with our busy times? An understanding of what suffers will enable us to concentrate on the most important features of service and support delivery when we are coping.

2. Recognize when the limiting stage for capacity is being reached. Often this can be seen in response centers through the number of calls waiting or being lost from the telephone call management system. In a physical environment, customers may be waiting in line in a service center. Also, we realize customers are not being visited within the target times by service staff.

3. Decide on policies for limiting service provision. These may include a prioritizing system for responding to requests. Level of service contract is commonly used for this purpose. Different service contracts may promise alternative response times with the premium contract having the shortest times. These might be given the highest priority in the busy times. Alternatively, the highest priority goes to the most important customers who need to be retained at all cost.

4. Develop information systems. These give frontline people the opportunity to give customers an explanation of what is happening and what will happen. British Airways has improved the way in which it keeps passengers informed of reasons for unexpected waiting; for example, extra security checks or air traffic congestion, and the length of time passengers can expect to be delayed.

5. Encourage customers to tell us when service is poor. This service could be as a result of high demand. We should look to compensate them for the failure as quickly as possible.

The message from these stages is that the more we recognize that there will be times when we are under pressure and have developed ways of dealing with it the greater the chance to keep customers. Moreover, we are taking the positive step of trying to keep customers.

Using Resources to Best Effect: Escalation

Allied to coping strategies is the issue of how we can best use all our resources when things go wrong. We have been talking about the effects of not having resources to meet demand that causes problems with customer satisfaction; however, there is another area that holds dangers, which is when one part of the delivery system runs out of resources through not having sufficient skills or knowledge to do the job.

The way to deal with this situation is to develop a clear escalation approach that is triggered either by individuals or through a service event tracking system. The use of escalation procedures is common in the computer services industry, where inability to meet target times and close down one service or support job results in it being brought to the notice of the next level of management. If there is still no resolution within a set time, the information is escalated to the next level of management and so on up to the CEO level. Needless to say, in those customer service and support organizations that operate this type of escalation very few events reach the CEO! The pressure is on the service managers at the intervening levels to redeploy resources and to call on the skills and knowledge from the whole network.

Rather than the service management and staff activating an escalation procedure, we might encourage customers to contact us as things go wrong. The use of special telephone hotlines gives an immediate signal to the service managers that something is wrong. Resources may be held in reserve to deal with these circumstances or other resources used as in the normal escalation process.

The use of escalation procedures is a way of flexing the capacity of the total service and support network in a way that makes sure that it is focused on potential failure or responds to imminent customer complaint.

Measurement of Customer Satisfaction

Unless we are consistently measuring levels of customer satisfaction and their attitudes to service recovery, we will not know what the cost is to us and whether we are doing the right things to recover from service failures. There are some ways this can be done:

1. Gather information from the frontline people at the time of service either in a structured or unstructured way. The onus is on the service managers to encourage their staff to report failures. This method gives the best opportunity of responding quickly to failure and achieving customer satisfaction.

2. Encourage customers to call when things go wrong through publicity, cards left with the users, and the provision of a free call to a hotline.

3. Leave questionnaires with the customers at the time of a service visit. The response rate from this technique may be low, and it will fail to identify the really disgruntled customer whose only intention is to find another company to do future work.

4. Mail questionnaires with some inducement to complete them, such as all responses will be put into a drawing for a prize. This measure will increase the response rate and also send the message that the service company is keen to get feedback on customer satisfaction.

5. Call customers who have had contact with the service and support organization in the recent past. This plan also gives the opportunity to pick up customers who might not have replied to a mailed questionnaire and yet are dissatisfied.

6. Have managers call randomly selected customers. While the sample size may be low the impact on the service managers can be dramatic. It also gives customers a sense that the service and support management cares about what is happening to them. Organizations may carry out this work in-house or employ a specialized organization like TARP to carry out the work.

The results from customer satisfaction surveys can be used most powerfully when they are translated into a cost of lost sales, so the impact on revenue and profits is clear to the service management team. The process may be refined to gather results in a way that allows the measurement of the performance of individual service branches. This can be used in the appraisal of service managers and incorporated into their reward package. Managers quickly realize that performance in recovering from service failures has a great influence on the satisfaction rating they receive from their customers.

Empowering the Service Providers

Much is talked about the empowerment of frontline service providers to recognize service failure, to take ownership of the problem, and to resolve it. This can only work if the service providers:

- Know what they can do.

- Know where they can call on help from other parts of the organization.
- Are supported in their actions by frontline managers.

Knowing what to do.   If our staff is to know what to do in cases of service failure, they need to be trained. Sometimes service failure will be associated with events that occur from time-to-time for which a distinct recovery procedure can be developed. For instance, a lack of spares could result in a courier service being used to deliver spares to a site. Special transport could be arranged to deliver equipment that had been repaired but was over the due time.

Where service failure is not clearly identifiable, another form of training is needed. This is to enable the service providers to recognize the reaction of customers and then be able to establish the causes of dissatisfaction at the point of contact. This means development of interactive skills for technical people.

Knowing who can help.   Empowerment of service staff means they need to have a sense of what resources could be called on from their part of the organization to help them out. This entails the service and support staff having a wide view of the service and support organization and of the capabilities available, rather than a narrow specialist view.

Escalation procedures are one way of mobilizing assistance as things get out of hand. The frontline people are guided in their actions through the service and support structure. However, there are often cases of failure that do not warrant the use of escalation but that can be dealt with by the service team. Knowledge of the potential of the team becomes an important aspect of recovery. A team that is motivated to take responsibility for satisfying customers by anticipating and recovering from service failures will be more successful.

Managerial support.   Unless there is support from the service managers for initiative by staff to recover from service failures, staff will not take on the responsibility. The role of the frontline manager is to build the service team to work to the quick resolution of problems as they occur. This process encourages customers to say when things are going wrong.

Reassuring the customers. There is one final reason why we should pay attention to recovery strategies. We have already talked about the importance to profitability of retention of customers over a length of time. In the area of customer service and support one of the prime features we are selling is "peace of mind." It is worth asking ourselves what we mean by this. Is it simply an aphorism or does it also have a real economic content?

Christian Gronroos has proposed a framework for looking at the costs of service from the viewpoint of the service provider and the customers. So for our customer service and support organization the costs are:

- Associated with the normal service delivery.
- Associated with maintaining the relationship with the customer. These include selling and other administration costs.
- Associated with putting right things that go wrong.
- Associated with the psychological wear and tear on staff from dealing with customers. These will include the costs of burnout.

For the customers, the costs of the relationship with us as the customer service and support organization are:

- Costs that result from the price we charge.
- Costs associated with the administration of the normal relationship.
- Costs associated with getting mistakes put right.
- Psychological costs associated with the wear and tear on the customers from dealing with our organization.

The normal production and administrative costs are widely recognized in most organizations, even if they are not measured and reported. However, the cost of mistakes and the psychological costs are usually not acknowledged or measured. Those organizations who have instituted TQM programs may be making measurements of the costs of poor quality, and so have some indication of the cost of mistakes. However, these measurements are, for the most part, the customer service and support organization's costs and not the customers' costs. Overall, there is little account taken of psychological costs on both sides and of the customers' costs associated with correcting mistakes.

The area of recovery is the one that has the greatest impact on the psychological costs and the customers' costs of dealing with mistakes. Quality programs will help to reduce the number of error events. Recovery strategies will help to reduce the customers' costs of dealing with our mistakes and the psychological costs.

So if we have recovery strategies, we have reduced the overall costs to customers, especially psychological costs, so the customers feel reassured and have peace of mind.

KEY ACTIONS

1. Write down the ways in which you manage recovery. Are you satisfied? Are your customers satisfied?
2. List the costs of recovery. Are they available to all managers?
3. Write down your escalation procedures for major failure. Could they be improved? Are all frontline staff aware of them?

Chapter Fourteen

Internationalization: Managing the Network

Introduction

In this chapter we look at some of the aspects of customer service and support, including the issues for marketing and operations brought about by changes in the international regulations. We examine the networks and their integration, and the management of the international supply chain.

WHAT IS CHANGING IN THE INTERNATIONAL SCENE?

On the international scene there is the general increase in international trade by countries. This has brought with it opportunities for companies who manufacture products to sell into wider markets, but it also increases competition from foreign manufacturers within home markets. Both of these factors have implications for customer service and support in the after sales area. We have seen this global spread from companies in sectors dealing with, for example, computers, automobiles, machine tools, and also those dealing in domestic goods. Companies like IBM, Hewlett-Packard, Toyota, and Caterpillar have established global networks for the sale of products and also for customer service and support. This situation will continue to intensify so long as world trading agreements like the General Agreement on Tariffs and Trade (GATT) continue to exist.

The work by the consultants Pittiglio, Rabin, Todd, and McGrath (PRTM) has identified some implications for service and support organizations.

Physical Barriers

The international movement of goods is likely to become easier as trade agreements are formulated. There are implications here for the logistics systems. Companies may now be able to centralize stock holding by region rather than at the national level. We are seeing the implementation of systems to control the separate dispatch of spares and engineers to take advantage of these savings.

Technical Barriers

There is a slow movement to the creation of global standards, though this is very slow at present in the area of telecommunications and other high-tech industries. Harmonization will bring many opportunities to end excess inventory, complex documentation, and the need to design different training methods.

Monetary Barriers

In Europe movement toward a common currency or linked currencies has received a setback in the collapse of the ERM. Opportunities are, perhaps, limited in this area.

The Impact of Global Organizations

Multinational companies are pressuring their national suppliers. Many will be searching for suppliers who can support them on a regional basis, if not globally. The trend toward fewer long-term supply contracts may force service and support suppliers to form strategic alliances to meet these requirements.

Awareness of Service Excellence

Customers are now exposed to the best of service from across the globe. It is no longer sufficient to be the best in your backyard. Customers benchmark across countries and across service sectors to make their comparisons, and are becoming more adept at making their opinions known.

WHAT WILL THE CHANGES MEAN FOR CUSTOMER SERVICE AND SUPPORT?

The changes we have outlined will have implications for customer service and support in the structure of the network for service and support delivery, for the logistics supply chain system, and for the planning and control of consistency across the network. Issues that will have to be addressed at the strategic level and in the functional areas of marketing and operations are:

1. *Strategic issues.* The strategic issues will mean a reassessment of the basic questions:
    a. What is now the business?
    b. What do the changes in the political, economic, social, and technical environment now mean for us?
    c. Who are now our main competitors and are there changes in the power of suppliers and customers? Do the changed circumstances mean there are greater threats of new entrants or substitutes for what we are selling?
    d. What do we see as the basis of our competition in the new markets?
    e. What do we see as being our main strengths and weaknesses to prosper in the new environment? Do we see new opportunities for business or threats to our existing activities?

Failure to address these issues and assume that the influences on our business will be exactly the same as in the past will undoubtedly mean that firms will miss opportunities and be unprepared for the threats to their business.

2. *Marketing issues.* Some of the main issues for marketing are:
    a. Can we segment the markets in different ways for either the sale of products or selling and delivering customer service and support?
    b. Where can we take advantage from standardization of products that will reduce the variety of the service and support tasks?
    c. How can we best build partnerships with major customers for the supply of products and customer service and support?

    d. What channels should we use for the sale of products and customer service and support?
    e. Can we harmonize contacts?

The role of marketing is to understand the new market structures and the needs of the customers so that competitive advantage can be gained by getting closer to major customers and segmenting the new market in ways that allow a focus on resources to the best effect.

  3. *Service and support operational issues.* Some of the main service and support operational issues are:
    a. What is the best network structure to deliver customer service and support?
    b. How much can we integrate the network?
    c. What is the best way to manage the logistics supply chain for spares?
    d. What information systems do we need to support the network?
    e. What are the implications for the recruitment, training, and deployment of service and support staff?
    f. How can we get the most capacity flexibility from the network?
    g. Does a new network structure offer resource productivity gains leading to lower unit costs?
    h. How should quality consistency across the network be measured?
    i. How can we reduce risks of not achieving the goals of the new service operations task?

The role of the service and support operations managers is to create the new networks and to plan and control the service delivery to consistent standards of performance. The pressure for change will be greater on some providers of customer service and support than on others. However, it is fair to say that any organization that does not review its activities in light of the changes may be in danger. To take no action an organization would have to be sure that its competitive position was protected by some long-term competitive distinctiveness, or that it only wanted to operate in a niche market.

WHAT ARE THE OPTIONS FOR SERVICE AND SUPPORT NETWORKS?

The new international environment means that the network for the delivery of customer service and support has to be reviewed. The options are going to be driven first at the strategic level, because they mean a reassessment of how much we want to maintain in-house control over the whole operation in the face of growing service intensity. The structures for customer service and support that we discussed earlier still apply, although with more complexity.

When a decision is made to provide customer service and support through intermediaries as agents or dealers, we will have to consider how they can be supported and controlled. The issues will center on:

- The number and location of dealers.
- The relationship of dealers, whether they are independent businesses or franchises. How much they offer customer service and support on our products and our competitors' products.
- Training the dealers. There will be issues relating to the present skills of the dealers, their systems, and ways of delivering customer service and support.
- Dealer training of customers means addressing the ways in which dealers are themselves trained, the expectations of the customers in the region for training as part of the customer service and support activity.
- Supply of spares. We may wish dealers to hold their own stocks of spares or to manage the whole process ourselves.
- Backup support for dealers with information and specialists. This support will have a bearing on the location of backup specialists and the information and communications systems that are used.
- Tie in dealers with our information systems. We may choose to integrate dealers into our own information network or to leave them essentially independent.

Decisions in this area will depend on the service and support and how much penetration into new regions. If the decision is made to maintain a high level of in-house control over the new network by using mainly SAS and Regulars, consideration has to be given to:

- The distribution of service intensity across the new geographic area to be covered.
- The location of service and support centers.
- The location of SAS specialists and Regulars.
- Composition of the service and support teams and their skills and knowledge requirements.
- The degree of integration of the service and support centers.

Service Intensity

Probably in the early days of expansion into new markets, the service intensity will vary considerably. This may frustrate the ability to use an SAS/Regular structure because the service intensity in some areas is too low to warrant the setting up of service centers. If field service staff could be deployed from more remote locations within the response time demanded, then areas of low service intensity could be served from service centers in adjacent territories. If this is not possible, then in the early stages of expansion the companies would have to resort to the use of agents. The issues that arise when intermediaries are used then apply.

Location of Service and Support Resources

Where to position the mix of SAS specialists and Regulars is important in the efficient use of resources. Under a structure that treated each country as a separate and independent unit there would be a mix of each in each country. If the whole of the new territory is seen as a single network, there are options for redistribution of the resources. Specialists no longer need to be positioned in each country. One model is to set up a number of centers of specialist support to cover the full product range with one center being responsible for each product group. Regulars no longer need to be positioned by country but according to the level of service intensity. Both of these changes lead to improvements in the level of service and customer satisfaction as well as resource efficiencies. Computer companies like Hewlett-Packard have started to organize their selling and customer service and support on product group lines rather than across products to build up distinct differentiating competences in each of the sectors serviced by the product groups.

It is the same for support activities and response centers. These no longer need to be positioned in each country but could be aggregated into a single center or a reduced number of centers. The difficulties of language are very real, and at least one computer company we know abandoned a single European response center in favor of a small number of response centers, each to serve a limited number of countries.

Composition of Service and Support Teams

The possibilities of new locations and flexibility of the SAS/Regulars mix presents us with other possibilities for reviewing the composition of service teams. With a country structure the service teams may be organized so that all teams give service and support to all products. Alternatively, there may already be specialization into teams giving service and support to specific product or customer groups. Multi-product teams need multiskilling but give more resource flexibility, while specializing in one product group gives increased learning and efficiencies from doing the job better. It is for each organization to consider where the best trade-off for them lies. By extending the product group service and support model to the international scene, companies could hope for increases in effectiveness from product service and support teams for the wider geographical area.

The Level of Integration of the Network

A fully integrated network is only feasible if there is the possibility of central control through fully compatible information systems and the supply chain. The stages to full integration are likely to be:

1. We have essentially separate operations, if not for countries then for small regions.

2. We coordinate activities by trying to have common standards and integrating the supply of spares.

3. We integrate information systems.

4. We consolidate centers of excellence and smaller numbers of response centers.

5. We move staff freely across the network.

6. All activities are controlled from one center.

The move toward full integration will be tempered by consideration of customer needs in different geographic areas. While sometimes these national needs may be stronger than differences in types of customers, the tendency across Europe is likely to be toward a greater homogeneity of social preferences and segmentation by type of customer rather than by nationality. If so, the pressure for integration to get the best from service teams dedicated to one product group or type of customer and serving the whole region becomes stronger.

HOW CAN WE MANAGE THE SUPPLY CHAIN?

It is in the area of managing the logistics supply chain that many customer service and support operations have done most. The influence of JIT thinking has made a great difference to the management of materials. The trends have been toward greater centralization of the stocking of spares and a greater control of the levels of stocks held at points along the supply chain. The reduction or elimination of stocks at the service center level and a greater control over van spares have given benefits in service levels and costs associated with holding stocks. The implementation of the changes has been made possible by a combination of improvements in information systems, EDI, and transport.

Any customer service and support operation can learn much from the leaders in the field like Rank Xerox, Caterpillar, and ICL. They have set up specialist logistics operations to control the supply of spares to the service activity.

We can take the Rank Xerox experience as an example of supplying a customer service and support operation for Europe.

Before 1980, each operating company in each country used to place orders for spares directly on the manufacturing units. The level of inventories was at least 15 months' supply, and service levels for spares were not good. Over the last 10 years they improved their systems and location of stocks to supply Field Business Units (FBUs) of approximately the same service intensity. The result has been nine FBUs in the United Kingdom, four in Italy, and three in Spain. The move has been toward centralization of control with a single point for setting service levels, stock levels, and van kits. This system gives control over stocks at both a country level and for the FBUs. While the system is not a fully integrated system, it has gone a long way to deliver the benefits of high service levels and lower stocks.

Caterpillar, the manufacturers of earthmoving equipment, is a good example of a company who delivers its customer service and support through intermediaries, the Mercenary structure in our Military Model. It does not own any stocks within the dealer network, but has concentrated its logistics efforts on improving the service levels to dealers from centralized sites throughout the world, thereby allowing dealers to reduce their own stock levels. Service levels have been improved. Delivery times have come down from 17–19 days to 3–5 days and with 90 percent of all items ordered being at the dealers in 3 days. Current performance is better, with many items arriving at the dealers within a 48hours. This has been achieved by an increase in the order frequency from the dealers (from weekly to daily orders), improved systems and order processing, and worldwide visibility of stocks. The whole logistics service is designed to give coverage.

A third example of supplying parts over a wider geographical area is the "spares banks" operated by the express transport companies like Federal Express and DHL. These companies will hold stocks of spares for companies and distribute them as they are needed by customer service centers. The operation is geared toward the supply of high-value spares, where the cost of rapid transport like aircraft can be offset against the savings in inventory levels.

Getting the level of improvement in the management of the logistics supply chain needs systems, good working relationship with suppliers, and fast order taking and processing.

WHAT UPGRADES IN INFORMATION SYSTEMS ARE NEEDED?

Clearly, any degree of integration of customer service and support across a network relies on the information and communication systems. These apply in the areas including:

- Call handling from customers.
- Customer records.
- Remote monitoring of equipment.
- Supply of spares and integration of the supply chain from suppliers of materials.
- Escalation procedures using the full resources of the network.
- Measurement of performance.
- Transfer of advice.

A great problem faced by organizations in integrating systems is the incompatibility of software within existing systems at national locations. Unless this is overcome, integration is impossible. Communications networks are especially important in the support activity. The use of databases that give information on products and their performance in operation and customer history allows support activities to be delivered from anywhere in the network so long as there is no language barrier. This helps the centralization of specialists associated with product groups, which reduces costs, and improves the turn-around time of support problems because of the concentration of resources. It also has implications as we see later for balancing the capacity across the network.

WHAT IS THE AFFECT ON HUMAN RESOURCE POLICIES?

How much human resource policies are altered by a move to an international scale operation will depend largely on the network for customer service and support. There are two issues: whether we are using intermediaries or our own operation as the main providers of customer service and support, and whether we still have an essentially discrete provision of customer service and support in individual countries or integration of the service centers into a coherent network.

When customer service and support is delivered by way of intermediaries, the main issue is concerned with training and supporting the dealers. There is unlikely to be an involvement in the recruitment of staff, although job specifications may be suggested, especially for technical staff.

When we are delivering customer service and support ourselves, the position is different. If we have discrete operations for service and support delivery in the different countries and regions, the influence from the center may be limited, and personnel policies are more likely to be set by the separate units. The greater the integration of the network, the more the policies will address issues that affect the network as a whole. For instance, the question of mobility of staff across the network and the training of staff on a network rather than a regional basis starts to assume more importance. Such practices have implications for the spread of learning across the network and of the development of a culture for the whole business.

Our view of the present position is that the degree of international integration of networks is limited for the movement of people. Language problems often limit the possibilities, and cultural considerations affecting the delivery of service and support can also make organizations reluctant to use frontline people who do not conform to the culture of suppliers. We can see now the movement of personnel throughout the network is limited to managers and specialists mainly.

CAN AN INTERNATIONAL NETWORK HELP WITH CAPACITY MANAGEMENT?

Having a wide network does, in concept, allow us to think of getting greater flexibility from the total resources. Let us take the common case of a customer service and support operation that has a number of response centers located in different countries. If we have the communication systems, we are able to flow calls from one center to another to balance the load. We gain from this flow in the quality of our initial response, which becomes more reliable if not faster.

Clearly, we can also get productivity gains from the use of a network especially in the support activity where we do not need to visit the customer. If we need to maintain a 24-hour response on a global level, we can use response centers located in Europe, the USA, and the Far East, each operating a 12-hour day and transferring calls to one of the other centers out of hours. This ends the need to keep staff in each center for 24 hours a day.

We may gain further benefits from concentrating specialists in one center either globally or regionally, who are then available to the whole network. The international network is less likely to increase the capacity flexibility of the service activities. There may be some opportunity for transferring engineers temporarily to give additional resources. Whether we can transfer will depend on the costs compared to the value and whether the timing is right. Also, it is more likely to occur for the service of capital equipment rather than low cost equipment.

CAN WE MAINTAIN QUALITY?

Consistency of quality of delivery of customer service and support across an international network is, of course, important. When we have discrete operations in each region operated either by intermediaries or with our own resources, the quality of service may be geared more to expectation of the customers in that area rather than to wider standards, in which case we can perhaps leave the setting of standards to each regional area.

However, if our customer service and support is being judged by the consistency of delivery to common standards across the network, this fragmented approach to quality management will not be good enough. If we are providing service and support to another international company that does have an integrated network, there is the expectation that our service and support will meet the same standards wherever it is delivered. Providers of customer service and support as in other services have found that this requirement from their major customers has acted as a spur to their closer integration to improve consistency of service and support delivery.

What advice can we offer to service and support operations who find themselves in this position? Clearly there is a role for quality standards that can drive through common procedures for all areas of delivery and that take account of any local regulations. However, as with all quality programs, it is only part of the story, and we need to have in place other quality initiatives that drive quality improvement and motivate the frontline people. The use of competitions on an international scale can work sometimes to encourage a wider view of the network from staff at all levels within the organization.

HOW CAN WE DECREASE THE RISKS FROM EXPANSION?

Expansion of any business carries risks. Increase in capacity involves a cost that must be paid for with increased business. If we set up new service and support centers before there is the service intensity to pay for this capacity the operation will suffer a financial loss. We can reduce this expense by using intermediaries rather than by setting up our own operations.

Alternatively, we might take the view that we are willing to set up our own operation to learn, and we might discount some losses against the experience we gain by delivering customer service and support in a new region. In the long run the extra experience may give us a competitive advantage.

So there is a trade-off between a cautious expansion through the use of intermediaries, which carries with it a limited amount of learning about the new markets, and the higher risk commitment of resources into the new area, which leads to rapid learning. Which route is taken will depend on an assessment of the potential of the market we are entering. We would need to assess whether the service intensity will rise quickly to make it worth committing resources.

KEY ACTIONS

1. Write down the pressures on you that force internationalization.
2. List any physical, technical, or monetary barrier that is coming down. Do any of these pose a threat or offer an opportunity?
3. Draw out the structure you think is best for expansion. Are there risks and how could the risks be minimized?

Bibliography

Chapter 1

Albrecht, K.; and R. Zemke. *Service America, Doing Business in the New Economy*. Homewood IL: Business One Irwin, 1985.

Bowman, C. "Perceptions of Competitive Strategy, Realized Strategy, Consensus, and Performance." Ph.D. thesis, Cranfield Institute of Technology, Cranfield, Bedford, England, 1991.

Carlzon, J. *Moments of Truth*. Cambridge, MA: Ballinger, 1987.

Drucker, P. *The Practice of Management*. London: Heinemann, 1985.

Heskett, J. L.; W. E. Sasser; and C. W. L. Hart. *Service Breakthroughs: Changing the Rules of the Game*. New York; Free Press, 1990.

Johnson, G.; and K. Scholes. *Exploring Corporate Strategy*. Englewood Cliffs, NJ: Prentice Hall, 1988.

Lele, M. M.; and J. N. Sheth. *The Customer Is Key*. New York: John Wiley, 1987.

Levitt, T. "After the Sale Is Over." *Harvard Business Review*, September–October 1983.

Mathur, S. S. "How Firms Compete: A New Classification of Generic Strategies." *Journal of General Management* 14, no. 1, 1988.

Normann, R. *Service Management*. New York: John Wiley, 1984.

Peters, T. J.; and N. Austin. *A Passion for Excellence*. New York: Random House, 1985.

Peters, T.; and T. Waterman. *In Search of Excellence*. New York: Harper and Row, 1982.

Porter, M. E. *Competitive Advantage*. New York: Free Press, 1985.

Porter, M. E. *Competitive Strategy: Techniques for Analyzing Industries and Competition*. New York: Free Press, 1990.

Waterman H. R.; T. J. Peters; and J. R. Phillips. "Structure Is Not Organization." *Business Horizons*, June 1980.

Chapter 4

Christopher, M.; A. Payne; and D. Ballantyne. *Relationship Marketing*. London: Heinemann, 1991.

Kotler, P. *Marketing Management*. 6th ed. Englewood Cliffs, NJ: Prentice Hall, 1967.

Lovelock, C. H. *Services Marketing*. 2d ed. Englewood Cliffs, NJ: Prentice Hall, 1991.

McDonald, M. H. B.; and P. Morris. *The Marketing Plan—A Pictorial Guide for Managers*. London: Heinemann, 1989.

Chapter 5

Carlzon, J. *Moments of Truth*. Cambridge, MA: Ballinger, 1987.

Clark, G. R.: C. G. Armistead. "Improving Service Delivery." *Managing Service Quality*. Bedford, England: IFS, July 1991.

Johnston, R. "The Customer as Employee." Proceedings of the Operations Management Association Conference, United Kingdom, January 1989.

Naisbitt, J. *Megatrends*. London: MacDonald, 1984.

Normann, R. *Service Management*. New York: John Wiley, 1984.

Porter, M. E. *Competitive Advantage*. New York: Free Press, 1985.

Shostack, L. "Designing Services that Deliver." *Harvard Business Review*, 1984.

Chapter 6

Handy, C. B. *Understanding Organizations*. 3d ed. New York: Penguin Books, 1985.

Kakabadse, A.; R. Lidlow; and S. Vinnicome. *Working in Organizations*. New York: Penguin Books, 1988.

Lele, M. M.; and J. N. Sheth. *The Customer Is King*. New York: John Wiley, 1988.

Peters, T.; and N. Austin. *A Passion for Excellence*. New York: Random House, 1985.

Chapter 7

Lovelock, C. H. *Services Marketing*. 2d ed. Englewood Cliffs, NJ: Prentice Hall, 1991.

Richardson, C. "Staffing the Front Office." *Operational Research Insight* 4, no. 2, 1991.

Sasser, W. E. "Matching Supply and Demand in Service Industries." *Harvard Business Review*, November–December, 1979,

Chapter 8

Berry, L. L.; A. Parasuraman; and V. A. Zeutham, "Quality Counts in Services, Too." *Business Horizons*, May–June 1985.

Black, S. "Creating the Competitive Advantage." *TQM*, 1, no. 1, November 1988.

Clark, G. *Managing Service Quality*. Bedford, England: IFS, 1990.

Crosby, P. *Quality Is Free*. New York: McGraw-Hill, 1979.

Deming, W. E. *Out of the Crisis*. Cambridge: MIT Center for Advanced Engineering Study, 1986.

Garvin, D. *Managing Quality: The Strategic and Competitive Edge*. New York: Free Press, 1990.

Gronroos, C. "Facing the Challenge of Service Competition: Costs of Bad Service." Proceedings of the Workshop on Quality Management in Service, SQM, Brussels, May 1991.

Oakland, J. S. *Statistical Process Control*. London: Heinemann, 1986.

Oakland, J. S. *Total Quality Management*. Heinemann, 1989.

Schonberger, R. *Building a Chain of Customers*. New York: Free Press, 1990.

Chapter 9

Innes, J.; and F. Mitchell. *Activity-Based Costing*. London: The Chartered Institute of Management Accountants, 1990.

McLaughlin, C. P.; and S. Coffey. "Measuring Service Productivity." *International Journal of Service Industries Management*, 1, no. 1, 1990.

Norman, M.; and B. Stoker. *Data Envelopment Analysis*. New York: John Wiley, 1991.

Potts, G. W. "Raising Productivity in Customer Services." *Long Range Planning* 21, no. 2, 1988.

Chapter 10

Edwards, C.; J. Ward: and A. Bytheway. *The Essence of Information Systems*. United Kingdom: Prentice Hall, 1991.

Ives, B,; and M. R. Vitale. "After the Sale: Leveraging Maintenance with Information Technology." *MIS Quarterly*, March 1988.

Porter, M. E. *Competitive Advantage*. New York: Free Press, 1984.

Chapter 11

Christopher, M. *The Strategy of Distribution Management*. Aldershot, Hampshire, England: Gower, 1987.

Saunders, J. A.; J. A. Sharp; and S. F. Witt. *Practical Business Forecasting*. Aldershot, Hampshire, England: Gower, 1987.

Vollman, T. E.; W. L. Berry; and D. C. Whybark. *Manufacturing Planning and Control Systems*. Homewood, IL: Business One Irwin, 1984.

Chapter 12

Anderson, J. C.; and J. A. Narus. "A Model of Distributor Firm and Manufacturer Firm Working Partnerships." *Journal of Marketing,* January 1990.

Cavusgil, S. T. "The Importance of Distributor Training at Caterpillar." *Industrial Marketing Management* 19, 1990, pp. 1–9.

MacGrath, A. J.; and K. G. Hardy. "Gearing Manufacturer Support Programs to Distributors." *Industrial Marketing Management* 18, 1989, pp. 239–44.

Moore, R. A. "The Conflict Gap in International Channel Relationships." *Journal of Marketing Management* 6, no. 3, 1990, pp. 225–37.

Chapter 13

Gronroos, C. "Facing the Challenge of Service Competition: Cost of Bad Service." Proceedings of a Workshop on Quality Management in Service, Ed Wiele and Timmers, Strategic Quality Management Institute, Rotterdam, 1991.

Heskett, J. L.; W. E. Sasser; and C. W. L. Hart. *Service Breakthroughs.* New York: Free Press, 1990.

Lash, M. L. *The Complete Guide to Customer Service.* New York: John Wiley, 1989.

Chapter 14

Johnson, G.; and K. Scholes. *Exploring Corporate Strategy.* Englewood Cliffs, NJ: Prentice Hall, 1988.

Livingston, I. "Design for Service." Proceedings of the First International Conference on After Sales Support, London: IFS, 1988.

Loeb, J. "Europe 1992: The Implications for Field Service." *PTRM Insight* 2, no. 4, 1990.

Index

A

Access, telephone, 152
Accuracy, of costing, 171
Activity-Based Costing (ABC), 171, 202
  and inventory investment, 199
Adaptive box, 115–16
Aesthetics, 150
After sales service and support; *see also*
  Customer service and support
Agents; *see* Dealer network
Albrecht, K., 13–15
Allocation of resources, 134–35
Allowances, 219–20
Altering
  capacity, 130–33
  demand strategy, 133–35
Analysis, managerial competence,
  110–11
Annual
  hours agreement, 130
  Requirement Value, 199
Anticipation stocks, 195, 199
Anxiety box, 115–16
Appearance, of service personnel and
  equipment, 113
Applications advice, 43
Appraisal costs, 146
Automobile warranties, 56
Avis
  car rental, 70
  views on customer satisfaction, 235

B

Back room
  concept, 82–84
  and the Right First Time standard,
    146
Bain & Company, 233
Bar codes, 185
Barriers
  to entry by competitors, 182

Barriers—*Contd.*
  to improvement of resource
    productivity, 175–78
  to international trade, 245
Benchmarking, 155
Benefits, of customer service and
  support, 5–8
Berry, L. L., 151
Bill of material (BOM), 205–6
Black and Decker
  service center layout, 93
  siting of service facilities, 88
Bottlenecks, 177
Boundary spanners, 90
Bradford University, 156
Brainstorming, 158, 160
Branch performance, 172–73
Branding, 70
Break-even analysis, 75
Breakdowns, visits for, 138
Britax, customer service, 44
British Airways, 70
  use of transaction-based surveys,
    154
British Gas, 94
British Telecom, 94
Buffer stocks, 196
Burnout, 85
  and costs of service, 242
  dangers of, 115–17
  and increasing capacity, 130

C

Call
  avoidance, 184
  back, 43
  management, 188
Capacity
  balance with demand, 129
  explanation of, 124–25
  flexibility of, 127
  measurement of, 126

Capacity—*Contd.*
  scheduling programs, 185
Capacity management
  importance of, 123–24
  and international trade, 254–55
  of the telephone network, 86
Capital goods manufacturer, example,
  39
Capital productivity, 178
Carlzon, Jan
  on customer-oriented systems, 185
  on Moments of Truth, 80
  regarding customer care, 8
Caterpillar Corporation
  dealer network, 221
  design for serviceability, 49
  mercenary structure, customer
    service, 252
  Quality Programme, 158–59
  Service Engineering department,
    191–92
  service supply chain, 211
  specialist logistics operations, 251
  targets, disassembly time, 9
Centralized service functions, 49–50
Channels, of distribution, 224–25
Chase capacity strategy, 130–33, 237
Close to the customer, 49–50
Closing batch, of production, 204–5
Coach, roles of, 119–20
Comet, emphasis on after sales service,
  9
Commercial awareness, 110
Communication, element of service
  quality, 152
Company loyalty, reinforcement of, 90
Competence, 152
Competitive factors, 17–18
Complaint box, 115–16
Complexity of product, effect on
  service intensity, 30
Computer manufacturer, example,
  39–40
Conformance, to target dimensions,
  149
Constraints, on service tasks, 19–20

Consumer products manufacturer,
  example, 38
Contact points, 82–88
Continuous improvement, 156
Coping strategy, 135–36, 162
  and customer retention, 237–38
Cost
  of customer service and support,
    74–75, 242–43
  dealer administration, 227
  of downtime, to the customer,
    12–13
  of gathering data, 176
  of inventory, 194
  plus basis, paying for service and
    support, 57
  of spares, 199
Costing, accuracy of, 171
Courtesy, 152
  cars, 52
Covedale training, 119
Cranfield School of Management, 110
Credibility, 152
Criticality, of spares, 198–99
Crosby, Philip, 141
Culture, of the organization, 157
Customer
  access to engineers, at Hewlett-
    Packard, 210
  audits, 56
  awareness training, 85
  characteristics, 67
  complaints, monitoring of, 187, 227
  and cost of downtime, 12–13
  databases, 183
  dismissal of, 92
  focus groups, 155
  focused organization, 61
  friendly information systems, 93–94
  help line, 42–43
  loyalty, influenced by customer
    satisfaction, 232–33
  management systems, 186–87
  markets, 78
  motivation of, 92
  oriented systems, 185

Customer—*Contd.*
 participation, to increase capacity,
  130–31
 process flow, 96, 98–100
 and quality, 144–45
 recruitment of, 91–92
 relationship, building the, 3
 research, 153–55
 reservations or appointments,
  133–34
 response centers, 137
 responses, 67
 retention, and profitability,
  233–34
 role, in service delivery, 91–92
 satisfaction monitoring, 197–98
 service levels, 196–99
 training of, 92
 understanding the, 152
Customer satisfaction goals, at Rank
  Xerox, 156
Customer satisfaction index, 79
 and dealer profitability, 227
 measurement of, 239–40
Customer service
 dimensions, 17–18, 152
 triangle, discussion of, 13–15
Customer service and support
 basics of, 236–37
 benefits of, 5–8
 costs of, 74–75
 and customer perception of quality,
  153
 integration with product design,
  10–13
 and international trade, 247
 as a major business activity, 12–13
 and market sectors, 69
 marketing of, 60–62
 and Material Requirements
  Planning, 205
 measuring inputs for, 167
 measuring outputs from, 166–67
 military model of, 23–30
 overview, 1–5
 paying for, 57

Customer service and support—*Contd.*
 positioning of, 69; *see also*
  Positioning; Positioning maps
 pricing of, 73–76
 process flow for, 177
 product mix, 62–65, 175
 reasons for, 53–57
 scope of, 8
 setting priorities, 57–58
 type, effect on service intensity,
  31–32
 value of, 74
Customer training, 54–55

D
Data Envelope Analysis (DEA), 172–73
Dead on arrivals (DOA), 187
Dealer network
 building a relationship with, 221–22
 and customer complaints, 227
 evaluation of, 226–27
 importance of contact people with,
  222
 and the international environment,
  248–51
 and international sales, 217
 and lack of service capacity, 219
 management of, 219–23
 minimizing network disputes,
  224–25
 motivation of, 225–26
 and performance expectations,
  223–24
 providing expertise to, 221
 reasons for, 217–19
 selection of, 225
 and spare parts inventory, 228
 training of, 226
Dealers' conference, 226–27
Decisional role, 106
Decrease service standards, to increase
  capacity, 132
Demand
 balance with capacity, 129
 dimensions of, 19
 elements of, 127–28

Demand—*Contd.*
  forecasting, 128–29
  forecasts, and inventory, 195
  patterns of, 127–29
Deming, W. Edwards, on systems and
  processes, 81
Density, of channels of distribution,
  224–25
Dependence on other products, effect
  on service intensity, 30
Design techniques, 158
Development, of the quality system,
  160–62
DHL, spares banks, 252
Dimensions
  of product quality, 148–51
  of service quality, 151–53
  of time, 42–45
Discretion, and systems driven
  organization, 115
Dismissal, of customers, 92
Disney World, 107–8
Distribution channels, 72–73
Distributor margins, 219–20
Domestic goods manufacturer,
  example, 38
Durability, 149–50

E
Earthmoving equipment industry, case
  study, 229–30
Economic Order Quantity (EOQ),
  199–200
Economies of scale, 174
EDI links, 214
Effective capacity, 126
  and transfer of resources, 131–32
Effectiveness, 169
  of teams, 118–19
Efficiency, 169–70
  targets, 19
Eight dimensions of strategic quality,
  148–51
800 telephone numbers, 42
80–20 rule, 199

Electronic Point of Sale (EPOS) system,
  94
Elements, of demand, 127–28
Employee
  markets, 78
  morale, and quality, 145–46
  surveys, 155
  value of, 103–5
Empowerment, 114–15
  of service providers, 240–43
Enemies, defined, 24, 28
Engineer data, 185
Environmental awareness, 110
Equipment, decisions regarding, 94–95
ERM, 245
Escalation approach, resource
  allocation, 238–39
Evaluation, of the dealer network,
  226–27
Exact time, of arrival, 47
Exponential smoothing, 208
Extended guarantees, 55–56

F
Face-to-face
  customer contact, 84–85
  questionnaires, 77
Facilities, impact on perceived quality,
  93
Failure costs, 146
Features, 148
Federal Express, spares banks, 252
Field Business Units (FBUs), 251–52
Financial systems, 186
First response, 42
First-time fix, 95
Flexibility, of capacity, 127
Flexible working hours, 130
Fluctuation stocks, 195–96
Focus groups, 155
Ford Motor Company, use of Statistical
  Process Control (SPC), 161
Forecasting
  constant, 208
  demand, 128–29, 208–9
Forming, 118

Forrester Effect, 211–12
Front office concept, 82–84
Frustration box, 115–16

G
Garvin, David, 148
General Agreement on Tariffs and
  Trade (GATT), 244
General surveys, 153–54
Georgia Light and Power, initial
  response policy, 43–44
Global organizations, and
  international trade, 245
Goffin, Keith, 49
Golden moment, 85
Gronroos, Christian
  and costs of service, 242–43
  and relationship costs, 144–45
Groups of customers, differences
  between, 65–66

H
Handheld terminals, 184
Hartford boiler inspection service, 56
Harvard Business School, 144, 148
Help lines, effect on service intensity,
  32
Hewlett-Packard
  customer access to engineers, 210
  product group line organization,
    249–50
  treatment of employees, 105
  use of job specifications, 188
  use of Just-in-Time approach, 210
  use of sales-service database, 185
Hi-Tech, Hi-Touch, 94
High in-house control, 35–36
High strike rates, 203
Human resource policies, and
  international trade, 253–54
Hygiene factors, 17–18

I
ICL, specialist logistics operations, 251
In-house control, 34–37
  and choice of military structure,
    35–37

Incident repair productivity, 171
Increase capacity, by decrease in
  service standards, 132
Independent customer profiles, by
  segment, 67–68
Industry rivalry, and management
  information system, 183
Influencer markets, 78
Information
  requirements, and the product life
    cycle, 180–81
  systems, and customer records, 113
Informational role, 106
Initial response, principals of, 45
Initiative, 110
Input costs, 169
Input/output measures, 169
Intermediaries; see Dealer network
Internal support, effect on service
  intensity, 33
International
  sales, and dealer network, 217
  supply chain, 244
International trade
  barriers to, 245
  and capacity management, 254–55
  and dealer networks, 248–51
  demands on the management
    information system, 253
  and human resource policies, 253–54
  marketing issues, 246
  and operational issues, 247
  and quality, 255–56
  and risks, 256
  strategic issues, 246
Interpersonal
  role, 106
  skills, 113
Interviews, 77
Inventory
  and Activity-Based Costing (ABC),
    199, 202
  categories of, 195, 198
  committing to production, 209–10
  cost of, 194
  and criticality of spares, 198–99

Inventory—*Contd.*
  and customer service levels, 196–99
  and the dealer network, 228
  and demand forecasts, 195
  and Just-in-Time (JIT) philosophy,
    210
  management, 201–10
  need for, 194–95
  overview, 193
  turns, of the total supply chain, 214
Ives, 188–89

J
Judgement, 111
Just-in-Time (JIT)
  and cost of inventory, 194
  and inventory management, 210

K
Key operator training, 92
Knowledge, skills, abilities (KSA) mix,
    113–14

L
Labor costs, and incident repair
    productivity, 171
Lead time, order replenishment, 206
Leadership, 111
Length, of channels of distribution,
    224–25
Level of capacity strategy, 133–35, 237
Levitt, Ted, on relationship between
    purchasers and vendors, 7
Lifetime costs, 6
  effect on service intensity, 30
Line of visibility, 99
Loan machine, 52
Logistics
  operations, for international trade,
    251–52
  productivity, 172
Long lead times, 206–7
Long-term income, and quality, 145
Lot-size stocks, 195, 199–200
Lovelock, Christopher, 112

Low
  in-house control, 37
  service income, and use of dealers,
    218–19

M
Mail questionnaires, 77
Making to order, 211, 213
Making to stock, 211, 213
Management
  control, 111
  of inventory, 201–10
  of the service supply chain, 211–15
  support, for service providers,
    241–42
Management information system
  as barrier to entry by competitors,
    182
  customer management systems,
    186–87
  customer-oriented systems, 185
  development of, 182–86
  financial systems, 186
  and industry rivalry, 183
  and international networks, 253
  overview, 180
  quality systems, 187
  resource management, 187
  sales-service database, at
    Hewlett-Packard, 185
  and supplier's schedules, 184
  time advantage of, 184–86
Managerial
  competences, 110–12
  roles, 106–7
Manufacturer's rights, to realistic
    controls, 222–23
Manufacturing Resource Planning,
    and scheduling, 203
Manufacturing-service interface, 202–7
Market
  intelligence systems, 185
  segmentation, 66–68
Marketing
  customer service and support, 60–62
  issues, and international trade, 246

Marketing—*Contd.*
  mix, 62–63, 71
  process, 63–65
  and quality image, 145
  research, 76–78
  at simplest level, 62
Marks and Spencer
  and financial services, 56
  treatment of employees, 105
  use of United Kingdom suppliers,
    201
Master Production Schedule (MPS),
    203–4
Master schedule, 202–3
Material efficiency, 171
Material Requirements Planning
    (MRP), use by service and support,
    205
Maximizing uptime, 50–53
Maximum value, from purchase, 6
Mean Time Between Failure (MTBF)
  in the electronics sector, 9
  and management information
    systems, 187
  measure of reliability, 50–51
  and product liability, 171
  and service contracts, 149
Mean Time To Repair (MTTR), 47–49
  and incident repair productivity, 171
Measurement, of customer
    satisfaction, 239–40
Measuring
  inputs, to customer service and
    support, 167
  outputs, from customer service and
    support, 166–67
Megatrends, 94
Mercenaries
  defined, 24, 27–28
  structure at Caterpillar Corporation,
    252
Microsoft, 86
Military model
  of customer service and support,
    23–30
  use of, 29–30

Minimizing network disputes, within
    the dealer network, 224–25
Mintzberg, Henry, 106–7
Mixed team approach, 138
Moments of truth, 8
Monetary barriers, to international
    trade, 245
Money back guarantees, 43
Monitoring, customer satisfaction,
    197–98
Motivation
  of customers, 92
  of the dealer network, 225–26
  of service teams, 177
MRP II; *see* Manufacturing Resource
    Planning
Multiple regression, 209

N
Naisbitt, John, 94
Network integration levels, and
    international trade, 250–51
Never fail computers, 45
Newness of a product, effect on service
    intensity, 30
Nissan, United Kingdom chain, 220
Normann, Richard, on Moments of
    Truth, 80
Norming, 119
Norris, Peter, 110
Number of products in the field, 34
Numerical analysis, 111

O
Oakland, John, 156
Off-site and support productivity, 171
On-line terminals, and banking, 186
One stop shopping, 183
Operational issues, and international
    trade, 247
Operations management, and trade-
    offs, 164–65
Order replenishment lead time, 206
Organization
  culture, 157
  of service delivery, 176

Otis Elevator, 189, 191
OTISLINE, 189
Output/input measures, 168
Overseas dealer, selection of, 225
Overtime burden, reduction of,
    130

P
Paper contact, 87–88
Parasuraman, A., 151
Pareto rule, 199
Part-time people, to increase capacity,
    130
Partial measures, of productivity, 167
Patterns of demand, 127–29
People and delivery process, 76
Perceived
    added value (PAV), 15–16
    quality, 150
Performance, 148
    expectations and the dealer network,
        223–24
Performing, 119
Periodic review stock control systems,
    205–7
Peters, Tom, 185
    on roles of the coach, 119–20, 122
Phone questionnaires, 77
Physical barriers, to trade, 245
Pipeline stocks, 195, 200–201
Pittiglio, Rabin, Todd, and McGrath
    (PRTM), 244
Planned
    inventory, 201
    maintenance, 53
Planning and organizing, 111
Plant within a plant, 204
Porter's five force model, 182–86
Positioning, 66–68
    maps, 70–71
Potential capacity, 126
Prebooking, 133–34
Predictive
    maintenance and uptime, 52–53
    systems, 184
Prevention costs, 146

Preventive maintenance
    contracts, 133
    effect on service intensity, 31, 34
    efficiency measures for, 170
    and uptime, 51
    visits for, 137
Problem analysis, 110
Process
    customer service and support, 153
    flow, service and support delivery,
        177
    statistics, 158
Product
    effect on service intensity, 30–31
    mix, customer service and support,
        62–65
    reliability, 187
Product design
    and customer perception of quality,
        153
    for ease of use, 55
    effect on service intensity, 33–34
    integration with customer service
        and support, 10–13
Product liability
    legislation, 54–55
    and MTBF, 171
Product life cycle, and information
    requirements, 180–81
Product Quality, dimensions of,
    148–51
Product/service/support package,
    71–72
Production of documents, and word
    processors, 87–88
Productivity
    defined, 165
    index, 177
    and trade-offs with quality, 164–65
Profit Impact of Market Share (PIMS),
    144–45
Profitability, and customer retention,
    233–34
Purchase price
    definition of, 10
    effect on service intensity, 30

Q
Qualified sales leads, 185
Quality
    action team meeting, 99–100
    circles, 158
    costs, 146, 185
    and customers, 144–45
    definition of, 147
    and employee morale, 145–46
    image, and marketing, 145
    information systems, 187
    and international trade, 255–56
    reputation, and dealer network,
        221–22
    setting standards for, 153–55
    system, development of, 160–62
    techniques, 158
    and trade-offs with resource
        productivity, 164–65
Quality Function Deployment (QFD),
    158
Quality Programme, at Caterpillar
    Corporation, 158–59
Quality Triangle, 156–57, 160–62
Questionnaires, 77
Queuing, 134, 137

R
Range flexibility, 127
Rank Xerox
    customer satisfaction goals, 156
    development of sales leads, 185
    emphasis on serviceability, 9
    specialist logistics operations, 251–52
    use of benchmarking programs, 155
Ratner, Gerald, 145
Reactive service, 53
Recruitment
    costs, for service providers, 90
    of customers, 91–92
Reducing
    quality costs, 146
    service intensity, 134
    variability, 149
Redundancy, 45
Referral markets, 78

Regression models, 209
Regulars
    defined, 24–25
    and international networks, 249–50
Relationship
    costs, 144–45
    marketing, 63, 78
Reliability, 149
    increasing, 50–51
    index, 10, 12
    in service quality, 151
Remote Elevator Monitoring (REM),
    191
Remote sensing and diagnosis
    effect on service intensity, 32
    and effective capacity, 134
    and resource productivity, 178
    and uptime, 52–53
Reorder point stock control system,
    203, 205–7
Repair productivity, 171
Replace or repair, 52
Reserving slots, 133–34
Resource management, and
        management information systems,
        187
Resource productivity
    complexity of measurement, 168–69
    difficulty of managing, 165
    and frontline staff, 178
    improvement of, 173–78
    levels for measurement, 167–70
    and motivation of service teams, 177
    and trade-offs with quality, 164–65
    and variation in demand, 175
Resources
    allocation and scheduling of, 134–35,
        238–39
    control and planning of, 136–40
    service and support organisation,
        89–96
Response
    flexibility, 127
    time, 161
Responsiveness, 151
Retailer's viewpoint, 228

Retention of customers, and
    profitability, 233–34
Revenue yield, 172
Right First Time standard, 146
Risks, and international trade, 256
Robustness, of design, 150
Role playing, and telephone training,
    86
Route planners, 137
Ruggedized products, for adverse
    conditions, 150

S
Safety stocks, 196, 206–7
Sales-service database, at Hewlett-
    Packard, 185
SAS
    defined, 24–25
    and international networks, 249–50
SAS airline, 80
Scheduling of resources, 134–35
Schonberger, R., 151
Scope, of customer service and
    support, 8
Scripts, for communication, 113
Seasonal
    adjustment, exponential smoothing,
        208
    stocks, 199
Secondary information, market
    research, 77–78
Security, 152
Selection, of the dealer network, 225
Self-monitoring, by service providers,
    114
Selling skills, 113
Separate teams approach, 138
Service
    capacity, and need for dealer
        network, 219
    engineering, at Caterpillar
        Corporation, 191–92
    excellence, and international trade,
        245
    facilities, siting of, 88
    intensity, influences on, 30–34

Service—Contd.
    kits, 203
    quality, dimensions of, 151–53
    standards, and effective capacity,
        132
    task, defined, 16
    times, decreasing, 47–49
    trinity, 112
Service and support
    manager, 105–9
    organisation, resources of, 89–96
    personnel and service intensity,
        32–33
Service delivery
    customer role in, 91–92
    system design, 107–8
Service Delivery Triangle, introduction
    of, 81
Service level
    definitons of, 196–99
    trade-offs, 46–47
Service providers, 89–90
    empowerment of, 240–43
    need for training, 241
Service recovery
    developing strategies for, 235–43
    need for, 231–32, 242–43
Service supply chain, 193
    managing the, 211–15
Service team, 117–20
    audits, 122
    loyalty, reinforcement of, 90
Serviceability, 150
Setting priorities, customer service and
    support, 57–58
Sharing capacity, 132
Simple
    card system, inventory control, 206
    moving average, 208
    rating scales, 154
Smile campaign, failure of, 104
Spare parts inventories; see Inventory
Spares banks, 252
Specialist logistics operations, for
    international trade, 251–52
Split-level service, 47–48

Staff productivity, 172
Statistical Process Control (SPC), 158
  at the Ford Motor Company, 161
Stock cover, measure of, 222
Storming, 118
Strategy
  compass, 15–16
  issues, and international trade, 246
  for service recovery, 235–43
Strong arm tactics, control of dealer
    network, 220
Subcontractors, use to increase
    capacity, 132
Subordinate development, 111
Substitute products or services, threat
    of, 182–83
Supplier markets, 78
Supplier's schedules, and
    management information system,
    184
Supply chain
  and international trade, 251
  inventory turns, 214
  management of, 95
Support
  activities, 138–39
  costs, for service providers, 90
SWOT Analysis, 69–70

T
Tally charts, 158
Tangibles, 152
Target waiting time, 137
Team building, 109
  effectiveness of teams, 118–19
  the service team, 117–20
Team work, 111, 114
Technical
  barriers, to international trade, 245
  skills, 113
Technical Assistance Research
    Program Inc. (TARP), and
    customer satisfaction, 232–33, 240
Telephone
  contact, 85–87
  hotlines, 239

Telephone—*Contd.*
  network, capacity management of,
    86
Territorials, defined, 24, 26
Thriving on Chaos, 185
Time
  advantage, management
    information system, 184–86
  based efficiency measures, 170
  dimensions of, 42–45
  management, 113
Toll-free telephone numbers, 42
Total
  service revenue, 6
  supply chain, inventory turns, 214
Total Quality Management
  meaning of, 147
  overview, 141–43
Trade-offs
  between quality and productivity,
    164–65
  in service level, 46–47
Trade surveys, 77
Training
  costs, for service providers, 90
  of customers, 92
  for the dealer network, 226
  of service providers, 241
Transaction-based surveys, 154
Transfer of resources, to increase
    effective capacity, 131–32
Transportation stocks, 200–201
Traveling time, allocating for, 137
Trigger-input-process output (TIPO)
    model, 188–89
Trigg's Tracking Signal, 208
Two-bin system, inventory control, 206
Type of warranty, effect on service
    intensity, 31

U
Understanding the customer, 152
Unplanned inventory, 201
Uptime, maximizing, 50–53
Use, 169
User groups, 91

Users, effect on service intensity, 32

V
Value
chain, 96–97
of customer service and support, 74
Value-Added Resellers (VARs), 218
Van stocks, 198
Variation, in demand, 128
and resource productivity, 175
Variety, of demand, 127–28
Vertical integration, 211
Visits
for breakdowns, 138
for preventive maintenance, 137
Vitale, M. R., 188–89
Volume, of demand, 127

Volvo, and dealer profitability, 227

W
Warranty claims, 43
and customer training, 55
and management information
systems, 187
Word-of-mouth publicity, 233
Word processors, and production of
documents, 87–88
Work measurement, 170
Workshop repair, 139

Z
Zeithaml, V. A., 151
Zemke, R., 13–15
Zero defects, 156